No Stars in Jefferson Park

No Stars in Jefferson Park

A MEMOIR

Maggie Andersen

NORTHWESTERN UNIVERSITY PRESS
EVANSTON, ILLINOIS

Northwestern University Press
www.nupress.northwestern.edu

Copyright © 2026 by Maggie Andersen. Published 2026 by Northwestern University Press. All rights reserved.

Printed in the United States of America

10 9 8 7 6 5 4 3 2 1

Library of Congress Cataloging-in-Publication Data

Names: Andersen, Maggie, author.
Title: No stars in Jefferson Park : a memoir / Maggie Andersen.
Description: Evanston : Northwestern University Press, 2026.
Identifiers: LCCN 2025028927 | ISBN 9780810149519 (paperback) | ISBN 9780810149526 (ebook)
Subjects: LCSH: Andersen, Maggie. | Women authors, American—Illinois—Chicago—Biography. | Authors, American—Illinois—Chicago—Biography. | Actresses—Illinois—Chicago—Biography. | Actors—Illinois—Chicago—Biography. | Theater—Illinois—Chicago. | Gift Theatre—History. | Jefferson Park (Chicago, Ill.)—Biography.
Classification: LCC PN2287.A595 A3 2026 | DDC 792.0977311—dc23/eng/20250708
LC record available at https://lccn.loc.gov/2025028927

For my grandmother, Charmaine Gladych,
who took me to the theater

To the best of my ability, I have re-created events, locales, and people from my memories of them. In order to maintain the anonymity of others, in some instances I have changed the names of individuals. I have also conflated some characters and scenes. This book was written by memory, and mine is imperfect. However, I've done my best to be faithful to my experiences, and when possible, have consulted others who were also present during that time.

No Stars in Jefferson Park

PROLOGUE

2012

We never want the men who loved us young to think of us as old. Or worse, ugly.

I'm wearing a white cotton dress with a scarf looped around my neck in an effort to look sophisticated, and when I exit the theater and he says I look like an Italian model, I admit, it makes me happy. Because I am not tall, and nothing about me is conventionally attractive, but he says I look like an Italian model, and hyperbole is his kindness.

"Wanna go for a drink?" he asks.

"Of course I do," I say.

We are in Chicago, but probably not the Chicago you're thinking of. We are in Jefferson Park, which is one of my many Chicagos. Jefferson Park is like a scrap of small-town Wisconsin or Michigan sewn into the patchwork of Chicago. There's a Blue Line stop that'll get you to Wicker Park in fifteen minutes, but somehow, the neighborhood preserves its air of provinciality. The time-machine taverns, the Polish delis and bakeries, the law offices in frame houses and optometrists in old barns. This is not usually where Chicago transplants live; it's a neighborhood for those who have been here awhile, mostly city workers, white and Latino. The Gale Street Inn, an old-fashioned supper club that serves ribs and crab legs, is probably the most famous landmark, and the Gift Theatre, our theater, is just down the block.

As I push Mike in his bulky wheelchair across a busy street now, I talk to the back of his head. He's sporting a classic taper these days, and has been good-looking since college, after an ugly-duckling phase in high school. He grew up in Jefferson Park when it was still almost entirely white, a sub-suburb, solidly middle-class and very Catholic. When he grew up here, he did not need a wheelchair.

I grew up across the city in a neighborhood called Ravenswood, a port-of-entry neighborhood (at the time) that was not just white. I grew up in a chaotic and noisy family building and he in a small ranch house with an aboveground pool in the backyard. It wasn't that he was wealthy, but he was an only child whose parents gave him almost anything he wanted. By the time we met, doing a play together in high school, we were both fairly obsessed with theater—it wasn't just a social outlet or an extracurricular activity for us. I suspect my obsession has something to do with my grandmother taking me to storefront theater all my life. She lived in the apartment above us and didn't have a lot, but what she had, she spent on art. And Mike? I don't know. He was born with it, I guess. His dream had almost always been to be a famous actor. That, and to start a theater in Jefferson Park, one of the neighborhoods in Chicago that didn't have any. His neighborhood had bars, PTAs and churches, and big backyards for family barbecues, but it did not have theater before us. His neighborhood was one of boys who excelled in sports and seemed to be naturally good at roughhousing with children, drinking cheap beer, and making small talk. He had always been a misfit there, and maybe that's why he wanted to change it.

Inside the bar, we join our old friends, Lynda and Paulie, who have saved us an accessible table and ordered us fancy beers. We started the Gift Theatre with them a long time ago, back when we were still nomadic, before we found our permanent home. Mike and I were nicknamed the "Chicago hillbillies" (read: white kids who didn't grow up with money) and they were transplants, Paul from Queens and Lynda from South Boston. Paul always looks much younger than he actually is—maybe it's his full head of curls. I prefer when he cuts his hair short, but he seems to like it long and spilling all around his face. Paul left New York at eighteen to escape an overbearing Italian family. Lynda, sitting next to him, also appears younger than her forty-plus years. She wears stylish eyeglasses and thrift-store clothes, and her hair is usually just slightly graying at the temples because she's always proudly trying to save a buck. She is one credit short of a college degree and left Boston a long time ago to escape a long line of veteran alcoholics. Anytime I've seen either of them onstage, I have known they were put on this earth to be actors, and just when you think they've emptied the emotional tank, they'll somehow find a way to go deeper. They're the friends we chose as adults, and yet we can't remember our lives without them; the instinct of friendship has never left us. We have known one another's hearts dead and fully alive, and we pay close attention to life, which means we suffer more sometimes. We cry in front of each other without thinking and laugh together without trying.

As we're placing our order for a third round of drinks, a fellow bar patron pauses at our table. He looks at Mike's wheelchair with reverence and says, "Thank you for your service, sir. I, too, served my country." Mike winces a little before deciding to shake hands and keep his mouth shut.

"God bless America," Mike says, and they clink beer bottles.

I squeeze Mike's arm because I still feel inextricably connected to his disability, formed by it, protective of it, and haunted by it.

"I didn't really serve," Mike whispers to the waitress with a wink.

"I didn't think so," she says, laughing nervously.

"See, he used to be a lumberjack," Paul says.

"Wood-chopping competition," Lynda explains.

When we all laugh together like this, it makes everyone want to be near us, but Mike isn't in the mood for jokes tonight: He's in the mood for ghost stories.

"I don't even really remember what happened," Mike says. "Only Maggie really knows."

"Oh my God," Lynda says. "I can't do this tonight. I'm going outside for a cigarette. I'm sorry. I just can't tonight. Too much."

"I know the gist of what happened to you," the waitress says. "I mean, you're kind of a celebrity, aren't you?"

A flush rises to his face and I wonder: Does he still doubt praise and accolades because of his disability?

"Fuck them," I want to say. "Look at me," I want to say to him. "This does not define you."

"Tell her the story," Mike says. "Go ahead, Mag. Tell her the story."

Now I can see he's slightly drunk and in the mood for war stories. The music box creaks open, and all the secrets and sadness and beauty come spilling out.

CHAPTER 1
2003

Dear Mike,

I'll tell you again what happened. I'll tell you how I remember it. When I awoke that morning in our queen-sized bed, I did not appreciate the freckles on your shoulders or tell you that I felt grateful for your greasy scent on the sheets. I didn't thank you for thinking I was cool when I was clearly so far from it. I didn't thank you for teaching me that the artist's life can be for working-class kids too or for having energetic sex with me before I understood the beauty of a bikini wax. Instead of thanking you for loving me exactly as I was, I bolted out of bed at eight in the morning and ran for the shower, yelling, "Wake up, Thornton! Time for the Saint Patrick's Day parade!"

For the past few months, we had been busy with a little play called *County Fair*, but that had ended now. We had the day to drink away, and a free weekend was a luxury for us—no rehearsals, no performances. We were going to breakfast in the neighborhood where I had grown up and I could immerse myself in a familiar culture where nobody competed for theater reviews or auditions.

I hadn't seen my old friends in so long; I'd been sealed inside the National Pastime Theater for three months, playing an Iowa farm girl with parents who were splitting up. I hurried to the shower, turned it up steaming hot, and sang Irish folk songs so the whole block might hear my newfound freedom. "Low lie the fields of Athenry . . ."

While I lathered my arms and breasts with sweet-smelling oils, you yanked open the shower curtain and smiled approvingly. Now you were awake. But I didn't kiss you or ask you to join me; I splashed water at your face and pulled the curtain closed.

We drove toward the center of the city and picked up Paulie and Lynda, who said they wanted to see a "real" Chicago Saint Patrick's Day. Paul looked more California than Chicago with his golden skin and surfer curls, but Lynda blended in with her Boston Celtics T-shirt and DIY rainbow earrings. You and I were wearing kelly-green T-shirts and blue jeans, shamrock beads dangling from our necks, and big sunglasses obscuring our faces. We sang the entire way, and when you sang Irish folk songs, I would've driven anywhere with you. When you sang Irish, I could've driven right off a cliff. "So be easy and free when you're drinking with me. I'm a man you don't meet every day . . ." We drove through industrial corridors until we could see the skyline gleaming in the sun. We hadn't seen a sunny parade day since childhood, when I rode on political floats with my father and you played in a tin-whistle band.

We pulled up to a Lakeview greystone where a crowd of people in cable-knit sweaters sat on the front steps smoking cigarettes and drinking beer. Inside, there were more people and a long line for the only bathroom. My childhood friend kissed me on the cheek and shook your hand. He'd laid out a long table of scrambled eggs and crispy bacon, rice and beans, pecan pancakes. We piled our plates high, went to the keg and filled our cups. I said hello as we weaved through the crowd and made sure everyone remembered you. They had seen our plays and our names in the papers, our commercials on TV. I asked about their wedding plans and their babies. In this environment, I was the powerful one, and you were proud of me. In this room, energy was valued over elegance and street smarts over academic.

"Are you queen of the Saint Patrick's Day parade?" you asked.

I stuck out my tongue and crossed my eyes. "I'm so pretty, right?"

You laughed in spite of yourself, then looked at Paul and Lynda and said, "My God she's a monster."

My sisters and their significant others, my coed softball team, my life before you. We all toasted one another, and then floated down to the Brown Line station where we all herded onto the same elevated train car, loud and stinking of booze. I felt sorry for the families on the train, those poor passengers who had to endure us. My electricians and boilermakers were happy to have a Saturday off, and my doctors and lawyers were just happy to return to their working-class traditions. My college boyfriend and I held hands as we tried to keep our balance on an old train. Or maybe it was just me. You were actually a little more yourself inside a role, but I wondered how we could tell good stories if we didn't get out into the world sometimes.

We got off the train at Clark and Lake, and made our way down to Columbus. The river sparkled green, the bagpipers riled the crowd with fight songs, the Chicago skyline dwarfed the mobs below. You bought me a Kiss Me, I'm Irish button from a souvenir stand just for an excuse to make out with me. At some point, I ran off to the art museum where I worked so I could use a clean bathroom, and when I returned to our group, you were gone. I spotted my aunt in the parade, marching with a flask in her hand and her husband on her arm, so I jumped a wooden sawhorse and some policemen shouted after me. I blended into the march, waved at the television cameras, and smiled my headshot smile. That is the last documented image of me that day, and I was happy. I can't look at the pictures of you because I'm afraid that there's something I missed, something I should've seen but didn't.

At the end of the parade route, I went to Cal's, the combination bar and package liquor store where we always met if we lost each other, and I couldn't find my driver's license. I argued with the bouncer that I was twenty-five years old, goddamn it. Didn't I look it? But I didn't look it, then. You came to my rescue, of course. From behind, you said, "I knew I'd find you here. You gave me your wallet to hold, you dummy." We crowded around a window table with the friends that were left, and smoked cigarettes like they wouldn't kill us. Paulie loved our people, he said. He loved us and our families, my girlfriends too; we made him feel at home. He especially loved Tabitha and Shannon, friends from my all-girls Catholic high school who lived on the Northwest Side, were well read and brilliant but allergic to pretension, and were most comfortable in bars where they intimidated everyone with their acerbic wits. Admittedly, they were a little suspicious of artists, but they had always been soft for me and Mike, and we for them. Paul told stories about his Uncle Vito in Queens, and Lynda told some about her father, the king of the VFW hall.

"How about going back to our neighborhood?" you suggested. "Can Paulie and Lynda sleep over?" You never wanted the party to end.

We hailed a cab and took it to the Irish American Heritage Center. Time for corned beef and cabbage, and a set of traditional music. The place was so slammed, we couldn't find anywhere to sit or stand. The house band knew both our families and, as soon as they spotted us, started playing our most frequently requested folk song.

"Oh boy, Thornton," I said. "You'd better dance with me now."

And you did, of course, with the showmanship you were known for. You grabbed me up in your arms and led me around the dance floor by the small of my back as the tenor sang about wandering the hills and the rusty old mill. The song was called "When You and I Were Young, Maggie," and we sang it to each other while an audience looked on. It must've looked pretty silly, two twentysomethings singing about being old and gray, but we sang with all our hearts. "But to me you're as fair as you were, Maggie, when you and I were young . . ." You dipped me gracefully at the end of the song and smiled into my face.

"Now I'm going to get a beer," you said, and I laughed.

We stood in line for a drink, then found a booth on the dance floor. "God, my neck hurts," you said suddenly, but the Heritage Center was buzzing and I could barely hear you. I pulled an aspirin from my purse and handed it to you, who washed it down with beer.

"Can you give me a massage?" you asked, so I did.

"Can we go now?" you asked. "My neck is really killing me."

I knew you must be in pain if you wanted to leave before closing—I should get you home to bed. I called out that we were leaving. Goodnight, Paulie and Lynda called from the dance floor, where they stomped around until his hair was in his eyes and her glasses were falling off. We stepped out into the night that had gotten cold and dark, and all we could hear was the singing getting farther and farther away.

Just as we started down the stairs, I saw our friend Connolly parking. He'd been on his way to meet us. Connolly was ten years older than us, a big bear of a man with a giant head whose eyes went squinty when he smiled. At the time, he was on a sobriety kick because he was devoutly Catholic, went to church every Sunday, and sometimes just felt guilty about his incredible fondness for whiskey.

"Can you take us home?" I asked. "Mike isn't feeling well."

You stood with your palms down on the hood of his Cavalier, as if you were under arrest. You took deliberate, deep breaths, and shook your head back and forth. Connolly asked if you were going to blow chunks and I said I didn't think so. You eased slowly into the passenger's seat and said softly to your friend, "Just drive."

I leaned forward in the back seat asking, "Babe, what's wrong with you?"

When we pulled up in front of our bungalow, you looked afraid. You said, "I can't go in there."

"I'll take you to bed," I said. "I'll take care of you. You just drank too much, that's all."

"Mag. I cannot feel my hands."

With that, Connolly sped away from 5254 North Lieb Street, and you began a long, steady moan. I couldn't believe these sounds were coming from you, the man of incredible laughter. Connolly told us that he had had a panic attack once and this is what it felt like. His neck hurt, his arms went numb, and he thought he was having a heart attack, but it was really just anxiety. I rubbed the back of your neck again, and now you asked me what was wrong.

"I don't know," I said. "But we're going to see a doctor and he'll be able to tell you exactly."

We looked out the window at the strip of Irish bars along the Kennedy Expressway. Kids billowing in and out, beer bottles in their hands, beads around their necks, shamrock stickers plastered all over their freckled faces, and tweed caps covering their sweaty heads. We had been them just an hour ago. Connolly screeched up to the emergency room entrance of Resurrection, a Catholic hospital.

"I can't open the door," you said, panicking. "My arms are totally numb now."

I scampered out to open the door for you and started toward the sliding glass doors with the weight of you on my arm. Me five foot two, and you six foot two. The security guard took one look at us, ran for a wheelchair, and you collapsed into it. I told him you couldn't feel your arms, but he had already swept you away. I went inside to fill out the paperwork.

"And who are you?"

"His girlfriend."

"Insurance?"

"Yes, Actors' Equity. His card is in his wallet."

"Profession?"

"Actor."

"Symptoms?"

"Neck pain and numbness in the arms."

"Last time he was here?"

"Not sure. He was at a hospital in Wisconsin last summer for a bug bite that swelled up."

"Date of birth?"

"March 3, 1979. He just turned twenty-four."

"Social Security number?"

"I don't know. I'm sorry."

"Thank you. Please have a seat."

"It's just a panic attack, isn't it?"

"I'm sorry ma'am, I just don't know."

I called your parents from a pay phone; your father's voice was gravel.

"It might be nothing," I said. "But I thought I should let you know."

I went outside to smoke a cigarette and then your parents came reeling toward me. A nurse signaled through the window with annoyance; they were going to let us see you now, she said. Connolly decided to stay behind in the waiting room. I pushed through a padded door and headed down a hallway of crucifixes and biblical passages. Okay, Thornton, I thought. From now on, no more drinking, no more cigarettes, and we're going on a diet. We'll go to bed early, we'll try yoga and organic everything.

I was the one who saw you first, much paler than before under all that fluorescent light. Restrained in what looked like a dental chair, gulping for air. All of the doctors yelling, "Thornton! Critical!" I had always dreamed of Thornton being my last name; it complemented my first name so nicely. Thornton as in *The Quiet Man*. I always gave your name when I made reservations, and you always smiled when I said it.

"Thornton! Critical!"

"I can't breathe," you mouthed to me, fear flashing in your eyes.

Your parents rushed in behind me, your father already hiccupping tears. I held your hand and said, "Don't be afraid. It's going to be okay." Even though I wasn't at all sure of that. The doctors rushed around and didn't seem to have time to explain. "He needs to be intubated!" one of them cried out. Your mother asked what that meant. Intubated meant you had to be put on a ventilator because you weren't capable of breathing for yourself anymore. Intubated meant they would have to empty the contents of your stomach and sedate you before they inserted breathing tubes. Intubated meant we had to leave you alone with the doctors and your dignity, so we did.

"Am I going to die?" you whispered to the doctor.

He was an honest man. He said, "I don't think so."

Back to the waiting room, where I sat beside your parents and Connolly, who talked and talked, but sounded like they were underwater. I focused on the television, blasting at midnight, until a doctor came for us. A thirty-something man with a shiny bald head, designer eyeglasses, and a perfectly manicured goatee. He asked us to follow him, and when he saw me, he said, "Family only."

"She *is* family," your mother said, the first time she had ever advocated for me.

We, the new family, trailed behind the doctor to a room bleached of color, the sterility of the place making me aware that my coat smelled of an awful blend of cigarettes and floral perfume. I tried to keep a distance from your mother, who doesn't like the smell of cigarettes, but she put her arm around me anyway. Your father stepped around to the other side and I held his giant hand. I was grateful for his crying and squeezed his fingers tightly.

The doctor said it like this: "We *believe* that Michael may have Guillain–Barré syndrome, which could mean temporary paralysis, up to one or two years, maybe. At this point, it's still a mystery, but it seems like a possibility, and we wanted to keep you informed. If this turns out to be the case, he may have to learn to walk all over again, but it *is* only temporary and he should recover sooner than later, a boy his age. We'll pray for Guillain–Barré, but we're going to run a series of tests. We've pretty much ruled out heart trouble and we do have him stabilized. Do you have any questions?"

I spilled out into the hall then without any of them and saw you lying on a portable bed; a suctioning tube slowly drained the contents of your stomach. Your cousin, the paramedic, rushed by in uniform (I'm still not sure how he found out we were there), gave me a quick kiss, and said, "Jesus Maggie, what'd you feed him?" You were so exposed, anyone could've seen you lying there. A man on the other side of the screechy curtain was yelling, "Nurse! Nurse! Can I have my breakfast now?" In a way, I wanted to laugh, and I wanted you to laugh with me, but your eyes were closed, tears leaking out the sides. The doctor came and touched my shoulder, assured me that you were on morphine and felt no more pain now. There wouldn't be any laughing today.

* * *

I stood in a hallway staring at you as the doctor grilled me about your personal life.

"Does he use cocaine?"

"No."

"A smoker?"

"Yes."

"How long?"

"Just a few years. Started in college."

"Has he lost a considerable amount of weight recently?"

"Have you looked at him?" I joked.

"Has he lost weight recently?"

"No."

"Does he play any sports?"

"Not really."

They asked if you drank energy drinks or took dietary supplements, again if you were a cocaine user, if you had engaged recently in full-contact sports. Occasionally, you drank vodka with Red Bull, I said. Once every few months, you pretended to diet, which meant you ate two meals a day instead of three, and drank more water. I insisted you had never tried cocaine, even though all those assholes on that movie set abused it. The only sport you had ever mastered was golf; your mother was too afraid of full-contact sports, especially after the ice-hockey incident in junior high, from which you still have a chin scar. I so enjoyed being a scholar of you that I momentarily forgot the purpose of the questions, the coma they had induced. The doctor asked if there had been any car accidents in the past six months, if anything unusual had happened today.

Wasn't it unusual that I had just read Susan Sontag's quote about the double passport only weeks before? "Everyone who is born holds dual citizenship, in the kingdom of the well and in the kingdom of the sick. Although we all prefer to use only the good passport, sooner or later each of us is obliged, at least for a spell, to identify ourselves as citizens of that other place."

"We drank a lot," I conceded guiltily. "He drinks a lot all the time."

"He's twenty-four," the doctor said. "Doesn't mean a thing. Anyway, try to think about head injuries, drug use, fistfights, anything you can think of that might be helpful. We, of course, won't tell his parents anything you don't want us to."

I told the doctors about Charlotte's then, about the night you ended up at the Northwest Side neighborhood bar after a *Cherry Docs* performance, and a group of neo-Nazis came in and took over the place. Do you remember this? You thought it was ironic because you were playing a neo-Nazi in *Cherry Docs*, and yet you had never seen one in real life. You said you watched as they went to the bathroom two and three at a time. Drugs, you thought. But later in the night, you found their propaganda plastered all over the stalls. You ripped down the posters, crumpled them into a wad, and carried it to Asha, your favorite Polish bartender.

"Throw this shit away," you said.

And when you left the bar at 2 A.M., the Nazis waited for you in the alley and knocked you down on the asphalt. Then you rolled over and they kicked and punched you in the back of the head repeatedly. Whenever I imagine this, I remember that you were wearing a leather jacket in those days, and had a swastika temporarily tattooed on the back of your neck for the play. You *looked* just like one of them.

"How long ago was this?" the doctor asked.

"Several months ago, I guess."

The doctor took the note and started to walk away, then spun around with an afterthought. "Maggie," he said. "What you and Mr. Connolly did today was very smart and very brave. You saved Michael's life. If he had gone home tonight, he most certainly would've died in his sleep."

Then he returned to your parents and I stayed where I was, unmoving, as nurses and doctors hurried around me, calling out urgent medical orders. You slept without snoring, slipped silently into morphine dreams, and I had no idea who I was.

There were babies in bubbles and seniors with bad hearts. More yelling, more code blues, more criticals. A tan, blond middle-aged woman sobbed while explaining to a doctor that her mother had the heart attack on the airplane; they had to make an emergency landing.

Back in the waiting room, I pushed two chairs together, laid my head on one, scrunched my feet up on the other, and let my torso sag in between. Connolly patted my head while he read a magazine. I squeezed my eyes closed and thought I heard you laughing. I thought I heard you regaling the nurses with your most off-color jokes. I thought I heard you say, "Come on, Bruiser, let's go home now. I'm sober; I can drive." But every time I looked up, I only saw your mother multiplying into more and more of her sisters, who had come to the waiting room to comfort her. Your father's red-rimmed eyes were lifeless as he embraced them. The Irish song I'd been singing in the shower—"The Fields of Athenry"—it played on in my mind. *By a lonely prison cell, I heard a young girl calling, "Michael, they have taken you away . . ."*

Our flannel sheets, our unmade bed: You could've died beside me. That was the only thing I could hold on to. This was March 15, 2003. *Beware the Ides of March.* I was twenty-five years old and you were twenty-four. At five o'clock in the morning, I called my parents. I told them something terrible had happened.

CHAPTER 2

2001

We had started the Gift Theatre just two years before that terrible Saint Patrick's Day. Mike had been dreaming of his own theater company since we first met each other doing musicals at my all-girls high school. (He had come from the neighboring boys' school.) While it was true that I'd landed the best roles back then, and performed at the statewide festivals, Mike was the kid who had courted a mentor outside of our high school program. At fifteen, he convinced his father to drive him to Victory Gardens for a Performing Shakespeare class where, every week, he studied with professional actors. In the land of high school, most kids thought Mike was a weird asshole, and I did too, but also, I thought he was cool. At seventeen, he would rent out the theater at the community college and cast the two of us in all the husband and wife roles. Mike referred to my dockworker boyfriend as "Shakespeare" in a way meant to diminish him. He snuck handwritten poems into my backpack, but we didn't date back then. Before he graduated from high school, Mike promised he would one day start a theater company, and that I would always have a place in it. The difference between me and the rest of our classmates? I believed him.

Off I went to the commuter college, per my parents' wishes, where I'd been awarded a full-ride scholarship. Despite my initial disappointment, I made the best of it, declaring an English major and a theater minor, performing in university plays directed by real Chicago directors, and working a series of bizarre jobs and internships while dating the dockworker. I started an internal newsletter at the Chicago Transit Authority, wrote restaurant reviews for *Barfly*, and worked as a public relations assistant for my local Democratic organization during a particularly intense political campaign. I needed the paychecks, but also hoped I would someday love my job in a way my parents didn't love theirs. I couldn't have appreciated at the time that these bus drivers and bartenders and politicians were also shaping my understanding of the world and my future artistic life.

While I was shuffling back and forth between the University of Illinois Chicago and my parents' apartment and various gigs, Mike studied acting, on scholarship, at the University of Iowa, a Big Ten school with a huge arts endowment. His parents bought him expensive headshots, paid for his apartment, car, and credit-card bills. None of us understood it. My parents and friends all thought Mike should get a job, and sometimes, so did I.

This lack of a job did allow him time to write ambitious screenplays though, so when he came home from college for breaks, we spent all of that time making indie movies together and submitting them to contests, which we often won. When he went back to school, he had flings with the graduate students, and called me from their apartments, drunk, in the middle of the night. I liked hearing about all the things he was learning. One night, he drunk-dialed me after Grotowski class.

"Can I read you something real quick?" he asked.

"Yes," I said, half asleep.

"Acting is a particularly thankless art. It dies with the actor," Mike recited. "Nothing survives him but the reviews, which do not usually do him justice anyway, whether he is good or bad. So the only source of satisfaction left to him is the audience's reactions. The actor, in this special process of discipline . . . is not afraid to go beyond all normally acceptable limits . . . The actor makes a total gift of himself."

"A gift of himself," I repeated. "I like it."

"How about the Gift?" Mike asked. "For the name of the theater company."

". . ."

"Artistic Director: Michael Patrick Thornton."

"I love it."

"Me too. And also, I love you."

"Okay."
"I really do."
"I know."
"When doth thouest break up with Master Shakespeare?"
"I'm not breaking up with him, Mike."
"Okay. Had to try. Have a good day at school tomorrow."

* * *

In my final year of undergrad, I was awarded a fellowship to study Irish drama and literature for one semester at Trinity College Dublin. My first taste of solo travel was transformative, of course, and I was an eager student. In Dublin, I rode the DART to the places where James Joyce had lived. I read contemporary poetry as I looked out the train window and daydreamed. Back on campus, I wandered around the library and looked at the Book of Kells whenever I wanted. I saw plays every week with my class, and when we interviewed the artistic director at the Abbey, he may as well have been a prophet. He spoke about his theater as an arena of art and ideas, and explained how theater in Ireland was for every class of people and not just for the highly educated and very rich.

He gave a lecture about William Butler Yeats and Lady Gregory, and perhaps because I had told him where I was from, he looked straight at me when he told us about her affection for the Hull House Players from Chicago. "Don't engage professional players," Lady Gregory counseled the theater producers. "They have been spoiled for your purpose. Engage and train, as we of the Abbey have done, amateurs." She advised the Hull House Players to train shopgirls and schoolteachers, counterjumpers and thieves, but never, never professionals. "And prepare," Lady Gregory said, "to have your hearts broken."

I found myself scribbling postcards to Mike to tell him everything because he was the only person I knew who would care. And when I came home from Ireland with new eyes, I started taking the bus every weekend to see him, to sleep in a twin bed with him, to enmesh my life with his.

I took the bus from the shitty Greyhound station on the South Side of Chicago, walking distance from my own university, to a pastoral campus in Iowa City. I walked down the pedestrian mall to see

Mike's plays in the theater that opened out onto the river. We went to cast parties with Will Nedved, who was tall, gay and handsome, bright-eyed and ambitious. Mike and Will were called "the gems" of the university, the former a promising actor, the latter a promising playwright, and Mike called Will "co-artistic director" of the Gift long before we even got started. The three of us sang showtunes at the top of our lungs and dreamed about making art together in Chicago, just like the Hull House Players.

* * *

It was my professor, a theater director named Dexter Bullard, who encouraged me to apply for the training program at Steppenwolf Theatre. In acting class one day, he said that I was equal parts "raw and refined," and that it was a potent combination. I wasn't totally sure what he meant at the time, but suspected it had something to do with the way I could hold my own in a room of theater kids as well as in a room of angry young men who didn't go to college. I'd often felt I half belonged in each of the places, yet never like I truly belonged anywhere.

An excerpt from my application essay:

> My mother and grandmother went to the theater on Thursday nights. Usually, when they came home from work, they looked sallow and tired, in winter and in spring. They slouched at my grandmother's dining room table in the apartment above ours, tapped their cigarette ashes lazily into a round glass ashtray, and yawned as they tried to outwit each other in the post-dinner game of Scrabble. But on theater nights, they came home late and sat up on their knees, recalling the actors as if they were old friends.
>
> "Rondi was terrific," my grandmother said.
>
> "She always is," my mother agreed. "What about Fran?"
>
> "Who's Rondi?" I asked. "Who's Fran?"
>
> "The actors," my mother said. "The actors from the play."
>
> They looked bright and young and animated. I sat on my grandmother's lap and did my best accents and impersonations while they were still in the mood for entertainment.

"I have always hated my father," I said in a British accent, quoting Fahrenheit 451.

"She's good!" my grandmother said to my mother. "She's really gonna be something."

My mother and grandmother were both terrified of public speaking; neither of them had ever had any desire to perform, but they made me want to try. On Thursday nights, after work, they took the elevated train to the Steppenwolf Theatre on Halsted, the actor's theater, an ensemble of Chicago artists in a neighborhood my father warned against. In the eighties and nineties, it was still all public housing, bookies, and hookers.

"Laur," he'd say to my mother, handing her a canister of pepper spray. "I'm not fuckin' around. It's dangerous over there."

For as long as I can remember, I've wanted to be a part of that world, that nighttime city magic that made the old look young again.

I was called in for an audition, and though I didn't make the final cut, the director of the program did call me to say that my application essay was the best he'd ever read. At the age of twenty-one, I graduated from college, a little bit aimless, but deeply in love. Mike, always a singularly focused doer, dropped out of school to move back to Chicago and pursue his professional acting career, and me.

* * *

We took a trip to Ireland together and traveled across the country to visit both our families. I showed Mike around Trinity, the theaters in Dublin and Galway, and we made love for the first time in a garden house near the Abbey. We had no responsibilities then, traveled on the cheap, and our dreams seemed to color even the laundry hanging on clotheslines. I felt I had something to offer when we walked with his uncles in the woods and played imagination games with the children. I also felt I had something to offer in the lobby after a show when it was time to discuss it. This was a particularly gratifying mix for a heart that was so conflicted between the pull of family and the insatiable hunger for an artistic life.

Mike and I took a two-person play to San Antonio, Texas, where we lived for a few weeks with a Mexican family. He got cast in shows in Chicago that I went to see with Tabitha and Shannon. (I always traveled with an entourage in those days.) We saw him in Shakespeare at the Ivanhoe, *Flanagan's Wake* at the Royal George. We befriended his castmates and he bought us drinks all over the city on his credit card. I was an excellent sidekick.

But sidekick wasn't quite good enough. I worked a string of jobs after graduation and none of them felt meaningful. Not writing copy for a manufacturing company that made Zambonis, not the admin job for *Playboy* magazine, certainly not the suburban newspaper job I worked at the time where I mostly wrote obituaries. Mike didn't have a job, or even the pressure to get one, so he took me out for lunch a few times a week, watched me cry over my grilled cheese, tried to convince me to quit my job, and half listened about the obituaries I was writing. One day, while I was busy thinking about dead people, he was accepted to the training program at Steppenwolf, the same one that had rejected me.

* * *

We started the Gift Theatre with some of the actors Mike met in the program. I was twenty-three years old and still living with my parents, in their apartment without central air. My father was a police officer who worked in the youth division, planning summer camps for "at risk" kids, and my mother was a part-time secretary. We lived together, with my sisters and my grandma and my aunties, in our family three-flat, where I had lived since infancy, and when I walked from our apartment to the Brown Line el station, I could've done it with my eyes closed. On the day the Gift Theatre began, I rode the train away from my neighborhood, before all the restaurants and wine bars cropped up, before our taverns all got facelifts. It's true that I loved the new coffee shops and art galleries, but I also hated the yuppies moving in who thought they were better than my family.

Belmont and Clark: That's where I would get off. When I was in high school, in the nineties, it was gay nightclubs, brightly colored mohawks, and a punk-rock music scene. I used to take the Brown Line there to buy my CDs at Wax Trax. Now I was on my way to start a theater company, and it was still a secret—it was all so impossibly romantic. For the first time, I had friends who weren't born in Chicago, who lived in apartments I had never seen, and in neighborhoods I didn't know by heart. They didn't have cars or families here, nothing to fall back on. They would become part of my personal constellation, my hopelessly emotional geography. I got off the train and walked to Brendan Donaldson's apartment. Mike had met him at the School at Steppenwolf just six weeks prior, and told me about him on the very first day.

"There's this weird kid, Brendan," Mike said. "He's really good. I think he's gonna be the next John Malkovich."

Brendan Donaldson: couldn't even get into the bars in Chicago yet. Like Mike, he had dropped out of college to be a professional actor. A cigarette-skinny twenty-year-old boy with a pretty, chiseled face, a Southern boy without an accent. Mike told me that, during a particularly psychological acting exercise, they'd been asked to recreate a day in their high school lives. Brendan pantomimed his high school morning shower and really took his time with it, but ended up panicking and begging his parents not to make him go to school because everyone there made fun of him. This made me always want to be near him, so when he buzzed me up, I wrapped my arms around him tightly.

Soon the room was crowded with a mix of artists who had been groomed for and felt entitled to this kind of life, and a few Midwestern types, like me, who just wanted to make their parents proud. Their moms and dads who worked so hard and thought the actor's life was a little much. When I took a voice class in college and the instructor encouraged me to tone down my Chicago accent, my mother said, "How pretentious." Who did I think I was? I had no idea, but I loved Chicago, the way it let me be so fully myself, even the ugliest parts, and the theater, because it reminded me I had the potential to be someone else entirely. And then there was Mike, who somehow allowed for both.

Mike chose Brendan's apartment because it was centrally located, but also, he and I were still living with our parents. One of the actresses lived in a high-end condo downtown with her wealthy husband, but most of them lived together in basement apartments or alone in crappy studios. I distributed the scripts for *Boys' Life*, by

Howard Korder, and the apartment buzzed with the energy of young actors who wanted stage lights and applause more than financial security or families. They wanted to be different from their parents; they wanted to be interesting, they didn't know yet how interesting their parents were. The play was about a trio of men navigating their twenties, and the poor women who had to bear witness. The critics called it "a flawless comedy." William H. Macy had directed a wildly successful world premiere in the 1990s and now we were going to remount it.

Many groups had done this before us, so we weren't original, but we didn't fully know that. So many ensembles have thought they were the next big thing, that they could be the next Steppenwolf, that ensemble of actor's actors, which started in a church basement and ended up putting Chicago on the map of world theaters. In our minds, we were the first ensemble to emulate them, but I know now that some hungry group of twentysomethings does this every summer. They graduate from college, move to Chicago, and put on a show. We may not have been business savvy, but we had a sense of urgency. If I knew then how many companies had failed, how intense our competition was, I might not have stayed in the room, but I like to think I would've. Sitting on a milk crate full of records, I waited for Mike to arrive. Yes, I was irritated that he was late. Yes, I was anxious about performing with actors who seemed like they knew things I didn't, but Brendan was an awkward host and he needed my help, now.

Everyone knew I'd known the neighborhood guys in the room for years now and the Steppenwolf cohort for a few months, so they expected me to bridge the gaps, and I enjoyed the role. I asked the Steppenwolf cohort about their classes. Paulie, Lynda, and Brendan had all met Mike at the School just weeks ago. Every year, Steppenwolf held auditions in Los Angeles, Chicago, and New York, and from that pool, they accepted about fifteen students. The chosen actors took improv workshops with Sheldon Patinkin in the morning and did Meisner scene study in the afternoon with Mary Ann Thebus. In improv, they learned how to be funny without scripts, and in Meisner, how to focus on the other actors in the scene more than themselves. There's a repetition exercise, central to the Meisner technique, that's believed to be crucial in getting an actor out of their head. This means that Mary Ann acted as part psychologist, part parent, part instructor. This also means many of the students ended up making out with each other in her class. She made these grown men and women cry with her honest assessments of their talent, and after class, they got drunk with each other in Lincoln Park bars that they would never go to once they officially moved to Chicago.

Even though the School stories were juicy, I never forgot to ask the untrained actors about their jobs. Connolly was there with his squinty Irish eyes and his big giant head. He'd been working as a collections agent for the past several years while doing improv on the weekends. After all those years of improvising, he had a tendency to always be on and very loud and very funny, so that when he abruptly shifted into his soft voice, you felt like you could see right through his soul. Connolly had grown up an artist and misfit in Jefferson Park, just like Mike. He had an endearingly childish sense of humor and wonder. His older brother once told me that, in the summers of their childhood, Connolly would put on homemade capes, climb to the top of the garage, and tell himself he could fly. One day, the older brother heard a thud and his weird younger brother say, "Ouch." Then: "I tried." Connolly had only started pursuing an acting career in his thirties, and I'm convinced that the young people who had the luxury of playing theater games all day benefited from him as much as he did from them.

After introducing everyone, I looked at my lines again. I started to feel annoyed that Mike had asked me to read a character that only existed for one scene, but it was absurd of me to want more. I hadn't acted since I graduated from college, and even then, I only took a couple of classes, did a couple of amateur shows. I had been an English major, after all. While many people in the room had spent years in conservatory programs doing psychological acting exercises, I had been learning how to write, so when I looked at a script, I sometimes thought more about rewriting it or responding to it than I did about performing. Nobody in the room was a professional, but some were more seasoned, and I was not one of them. Brendan passed out glasses of ice water because the apartment was getting unbearably hot.

At some point, I looked up from my script to see this room of actors who would soon become my ensemble, the people who made the dingy dressing rooms feel like some kind of home. Eventually, I would cast them all as my family inside the theater. Brendan was my little brother, even then, even though he was from an upper-middle-class Southern family, raised by elegant women who were nothing like me. He wore a T-shirt that said *I Hate Vegetables* even though he'd been a vegetarian for years, and smiled uncertainly at me as he tried to be a grown-up. Connolly was my favorite uncle, looking out the window at the arcades and sex shops as if he'd seen it all. Some of these actors moved away from Chicago a long time ago, and some still live here now, but on that oppressively hot day, we couldn't have imagined our future successes and disappointments, all the love affairs and funerals to come.

The doorbell rang and Brendan hit the buzzer. Mike came bounding up the stairs because he always did make an entrance. He always did take stairs two at a time. I love to remember him walking because he always did it with such flair. All of a sudden, he was there, all six feet and two inches of him, all two hundred and twenty pounds. He towered over all of us, and even with the extra weight, he was handsome. The actors bombarded Mike with questions about their characters and the room became a swirl of nervous energy. He answered all of their questions, then came over to kiss me.

"Thanks for helping," he said into my ear.

He had called me just hours before the reading, panicking, because he hadn't thought about scripts, so I drove to the library on my lunch break, picked up *Boy's Life*, and made several illegal copies. The play itself was an exploration of male friendship and the slow realization that growing up means growing apart from one another. The dialogue between the boy-men was near perfect, and while the women weren't written quite as well, I didn't mind at the time. After all, sneaking away from work and being Mike's assistant was more fulfilling than my current job, writing obituaries for minimum wage. I had always hoped that journalism would feel like writing, but most of the time, it felt, to me at least, like bothering people. Reading plays was more collaborative and I felt like I was part of something important: that nighttime magic of theater that made the old look young again.

Mike planted himself in a beanbag chair and looked around at each one of our faces.

"Let's put on a play," he said, and then he smiled. It could've been his dimples that allowed him to get away with such cheesiness. I don't know. But everyone smiled and opened their scripts.

Mike was twenty-two years old and totally pretentious, totally full of shit, but he had the ability to command a room, maybe because he had grown up an only child. His parents instilled in him early on that everything he said was profoundly important, and he tried to make sure it always was. He had the charisma and comic timing to play Jack, the Peter Pan of the play, the stay-at-home dad whose wife makes all the money and might or might not know that he flirts with joggers at the park while his son plays on the monkey bars.

"Take a deep breath," he said to us. "Have *fun*."

Mike looked down for a few seconds, then threw his head back and began the play.

"Do you remember the nineteen-seventies?" he asked, and suddenly he was just as high as he'd been the night before. He became a man full of resentments, and his transformations always excited me, like good jazz on a record player. The living room turned into a theater, a proscenium stage, blood-red velvet curtains. We put on the play in a studio apartment. Mike conjured the flawed character of Jack, and begged his single friends to describe their sex lives, insulted their girlfriends, crossed every single line. He did it so well that I was half in love with him and half anxious. I had seen him play child molesters and serial killers in college, but this one was somehow more disturbing. I didn't suspect he would ever become those things, but I knew he might become a Jack. The first scene crashed into the second.

Brendan played my ex-boyfriend, and cornered me in the "coat room" at a party, pleading with me for another chance. He was so earnest, so pathetic, and I knew then that this play had been partially chosen as a vehicle for him. I tried to resist, but he broke me down, and soon we were crawling toward each other on the dusty floor of a studio apartment. Mike read the stage directions: "They kiss." My body felt sort of electric and I began to worry about what Mike felt when he made out with his classmates in Meisner. The play stayed on track while the men struggled with their demons and the women struggled with the men. At the end of the play, Lynda, as Mike's stage wife, crossed the studio to sit beside him in a beanbag chair. She took off her glasses, put her head on his shoulder and he stared straight ahead.

In her thick Boston accent, she told him he wasn't the worst man in the world. "But you'd like to be," she said.

The line arrived like a fist, and when the tears came rushing out of Mike's eyes, I remembered why I loved him—he couldn't sustain the villain. We all clapped, felt a rush of pride together. A reading like that can be more magical than the show itself. The world comes alive with possibility. It's like love—you can never recreate the first time. It's like a first kiss—it can never happen again.

"I'm going to start a theater company," Mike said. "The Gift. I know some of you were planning to go home, wherever home is, at the end of summer. If you stay, you have a place here. I'm asking Sheldon to direct."

Sheldon Patinkin was one of the founders of Chicago's most famous comedy establishment, The Second City, a director at all the big houses, head of the theater department at Columbia College, and a legend in the theater community. He had recently published "the essentially accurate history" of The Second City with a foreword by Catherine O'Hara, in which he lovingly told the behind-the-scenes stories. Sheldon was also the improv teacher at Steppenwolf, but Mike had met him just a month ago. Most of the time, Mike's dreaming was charming, but this time, it just seemed ridiculous.

"Bring me the white pages," Mike said. (Yes, we still used phone books in the year 2002. No, we did not have cell phones.)

Brendan fetched him the phone book and I walked around the room, complimenting everyone on their performances, secure already in my role as company cheerleader.

"Found it," Mike announced. He dialed without hesitation.

"Sheldon," Mike said in his best businessman voice. "I'm here at Brendan Donaldson's apartment with some of the kids from school . . . Yeah . . . We just had a reading of *Boys' Life*."

We all stopped where we were and watched him.

"I know it's not *Sexual Perversity*, but it's gonna be great. Listen, man . . . I'd love it if you'd consider directing."

Mike fell silent and I looked out the window, tried to find stars in the sky.

"Next Saturday would be *wonderful*," Mike said, pumping his fist. "Thank you so much. See you in class tomorrow."

Mike hung up the phone and we held our breath.

"He said he'll listen to it next Saturday. We're gonna do this, guys. Let's go to the L&L and get drunk."

I was able to see the great acting in the room that night, even if I couldn't quite reach it yet myself. Looking down at all the neon signs, I promised myself that I would get better, that I would blow them all away with my talent. Otherwise, I was just Mike's girlfriend, which I already knew I was good at.

* * *

"Hey Bruiser," Mike said to me.

"Was I okay?" I asked.

"You were fine."

"I know I was fine, but was I good?"

"Of course you were," he laughed. "How was I?"

I told him at least seven of my favorite parts.

"Let's go to the bar," he said, smiling. "Let's celebrate, okay?"

I was lonely for the words he wouldn't say as he walked ahead of me down the stairs, but I followed him anyway. I knew he depended on me to keep his oversized ego in check, so I hurried to think of a note.

"You should sharpen your point of view on that scene with your wife," I said.

Then he turned around and grabbed me between the legs, smiling. "Thank you."

I swatted him away.

"Thank you," he said again, grabbing at me hungrily.

I took this for granted at the time—his ferocious, insatiable appetite.

When we entered the bar, everyone from the cast was there, even the ones who didn't particularly like to drink. The bartender, who looked like the lead singer of the Cure, filled a pitcher with strong German beer. We drank several before the night was over, and Mike and I held court, as we always did. He'd always been a mix of heady philosophy professor and irreverent frat boy, and I'd always been a curious mix myself. We made fun of everyone equally to show them we loved them, and I think they all knew we did. We made fun of Connolly, who had a hundred ideas for screenplays but had never actually written one, and Brendan, for the ironic wizard hat he was wearing. It was a family of misfits, and Mike and I were their parents.

Most of them were new to the city—they had come to us from Knoxville, Boston, Virginia Beach, Maine, and Winterset, Iowa, and without discussing it, Mike and I felt an obligation to make them feel at home in Chicago. We laughed with them, too loudly. We reenacted our favorite dramatic scenes, swapped stories about our favorite actors; we ached for plays to go on long after they'd ended, tried to clap the characters back into existence.

Mike raised his pint glass and said, "The only source of satisfaction left to him is the audience's reactions. The actor, in this special process of discipline and self-sacrifice, self-penetration, and molding, is not afraid to go beyond all normally acceptable limits—"

"The actor makes a gift of himself," I finished.

We all smashed our glasses together.

* * *

When we reemerged into the city after midnight, I still felt the gnawing insecurity. Maybe it was hearing about the other actors who had gotten their Equity (union) cards already after doing shows in Boston and New York. Mike and I walked down the street, past Manhole and Berlin. We walked past twenty-four-hour diners and Dunkin' Donuts, the still-crowded Belmont el station. We *walked*. We held hands and we *walked*.

"I'm just not sure I'm talented enough," I said.

"Give yourself a break," Mike said.

Then he gave me the cheesy pop quiz that he gave whenever he sensed my actor insecurity.

"Who's the smartest girl I know?"

"I am." I said this reluctantly.

"The prettiest?"

"Me."

"Who's my best friend in the world and the love of my life?"

"Me." By now I was smiling like an absolute dope.

He opened the car door for me.

I'm better, these days, at knowing if I'm good or if I'm bad at something, when I'm wrong and when I'm right, and I certainly don't expect my boyfriend to be the judge, but then I really wasn't sure, and Mike's opinion mattered because he was the smartest, most talented person I had met up until that point. He was a true artist, even then, and I loved the theater, and him, but they required so much that there was very little left for me.

* * *

We sped down the Kennedy Expressway that night with the windows rolled down, and Mike serenaded me at the top of his lungs. When the song ended, he said, "I guess Jesus is driving the car home tonight." I laughed, even though I felt slightly afraid. I mean, there was some sweet pleasure in all of this, right? I was being serenaded—we had our very own theater company in the city we loved most. I could not see yet that we looked just like the characters we played, flying down the expressway. The insecure young woman just out of school trying to figure out her place in the world, and the larger-than-life Peter Pan, delighting in his terrible choices. All I could think of was the actors I'd be working with, who were as good, or better, than any I'd ever seen. That perfect dialogue jumping off the page. Our slowly materializing story.

"I'm going to marry the shit outta you," Mike said to me. "I'm going to marry Maggie Andersen!" he cried out the window.

Then I held on to his thigh, felt his muscles tighten as he picked up speed.

"I think this is the happiest I'll ever be in my life," I said.

I was still thinking about obituaries.

CHAPTER 3

2003

In the waiting room, Mike's father, Frank Thornton, woke me and said they had ruled out Guillain–Barré syndrome. Mike had had a spinal tap, one of the most painful medical procedures, and hadn't felt a thing. He couldn't feel pain or temperature, anything below his neck. The doctors thought it might be a stroke of the spinal cord. They thought he might never walk again.

"What's a spinal stroke?" I asked.

Frankie was crying again.

"It's noon, baby. You've been here all night. I'll have someone take you home. Take a shower, take a nap. We'll call you if anything changes."

Frank Thornton, who had taken us out for pizza every Wednesday because he knew we didn't have any money. Francis Joseph Thornton, who had retired just the week before with thirty years on the job and one son in the world.

* * *

The next twenty-four hours are a blur, as they say. I know a few things: I went home and changed my clothes, called my places of employment and left messages. Previously, I had called in and said I was sick when I wasn't, told my boss I'd had a root canal when I hadn't, but this time I didn't lie. I called our friends on Monday morning. (Some of them left work early over the next few days to visit us at the hospital. Tabitha and Shannon brought coffee and doughnuts for the family room, and a care package just for me. Northwest Side women always know what to do, even the supposedly mean, hard-drinking ones.) Mike's childhood best friend, Rob Keleghan, came to take me back to the hospital on Monday afternoon, and I know that our living room was suddenly a sad place because Mike wasn't sitting on the couch playing video games or reading *The New Yorker*.

I didn't know how to prepare Rob Keleghan, who hadn't seen Mike yet. Rob had been a sweet and nerdy boy in high school, but in college, he went frat boy, and that identity seemed to be following him into early adulthood, so it was strange and sad to see in his eyes that he'd been crying all morning. He picked up my overnight bag, put his arm around my shoulders, and walked me down the stairs, gingerly. I felt like the widow already, even though I'd never been married, and Rob was taking the responsibility of me so seriously that I wanted to cry for him, this boy wearing a suit just a little too baggy.

We entered Resurrection Medical Center, and I said, "Michael Thornton," but this time we were given neon-orange ICU visitor's badges instead of front-row theater tickets. We rode the elevator up to a visitors' room where Mike's extended family urged his mother, Rita, to have some pizza or some fruit or some baked goods. Anything—just eat. The room was filled with trays of food and cops in uniform, cheap paintings, and paisley furniture.

"Maggie," one of his aunts said. "Make sure to wash your hands, and we can only go in a few at a time. Rob, can you wait, honey?"

Just then, Uncle Jerry came out of the room. Jerry was Frank's older brother who had infamously done two harrowing tours in Vietnam. "The priest is here," he announced, then he came over to kiss me.

"Sweetheart," he said in my ear. "This is worse than the war."

"We don't want him to know how bad it is," Mrs. Thornton said to me. "We don't want him to be scared. No crying in there, okay?"

I washed my hands and prepared to put on a show for my boyfriend. I walked toward the room feeling tightly pressed between his parents, trying not to hear the terrible coughs of the dying and the desperate sobbing of those they would leave behind. When I walked into Mike's private room, he opened his eyes and they really did light up for a second. His mother pretended to pout. "Why didn't your eyes light up like that for me?"

I hurried over to the side of the bed, kissed up and down his face.

"Is this hurting him?" I asked the nurse.

"No," she said. "You're fine."

I was fine, but he was barely breathing. His face was pale and covered in a film of sweat. The priest came into the room and as it turns out, he knew Mike's parents from the old neighborhood. I held Mike's hands that didn't move anymore as his parents whispered with the priest.

"Michael, I hope from now on you'll be joining me at church," his mother said, trying very hard to maintain her composure.

I could swear that he was rolling eyes at me, but no: They stayed closed as the priest read over him from a Bible. The priest blessed his head with the oil on his thick fingers. "Amen," I said and crossed myself even though I had a feeling I was done with God now. And then I was angry with myself for *not* believing. Maybe if I believed, his eyes would open again. What if they never looked at me again? The thought panicked me because no one had ever looked at me the way he had. He once looked at me naked and sprawled on the bed after the annual Christmas party and said softly, "You have the most beautiful body I have ever seen." He didn't stop looking for a long time.

* * *

The phone on the wall in the family room rang and Mrs. Thornton asked me to answer it. "I don't want to talk to anyone," she said.

I picked it up.

"Maggie?" Sheldon cried. "Are you there? What *happened*?"

I slid down to the floor.

"They just read last rites," I said.

Rob Keleghan, in his baggy suit, broke down sobbing.

* * *

I told Mike's mom I would stay bedside so she could get some sleep in the family room. The doctor said we had a few more days to wait and see. Frankie made arrangements to go out for a beer, which is what we all agreed he needed. I sat beside Mike and rubbed his hands with lotion.

"Sheldon called," I said. "He was crying."

I checked his face for a reaction.

"Robby was here. Selling houses like crazy. I think he's gonna be rich. But we will be too, don't worry."

Still nothing.

"I wonder who else got cast in the Pirandello play. You'd better hurry up and get better, right? I think rehearsals start pretty soon."

I paused.

"Yeah, I think I'll just stay here. I don't want to go back to the apartment without you."

I couldn't stop rambling because his silence scared me as much as all the beeping. It was the longest I'd ever gone without talking to Mike, and we'd been talking since I was seventeen, and now I was twenty-five years old. Sometimes I wasn't even sure if my opinions were worthwhile unless I tried them out on him first. I asked the nurses what the numbers on the monitors meant and one of them showed me how to suction the saliva from his mouth when he made that awful choking sound. The doctors were still saying spinal infarction—C4—severe paralysis, likely affecting all four limbs. They didn't know if he'd ever breathe on his own again, but I wanted to know about his mind. There was a time he felt threatened because I had a crush on a young scientist, and the next time we saw the guy, Mike knew a good deal about quantum physics. By the end of their conversation, the physicist said, "I thought you were an actor." Mike had a photographic memory, an uncanny ability to comprehend anything, and quickly. He was a thinker, and a good one, which was why I felt honored that he had chosen me.

The priest returned with Mrs. Thornton.

"A prayer before bedtime," she said.

Behind them, in the hallway, I saw my father.

"Your father's here to take you home, honey."

Al Andersen looked into the hospital room and I don't know what he saw. His daughter sitting beside her boyfriend on life support, I guess. The boyfriend he hadn't totally trusted, the boyfriend he hadn't wanted her to live with, alongside the priest he admired and feared.

"Hello, Father," he said. He entered the room and hugged Rita Thornton, then he turned and looked at me.

"Let's go home," my father said.

"I don't want to," I said, not moving my eyes from Mike.

I was an adult woman now, living on my own, working two jobs to make ends meet and still making time for a life in the theater. I had been happy in the apartment, sometimes; I couldn't go back to my parents. And yet I didn't want to be alone. But what if Mike didn't make it through the night?

"Go home, honey," Mrs. Thornton said. "We'll see you tomorrow bright and early."

"You haven't slept," my father said.

I bent in half to kiss my boyfriend.

My father came closer and it only made me crazy, to be pulled between these two men again, the art-filled life with Mike and the comfort and familiarity of my working-class family. My father pulled me away because I was making a scene now, crying loudly and saying, "It's not fair."

"I know, babe," he said. "Stop now. You're upsetting Rita."

I looked into the room once more and saw Mike's eyes fly open; he saw me leaving and he did look afraid. Then my father and I got lost in the hospital somehow, took a wrong turn, and ended up in a laundry room in the basement. Industrial-sized washing machines churned with soiled bedsheets and stained pillowcases.

"Think," my father said. "How do we get out?"

"How am I supposed to know?"

"Great. Now we're lost. What the fuck is goin' on around here?"

We didn't say much on the way home. I rolled down my window to get some air. We got stuck at several red lights, and my father turned the radio on and off compulsively. But when we arrived at his apartment, he did seem to relax a little. He led me to my mother, who had made up the couch in the basement with cartoon pillows and sheets.

I lay down in my jeans, and she covered me with two blankets.

"Right to sleep and not a peep," my father whispered: the comfort of my childhood.

Then he went upstairs to the kitchen and sat with my mother.

"How does he look?" she asked, when she thought I couldn't hear.

"Like he's gonna fuckin' die," my father said.

CHAPTER 4

2001

My father openly resented my decision to be an actor, and didn't understand my rehearsing five nights a week at the park where I'd once gone for summer camp. It didn't seem lucrative or professional, and he'd been working since the age of fourteen, shipped off to Vietnam at seventeen, and had his own apartment by the age of nineteen, so he viewed my acting career as an extended adolescence. I knew, though, somewhere in my dummy twenty-three-year-old heart, that working with Sheldon Patinkin would be a serious education.

We rehearsed *Boys' Life* with Sheldon in a rented park district room for several weeks. Usually I met him outside on a bench where he sat, legs crossed, smoking a cigarette, inhaling and exhaling slowly. He's one of the only people I've ever met who still made smoking look elegant. He was in his sixties at the time, but appeared ageless. His voice was smoke-damaged already, but no one could tell because he spoke so softly. His eyes were sometimes bloodshot from his steady diet of high-end pot, but strangers didn't know because he wore tinted glasses. After growing up in an upper-middle-class Jewish family on the West Side of Chicago, he never looked like he belonged among the crappy park district folding chairs and dingy linoleum floors, but, every day, he seemed genuinely happy to be with us. Every day, he kissed us on our foreheads.

Once in a while, he said to Mike, "How *much* did you drink last night? Take it easy."

One Saturday afternoon, one of our first days off book, he got impatient with me during scene work.

"Maggie, that line is supposed to be *funny*!"

Shortly after, he got impatient with Connolly, whose voice was usually several decibels too loud.

"You're at a ten," Sheldon said. "I need you at a seven."

"Lynda," he said. "This is the best I've ever seen you."

When we had exhausted his patience, or when he was stuck, he would say he had to "feed the meter" and we all knew what that meant. We worked the scenes over and over until the lines felt natural in our mouths, until we could find all the nuance in the language. After the first stumble-through, when he laughed at all the right parts, it felt like we'd won the lottery, but he also reminded us that, during the run, we shouldn't depend on laughter.

"You can't hear a smile," he said, then he looked at us to make sure we'd understood.

Mike suggested we all go to a bar that night and celebrate.

"Sheldon? Join us for a beer?"

"I don't drink beer," Sheldon said with disgust. "But if you offer me bourbon, I won't say no."

The Southport Corridor had almost completely gentrified by 2001, but we chose one of the remaining dive bars. The bartender, an unhealthily thin woman with a shock of red hair, sat on a barstool and filed her nails, pretending she didn't see us. I recognized the situation immediately, tried to get her attention anyway.

"No cosmos," she said without looking at me.

The attitude was a result of the neighborhood's recent gentrification, I knew; she was protecting herself and her customers. The working guys just wanted some peace and quiet after a long day, and they were more often getting interrupted by bourgeois types who complained about the liquor selection and the smoke. People who had raised families in the neighborhood suddenly felt like their way of life was being judged, or worse, like they weren't wanted, and like they weren't part of the beautification project. This had never happened in Mike's neighborhood, so he didn't completely get it.

"What the fuck?" he said to me.

“You know Mary Gladych, don’t you?” I asked the bartender.

“Mary?” She brightened. “How do you know Mary?”

“She’s my aunt,” I said. “You’re Cheryl, right? I’m Maggie Andersen, Al’s daughter”

Cheryl ended up buying us a round then. I told her who Sheldon was and she got his autograph for her son. I asked her if the yups were driving her nuts and she told me they were *mostly* harmless, then she told me a few of the sadder stories.

“Hey, life’s depressing,” she said. “We’re just doing the best we can.” Then she said, “Ah, fuck it,” and showed me pictures of her grandchildren.

Most of the time, in the company of actors, my working-class background made me feel inadequate. I became keenly aware, when I was around people who had not grown up in Chicago or kids who’d had help from their parents, of the educational gaps and financial disparities. But on that day, I was strangely proud of everything I had inherited, and Mike seemed to be too.

We sat at a long table, and while the others talked about the most revealing rehearsal moments and their favorite lines, I asked Sheldon about his life. He told me about starting his professional training as a young teenager and the profound sadness of being labeled an ingénue. He made jokes about his cousin, Mandy Patinkin, and still felt wounded by the No Jews Allowed signs of his adolescence.

“Those fucking pricks,” he said.

At the end of a night of appetizers, pizza, and pitchers of beer, we asked for the check, and Cheryl told us Sheldon had picked up the whole thing. We walked him to his car, and he hugged and kissed each one of us. Mike, Brendan, Lynda, Connolly, me.

“I love you all,” he said to us, at the corner of Addison and Southport.

He was exactly the director I needed at the time, one who would hold me to high standards, and take me seriously before I deserved it. After rehearsing for several weeks, we opened *Boys’ Life* at the Kinahan Theater in Hyde Park. We were so green, we hadn’t known that most theaters have to be rented at least a year in advance, but Sheldon’s name secured the University of Chicago space for us. He had started undergrad there at the age of fifteen, but more impressively, he had met Paul Sills at this very theater, and they had gone on together to form The Second City and *Second City Television* (*SCTV*). Sheldon and John Candy started The Second City Toronto, and forty years later, The Second City was a comedy mecca with locations all over North America and had launched the careers of actors like Bill Murray, Steve Carell, Keegan-Michael Key, and Tina Fey. Even though we were green, we knew we were walking on hallowed ground.

On opening night in December of 2001, Mike and I cut across the Gothic campus together, holding hands and wearing our game faces as we navigated icy cobblestone pathways. The campus was located in Hyde Park, inspired by the London park of the same name, and its first lecture hall had been erected in 1892. It was the picture of timeless elegance, with snow-frosted quads and towering limestone academic buildings, and our show posters were wrapped around the famous Oxford light poles. I obsessed over the architecture, but also worried that no one would come, or worse, that the world would come and I'd fail right in front of them.

We didn't say a word to each other as we walked through the lobby of chandeliers, stained glass, and arched doorways, decorated with black-and-white posters of Mike and Brendan. *Boys' Life, Directed by Sheldon Patinkin—Three Weekends Only!* In the poster, Mike and Brendan were laughing and young, totally untouched by real grief. Our logo, an outstretched hand, fit perfectly in the bottom left-hand corner. *The Gift Theatre Company.* I ran my finger across my name on the cast list, hoping this would be something I could show to my grandchildren, and I couldn't wait for my parents to see it, even though my father had been complaining about the drive to the South Side and the parking situation at U of C.

When we entered the two-hundred-seat black box theater, I inhaled. Mike and I looked at each other and smiled—it still smelled like sawdust and paint. Designers and actors scrambled around the theater with blue lighting gels and costumes slung over their shoulders. Sheldon sat in the last row with his director friend and former student David Cromer, who was currently directing on Broadway. The sound designer played cues from a booth ten feet above us. I was starting to feel nauseous, and Mike whispered to me, as if he could sense it: "You're a vessel for that character when you're not a bundle of neuroses." Then he went off to his private actor zone, where I knew I wasn't welcome. In the dressing room, Mike nervously cough-gagged, Brendan ate a giant falafel wrap, Connolly drank coffee from a stainless-steel thermos and read the newspaper, and Lynda took her time with her makeup. Beside her, on the vanity: an exploding bouquet from Sheldon, for all of us. I sat alone and wrote in my journal, tried to write a poem for Sheldon and capture the details of the campus. I wrote several times, "I am a vessel." (You remember I was twenty-three, right?) The stage manager stopped in and gave us a five-minute call.

Sheldon poked his head in and said, "Should I tell you who's here?"

"No," Mike said, firmly.

After blowing his final kisses, Sheldon disappeared, and it was our show now. There were no critics at the Gift's first show because we hadn't yet known how to properly invite them, but university students had come after seeing the posters all over campus. Competing actors had come in the hopes that we'd fail, and Hyde Parkers had come in the hopes that we'd succeed and they could say they knew us when. A few casting directors and agents had come, invited by Sheldon and eager to recruit new talent, and my extended family and Mike's had come, in the case that no one else did.

The audience volume seemed to rise in intensity. People laughed and unwrapped candy. Someone asked, "Now, who wrote this again?" The preshow music started to fade and the house lights dimmed. I wanted to kiss Mike, hard, but my urges felt childish compared to the complete concentration on his face. Brendan and Mike marched out to the stage, and I listened to the first scene, the one I had listened to so many times, but this time, there was a laugh track, an audience who was surprised by the lines that I was immune to now. The audience guffawed and the actors held naturally. I listened to Brendan, really listened to him, and as the scene progressed, I grew increasingly more nervous and excited to see him. Use it, I thought. Remember that she's lonely. But I didn't know loneliness then. I lived in a two-bedroom apartment with my mother, father, and both my sisters, and was rarely away from my boyfriend longer than a day. Life was chaotic, but never lonely. That would all come later. Brendan turned to look at me, and by the time he and I were in the room together with the coat pile on the bed, I didn't even know who I was. Some neurotic woman who had a slew of tics, a woman who had slept with him a few times, and who felt perfectly comfortable in this hideous patchwork dress.

In the middle of the scene, I gave a monologue about my life being a mess. I remembered the night before and tapped into the way I felt as Brendan and I lay on the floor of his studio apartment at dawn, singing our way through *Blood on the Tracks* while Mike paced the room, calling liquor stores and pizza joints, drunkenly insisting that somebody had to be able to deliver pizza and a six-pack of beer to him at this hour. "My life's a mess," I told Brendan, and I think that he believed me. When he pushed me down onto the bed, I clung to him; he was all I had now in this big room of strangers. The audience disappeared and I swam around with him in a sea of wool and fleece.

After my first and only scene, I watched the rest of the show through a slit in the curtains. The play moved quickly through several scenes, and I knew every choice Mike had made for his character; he always told me in bed late at night. When it came time for the final scene, the wedding, we rushed out to set the table. We half filled the rocks glasses with iced tea, dumped our real cigarette butts into the ashtrays, balled up some cloth napkins, and left the stage. When the lights came up, Brendan and Mike were wearing rumpled suits and looking fairly drunk. Their married friend came over to their table to shake hands, and the scene quickly escalated into a frenzy because Mike's character was a class-A dick who did nothing but make asshole comments about his friend's wife. Brendan left to dance the Hokey Pokey and Mike was left onstage alone. From where I was standing, the stage looked like a diorama. Lynda came out to tell Mike he wasn't the worst man in the world. Lights out. It was a good play, and I still believe that the eruption of applause was fully earned. We took our first bows, then a second. I squinted out into the audience and couldn't find a single empty seat. When my father stood and put his fingers in his mouth to whistle, Mike and Brendan held up their hands and pumped their fists. They looked out into the audience, laughing and exhilarated. We sold out the entire run, even without the critics.

After the show, my father said, "Hell of a show, guys. You didn't tell me Sheldon Patinkin was directing!"

* * *

In Sheldon's luxury apartment on Lake Shore Drive, we celebrated opening night. Not only did he lead us through our first professional production, he filled his refrigerator with fancy beer before the craft-beer craze had even come to Chicago. He put out his best cheeses, wine for tasting, his vintage glasses. When he passed around a gorgeous blue-and-white bowl rimmed with expertly rolled joints and I declined, he laughed.

He said, "I never would've guessed that about a woman who loves Bob Dylan as much as you do."

"But it's his lyrics I love," I said. "It's his love stories."

Sheldon revealed to us, that night, the cover of his new book, and when he showed us the photographs on his museum wall, we recognized many of the faces, and he told stories to accompany them. There he was holding a baby Anna Shapiro, hugging a young Eugene Levy, laughing with Catherine O'Hara, smoking a cigarette with John Mahoney, sitting between John Candy and his wife at a supper club. He detailed each one's talent but never mentioned his own. After we'd all eaten, he played Second City audition tapes and old episodes of *SCTV* in his viewing room. We all laughed, and as I sat there beside him on the couch, I let my head fall onto his shoulder. He looked straight ahead at the screen and smiled wistfully.

Throughout that rehearsal process and on the occasion of opening night, he modeled so many things for us: the value in taking young people seriously, an appreciation for beauty, the importance of being a good citizen of the theater world. He had always famously said it was better to be an asshole than a chickenshit, but I never once saw him as either.

CHAPTER 5

2003

I went back to the hospital the next morning and the next. President Bush announced the invasion of Iraq and we watched the images on television. A couple weeks after the stroke, a small man came to remove the feeding and breathing tubes. He warned us that Mike may not be able to speak at first; we didn't know yet if his mind had been affected. The man rolled Mike away and I thought of all we had taught each other. He had introduced me to Jerzy Grotowski, the Coen brothers, David Foster Wallace, and Ntozake Shange. I had introduced him to Maxim Gorky, Danny Hoch, and the heroes of the Harlem Renaissance. We had had long discussions about James Joyce, the Kennedys, and Christopher Hitchens. I was sometimes more articulate with Mike than I was in rehearsal rooms, especially if I was around actors from the Ivy League schools. Mike translated for me when I couldn't speak as beautifully as they did. Once I got frustrated in a rehearsal room and heard myself swearing like a David Mamet character. When one of the actresses in the room looked uncomfortable, Mike explained: "She's a yeller. She had to fight to be heard growing up."

Once Mike had been wheeled back into the room, the nurse touched his shoulder and said, "Michael, do you know who the president is?"

I waited; I held my breath.

"He's a monster," Mike whispered, and I knew his mind was still intact. It did not, it would not, die. The body was more trouble.

* * *

In a former life, when Mike and I used to watch movies in his parents' basement, we returned often to the 1992 film adaptation of Steinbeck's *Of Mice and Men*, starring Gary Sinise and John Malkovich, two of the founding members of Steppenwolf Theatre. Malkovich's Lennie was a sweet and lumbering simpleton who didn't know his own strength; Sinise's George was his guardian and protector. Lennie would get into trouble, and they would have to go together on the run.

While they camped out under the stars, Lennie would say, "Tell me—like you done before."

"Tell you what?"

"About the rabbits."

Then George would tell him in a once-upon-a-time voice about the life they would someday share, with a country house, hot meals on the table, and a band of pet rabbits. These friends of so many years could tell each other this unlikely fairy tale and convince themselves it was truth.

* * *

"You've got to get him to the Rehab Institute," Mary, the ICU nurse, whispered. "I could lose my job for saying that, but it's true. This floor isn't for Michael. He's a kid; he needs aggressive therapy. The people upstairs are all geriatrics. The truth? They're just not going to get any better."

Mary's brother had been injured in a diving accident when he was nineteen years old, and they had told him he would never walk again, but after a few weeks at the Rehab Institute, he did.

"Miracles happen there," she said, and then she left the room.

Mike looked at me from his bed, where he lay propped up on three pillows. His arms and legs still hadn't moved. His father called them the dead ducks.

"Sounds like RIC's the place," Mike said. I nodded in agreement.

Mrs. Thornton shook her head and fished around in her purse. "Her brother walks on a cane."

"Mom!" Mike cried.

"They saved your life here. I just don't agree that it's a second-rate hospital. I prefer a Catholic hospital. I like the priests."

"I promised I'd go back to church when this is over."

"Okay, honey. She gave me a brochure. I'll call and set up a tour."

"Mag, you go too."

"Michael Patrick, you have no faith in me."

"I want a second opinion, that's all."

The doctors prescribed aggressive therapy for recovery from spinal infarction, and I didn't completely understand what that meant, but the medical journals and survivor blogs said it was necessary. One blogger wrote, "I had a spinal stroke too. I was thirty-one years old. The cause was ultimately my birth control pills. After my stroke, the cardiologist told me I naturally had 'thick' blood and that the pill put me over the edge. With aggressive therapy, I learned to walk again, and my husband stood by me the whole time. He's my angel. I am almost 100% recovered, but sometimes I do wet the bed! The key is to get aggressive therapy right away." Aggressive therapy sounded awful, but I felt privileged to be part of the decision. I would be a good reporter, I would take notes, I had been trained for this, hadn't I? I would remember it all.

The following Friday, I waited on the front porch of our bungalow, watching fathers walk by, holding their daughters' hands, seeing them off to school, and I wanted Mike to have his chance. The church bells of Saint Constance rang out, and I hoped he would get into the Rehab Institute of Chicago. I had read there was a long waiting list. Please let him get better, I said to an abstract god.

Mrs. Thornton pulled up to the house and, when I got in the car, handed me a granola bar and a travel mug of hot tea. I couldn't wait to get downtown and see this miracle hospital, I told her. I told her I hoped Mike wouldn't have to stay at the rehab hospital too long because I just wanted him to come home. I hated sleeping in the apartment alone, I told her. But anyway, I hadn't been downtown in some time and the sun had finally emerged. The skyline made me feel like I was seeing the city for the first time: glass facades, art deco, and gleaming white. The tower of the Jewelers' Building and the Sears Tower antennae guided us, and we rocketed toward them now. These skyscrapers were all the realization of someone's impossible dream, I thought. While I was looking straight ahead, Mrs. Thornton pointed out her favorite churches along the way, and asked me what their names were.

"Saint Sylvester's," I said. "Saint Stan's. Saint Helen's is just over there. That one's Saint Nicholas, I think. That neighborhood's called the Ukrainian Village."

I loved playing tour guide, especially to Rita Thornton. I didn't know how to make a Christmas feast the way she did, but I knew the city we lived in in a way that she did not, and that made me feel like I had something to offer.

"You know," she said. "I don't really like downtown. Too many big buildings. You do have beautiful churches though."

The steeples looked European. They looked as old as hope.

"Do you pray for Michael, Maggie?" Mrs. Thornton asked.

"Every day I do."

She looked relieved then. She was a good driver, I realized that day. She steered us through the chaotic streets of downtown and parked at the Chicago Avenue firehouse, where Frankie knew a guy. We were walking toward the hospital when she said, "Now *this* is a nice area."

"Yeah," I answered. "Lakefront property."

"Did you and Michael come down here a lot?" Mrs. Thornton asked.

"We went to the Redhead Piano Bar for our last anniversary. The piano man played all our requests."

It made me sad, the way she listened so intently to details about her son's former life, trying to find clues.

"I would just hate to live in one of those big buildings," she said.

When we stopped in front of the hospital, a well-groomed woman in a pastel suit approached us. We must've looked confused. The valets scurried about, taking keys and parking handicapped vans. An old man got out of his van and onto his walking canes, struggled up to the hospital doors. If he could make a recovery, Mike could too. After all, Mike had youth on his side; that's what the doctors kept saying.

Mrs. Thornton was thin for fifty-five, but her khakis sagged on her since the stroke. Every day, she told me how many more pounds she had lost and then stretched her waistband to show me how roomy her pants were. I wasn't losing weight. I was still eating three meals a day and that made me feel like maybe I wasn't suffering enough.

The woman in the pastel suit shook our hands and introduced herself as Anne-Marie, our caseworker.

"Rita Thornton, Michael's mom."

"Maggie Andersen, his girlfriend."

"Maggie's our angel," Mrs. Thornton said.

These were the things I had always wanted her to say.

"Michael's very lucky," Anne-Marie said, but I didn't think so.

Mrs. Thornton continued. "We're trying to convince her to quit her job so she can be with Michael all the time."

She said that often in those days, and it always made me uncomfortable, even though I understood the sentiment and was honored to be one of the few people Mike actually wanted to see. However, something rankled me about the choices I was given as a woman in her mid-twenties: companion and caretaker, or overworked and underpaid. The caseworker showed us to the elevator bank where the doors took a long time to open and close, and inside, they were mirrored. She explained that this was a courtesy for the wheelchair drivers.

"We won't be needing a wheelchair," Mrs. Thornton said with self-assurance.

When we arrived on the fourth floor, we were greeted by kelly-green velvet couches and glossy medical journals on coffee tables. I circled the room and studied RIC's various awards and distinctions, success story after success story. The newspaper articles were perfectly framed and matted—this is where all the stars from the news had come. I had wondered what had happened to that football player who broke his neck in last year's playoffs, and to the cop who had been shot in the head while trying to protect his local bank. Well, they were here, learning how to walk again!

The caseworker took us up to the seventh floor, the spinal-cord injury floor, where there currently weren't any vacancies. The patients, we were told, ranged in age, and suffered from a variety of injuries. There was a teenage girl whose head and eyes rolled like a drunk's. She breathed noisily through a tube. Her mother pushed her around the floor and played Celine Dion on a small tape recorder. The more mobile patients sat around in a community lounge playing cards, and they all looked close to my age. One of the girls was especially pretty, and her legs stayed perfectly still while she wheeled around in her chair, dealing playing cards to her friends. I worried that Mike would fall in love with her. They would fall in love, I knew it, and he would feel like I didn't understand him anymore. They would rehabilitate together and move into our apartment. I resented the girl immediately, and started to wonder if Mike would use a wheelchair like her. Would he drool like some of them did? Would his legs be still like a statue's? It was then I realized: He was not going to be able to walk or dance or drive or give me piggyback rides or ride his bike. For a while, at least. For a little while. The caseworker asked if I was okay. Hold on, I thought. But just a few days ago, he was marching in a parade, climbing on and off of floats, and now he was going to be one of these people in a wheelchair? People being dealt lousy cards? People who got hit by drunk drivers and drove drunk themselves, who went skiing in the winter and surfing in the summer? People who got shot and stabbed and played football? In that moment, my life split in half. Everything would now be categorized as before or after this day.

Anne-Marie said she would take us down to the fifth floor now, the pediatrics ward, where they did have a couple of vacancies. We took the stairs because it felt like we owed it to the card players. I held on to the banister, and saw spots in front of my eyes. Anne-Marie showed us a corner room with an incredible view of Navy Pier—I could make out Chicago Shakespeare, where Mike had performed, and the Ferris wheel we had ridden together. But it was still a hospital room. When I looked down, I saw Lake Michigan in various shades of blue and green. The waves rolled back and forth.

"How long will he have to live here?" I asked.

"That all depends," Anne Marie said. "Could be two weeks, could be two months. The initial diagnosis is always two weeks. If he shows progress, we'll extend his stay."

Oh, he'll make progress, I thought. He'll be here for a year if he has to be. You just wait and see. You have no idea who you're fucking dealing with, Anne-Marie.

Back in the hallway of the fifth floor, I was greeted by children in small wheelchairs. Children were supposed to have full heads of hair and fully functioning legs, I thought. This floor was most definitely hell. One little girl hobbled around on bandaged feet and I asked Anne-Marie for her story.

"Oh, that's Alice," she said. "She was recently adopted from Russia. Did you hear about that fire on the North Shore? Those were her adopted parents."

"Are they dead?"

"Well, her father died saving her. Her mother's around here somewhere. You see, her toes are all burned off."

Alice: shoulder-length hair with straight-across bangs, olive skin.

"Hi, Alice," Anne-Marie said. When Alice said hello back, her voice sounded like my grandmother who smokes three packs a day.

Anne-Marie showed us the lounge where Mike would eat lunch from now on and have occupational therapy with Becky, who would teach him how to use his hands again. She would help him dress in the morning, reteach him to wash and shave. Currently, we were spoon-feeding him, but at RIC, they had special technology that might allow him to feed himself. The mission of RIC was to help him to reenter society "in his new state." Nearby, a pixie-looking therapist sat with a young boy with a bandaged head.

"Today is Monday," she said. "So what day is it?"

He looked out the window and traced shapes on the table.

"I don't know. I can't remember."

I recognized Nickelodeon on the flat-screen television. The therapist asked the boy what his name was. Again, he didn't know. My stomach knotted up, so I focused on a wall where I wouldn't see any more children. But on the wall, someone had painted a giant marquee that said *The Theatre* in cursive writing with little yellow light bulbs surrounding it. I pointed to the marquee and started to cry and, once I started, couldn't stop. The caseworker ushered us out quickly and said she would do her very best to get Mike a bed. She handed Mrs. Thornton a card and encouraged her to call with any questions. She raced through the rest of her routine, saying she would have the paperwork faxed and together they would navigate the insurance. Actors' Equity had one hell of a bill to pay, in the end.

"I don't want him to have a bed there!" I cried in the elevator.

"Not there, Mrs. Thornton! Please!"

She must remember this hysterical scene, even now. And this mother, whose only son lay paralyzed in a hospital room, hugged his girlfriend so tightly that she might stifle the animal sounds of pain.

The elevator operator let us out at the first floor and said quietly, "Have a nice day." He looked as if he wished he knew more English.

Mrs. Thornton said, "This is the best place for him, Mag, and you know it." Now the roles were reversed.

We drove back to Resurrection in silence, past the gloomy old churches and billboards. I looked into other cars at happy people who may as well have been from the moon. When we pulled up in front of the intensive care unit, the sun didn't matter anymore. Mrs. Thornton took my face in her hands and said, "You tell him all the good things, Mag."

I nodded.

"Okay," she said. "Good girl."

I charged into the hospital, past the front desk. The security guards all recognized me now; I didn't even need a visitor's badge anymore, didn't even need to sign in and out. After taking the elevator upstairs, I scrubbed my hands until they turned red, then went straight to Mike's room before I lost my nerve. I was going to tell him about the view, I was going to tell him there were pretty girls and it was okay if he ran away with one of them, just as long as he got better. I was going to report back on all of the success stories and tell him how the hospital was right in the middle of things. We could go to Emilio's for tapas, have dinner wherever he wanted, and we'd put it all on a credit card. So what? In the middle of my rehearsing, I didn't think to ask at the nurses' station if anyone was with him.

A few feet from his door, I squinted my eyes and looked closer. Through a crack in the door, I saw the backside of a woman, a thick, sturdy woman in blue scrubs. Sometimes my eyes played tricks on me in the hospital. Sometimes comatose patients looked like they were reaching out to me. I usually tried to avoid looking inside at all, but this was Mike's room. I was sleep-deprived, but I knew this was his. Had they transferred him? I wondered. And if so, why had they not told me? What was that woman doing standing over him like that? I opened the door a little more and saw that a therapist was trying to help him sit up in bed, and it was requiring all of her strength. His body swayed back and forth, confused and unsteady, his head rolled, and then he fell backward. He had no balance, no spatial sense of himself, couldn't even sit up on his own. His hospital gown had come undone in all the chaos; his eyes were screwed tightly shut.

"Are you okay?" the therapist asked.

"I feel nauseous," he said. He was pouring sweat from the exertion.

"Just give me a minute," she said. "I'll check your blood pressure now."

He lay awkwardly on the bed, his body twisted, and one of his legs kicked out wildly. Then it shook so hard that even his face vibrated. His eyes were still closed.

"Spasms," the therapist said. "Do they keep you up at night? We'll get you medication for that."

He had never told me about the spasms, and I couldn't stop staring. When he finally opened his eyes, they flashed with humiliation. "Mag!" he cried out, and I pulled the door quickly closed.

For the past ten days, I had only seen him in bed. The nurses gave him sponge baths there, changed the soiled Chux underneath him, and he asked us to leave when they did. I fed him small bites while he was propped up on pillows, nearly choked him a couple of times. So: This was why we were going to RIC. Now I understood. I went back to the waiting room and prepared my speech, knowing I had to tell him the truth without crying, knowing I had to sugarcoat it just a little.

At noon, I went back to see him. He looked at me with a defeated expression, then looked away. I sat down next to him, took his hand and kissed it, held my lips there, and hoped he could feel them. I kissed his sharp nose, his stubbly cheeks, his smooth, unwrinkled forehead. I had no idea what I could offer, but I had always been good at telling stories. "I'm gonna tell about the rabbits, George," I said. We moved into the Rehabilitation Institute a few days later.

CHAPTER 6

2003

We had held ensemble auditions for the Gift's second season just weeks before Mike's stroke. Jon Berry, an up-and-coming young director, had agreed to direct *Six Characters in Search of an Author*, one of our dream projects, as long as Mike played the role of the Director. (Everyone else would have to audition with the general public.) Mike had gone Equity shortly after *Boys' Life*, which means he was invited to join the union and had to be paid, unlike the rest of us. He had been performing at the bigger houses, while the rest of us did Gift shows for the love of it.

After the initial success of *Boys' Life*, we had produced *Orestes 2.0* at the Chopin, a legendary Polish theater in Wicker Park. Charles Mee, the playwright, had been crippled by polio as a child, and famously wrote fragmented, copy-and-paste plays that reflected his world back to him. This fever dream of a play mashed up interviews with poets and porn stars and housewives with an ancient Greek play as it told the story of Orestes and Electra, who murdered their mother. In the end, it felt like a circus of philosophical ideas played with youthful intensity, and of course, a group of recent college grads found the material thrilling, if only for its shock value. Mike chose this material for his directorial debut, cast Brendan as Orestes, me and Lynda as two of the evil nurses, and Connolly as one of the more heartbreaking soldiers. In Kerry Reid's review, she wrote that "a quartet of damaged soldiers and trio of sadistic nurses provide sharply defined choral commentary [on the central story] even when it's overlapping." Her review also provided a particularly helpful pull quote: "Thornton's assured ensemble delivers."

After *Orestes 2.0*, we swung to the other end of the spectrum just to show we could do it, I think, and produced a historical drama entitled *The Countess*, about the breakup of the art critic John Ruskin and his young wife. Mike cast Brendan as the homewrecker, and while the critic Justin Hayford didn't necessarily love the script, he wrote in his 2002 review, "Brendan Donaldson turns in a surprisingly affecting performance as Millais, speaking in a near monotone and delivering every line with mannered matter-of-factness yet communicating torrents of passion." To top off that first season, we did *County Fair*, a new play written by our co-artistic director, Will, Mike's playwright friend from the University of Iowa. I played a teenage hillbilly ingénue and Brendan my dead brother. Mary Shen Barnidge, a critic for the *Chicago Reader*, said the cast of *County Fair* "resisted the temptation to mock, portraying potential stereotypes with natural compassion and respect." To us, that was the highest compliment. We had momentum as a theater, and I wanted to stay on the ride. People had heard of us; they wanted to work with us and support us. *Six Characters in Search of an Author* was, I thought, the most perfect script we had chosen so far, and when the writing is that good, the acting hardly feels like work. Luigi Pirandello had written the script in 1921 and it was a gloriously inventive dramatization of the creative process. I wanted the role of the Stepdaughter, who laughed in men's faces and bossed around little boys, who called out falseness and resisted the idea of moral insanity. She had an urgent desire to control her own narrative and was the only one to successfully leave the group of Characters at the play's end. I wanted to be just like her.

Mike announced the news that the ensemble would have to audition for the guest director, along with the general public, at a Gift company retreat. We were all staying at a little cabin in Wisconsin that weekend, one with a fireplace and a farmhouse table. We woke early in the morning, shared bagels and coffee, then read scripts until two in the morning. By the end of the weekend, we had smoked a carton of cigarettes, drunk cases of beer, and we all had the same terrible cold. Mike had been pre-cast in *Six Characters*, he revealed after a couple beers, but the rest of the casting decisions were up to Jon Berry. Up until this point, we had cast shows ourselves, so when Mike made the announcement, I could feel everyone's discomfort.

"That's bullshit," I said, and the room went silent.

"The point of an ensemble," I said, "is that we work best with each other, so we get dibs *before* the general public. Have you read Steppenwolf's mission statement?"

"I have," Mike said. "Actually, I *attended* the School at Steppenwolf. However, our ensemble will appear more reputable if we bring in guest artists and work outside the company sometimes."

I was lazy about sending out headshots and auditioning outside of the Gift. Mike was attacking me for that, but also because I had publicly disagreed with him. I launched my full beer can at the sliding glass window and said, "This is no time for personal insults. I am not just your girlfriend. I'm a member of this company too." The beer spilled in streaks down the window. But the morning after my childish outburst, Mike announced that the ensemble would henceforth audition before the general public, and we documented it in our bylaws.

Jon Berry had seen me play the sadistic nurse in *Orestes 2.0* and the hillbilly ingénue in *County Fair*, and had waited outside the dressing room for me both times. "I'm so glad you haven't been typecast, dear," he said once. "You just get better with every show." I hoped my past performances would be enough for him to cast me. But when I showed up at the Griffin, a small storefront theater in Andersonville, a gay and lesbian neighborhood tinged with old-world Swedish charm, I felt a heightened sense of dread. I was up against my ensemble members with whom I had never competed, and all of the women wanted this role. I knew Mike was inside the theater, reading as the Director, and I had never auditioned for him so formally. I did my stretches in a room of ridiculously good-looking women, and tried to remember my last audition, what in the world had calmed me then. The next thing I knew, I was inside the theater with Mike and Berry. Mike sat on the set of the currently running show, wearing a waist-length rust-brown leather jacket and a new pair of jeans. He looked classically handsome and perfectly calm.

"Hello, Maggie," he said as if he were very happy to see me. But I couldn't enjoy the kinkiness—couldn't even pretend I was the new actress he was seeing for the first time. I couldn't relax because I was afraid that Berry would sense the truth about me, that I was a fraud with no formal training, that I had performed in almost every show so far and at some point, the subscribers would need a break. At some point, the critics would stop being so kind to me, right?

"Maggie," Berry said. "I would love for you to sing to us."

I thought as quickly as I could. "Sixteen Going on Seventeen" from *The Sound of Music*? I mean, I used to perform the gazebo scene with my sister. I used to dream in vignettes from *The Sound of Music* and wish for Rolf the Nazi to be my secret boyfriend. I always insisted on being Liesl and gave my sister notes on how to play Rolf.

"Okay," I said. "I'm ready."

In an unsteady voice, I sang about being sixteen and going on seventeen. I swear to God I heard Mike laughing. Berry leaned forward, smiling, nodding his head patiently. My knees knocked against each other and my mouth went dry, but still I went on singing about being totally unprepared to face a world of men.

"Great!" Berry interrupted. "Let's read a scene."

I wondered what Lynda had sung and knew I shouldn't have chosen the goddamn *Sound of Music*. When I held the script, my hands shook so violently that the words on the page blurred together. Mike, in an effort to help me, was especially playful during the reading, but I was stuck on the page. He nudged my chin up with his finger, looked me straight in the eyes, and said, "You're in search of a what?" But I couldn't shake the terror. He was so natural onstage, and I was trembling. We didn't even get through the scene.

"Thanks so much," Berry said. "We'll be in touch, Maggie."

As I exited stage left, I saw Mike looking down at the floor. I left the theater feeling two feet tall, and walked down Clark Street, where the world outside seemed irrelevant. Happy women holding hands and walking home with Swedish pastries, music blaring from local pickup joints. I got on the bus, surfed to the back row and sat down, listened to my headphones as I endured the evening traffic and watched the city go by slowly. Chicago looked gray and dirty, the snow had melted to reveal the curb litter, and I was going home alone. It was part of turning twenty-five, for me. No one was responsible for me anymore, I realized that year, a little later than most. Not fiscally and certainly not emotionally. Not my father or mother or Mike. And I was beginning to think I'd made some wrong turns along the way. I'd chosen a profession that made me crazy and a man who made me crazier, and I was getting tired of hearing myself complain about it.

When Mike came home late that night, I was angry to hear that Mary Fons, another company member and a friend of mine, had gotten the role. When he walked in, I was sitting in the dark, listening to "These Days" by Nico, a melancholic song about failure.

Mike flicked on the light.

"Ask if you can audition again," he said matter-of-factly. "He hasn't told her yet."

"Fuck you."

"Why are you yelling at me? What did *I* do?" But he wasn't really surprised; he was totally prepared for the argument.

He followed me, zigzagging around our small apartment as I called him a motherfucker, tried to blame him for my humiliation. I was angry because he wasn't sympathetic. I was angry because I could tell he was embarrassed of me. Ultimately, he was thinking of himself, the role he was slated to play, and his theater company's ambitious second season. But I knew him well enough to know that he also felt I was a reflection on him, and that I had disappointed him this time. Also, any time I failed, I took it out on him, because I knew that even when he felt insecure about an audition, which he rarely did, it never looked like what I had done tonight.

"I looked like an idiot," I said, and my voice broke.

And then his embarrassment disappeared, his tough love lost its force, and Mike Thornton hugged his girlfriend, who was a mess, a bundle of insecurities and nervous energy, maybe an actress, but maybe not.

"Bruiser," he said. "You kinda had a stroke up there tonight."

He started imitating me, shimmying around the room, shaking out his hands, making his teeth chatter.

"What song was that?" he asked incredulously. "Did you learn that at summer camp? Why didn't you just sing 'Happy Birthday'?"

I laughed harder and swatted at him. "It was *The Sound of Music*! Stop it!"

"Yeah, you totally stroked out," he said.

"Maggie," he said, sitting next to me on our couch. "I'll tell you again. I'm in love with you, but I'm even more in love with the future, the woman you'll become."

Before that night, I hadn't considered becoming that woman without him.

A few weeks after the stroke, I called Jon Berry to tell him Mike wouldn't be doing the show after all.

"I think you'd better find a replacement," I said. "Mike has some serious recovering to do."

Just a few weeks prior, my hands had shaken uncontrollably in front of this director, but after the stroke, I wasn't afraid of things like him anymore.

CHAPTER 7

2003

By the time Mike moved into RIC, our apartment and the Gift felt like a lifetime ago. The world outside the hospital felt like a performance, and we were now the passive spectators with shitty seats. During the week, I visited Mike at RIC, but there was a curfew because of morning therapy. On Saturday nights, we had sleepovers.

One Saturday night early on, I walked through the Gold Coast, where all the well-dressed, wealthy people lived. I carried a large deep-dish pizza, and the happy people looked like they may as well have been from outer space. Even on a cold night, Gibsons Steakhouse and Hugo's Frog Bar were full and the windows fogged romantically, while lines snaked down the block for Bar Chicago. The skyline seemed to be a spotlight for all of that health and money, for all of that good fortune. But on a darker street just a few blocks down, the luck seemed to change. At the number one rehabilitation hospital in the country, the patients used wheelchairs, walkers, and metal crutches, but they could still hear the soundtrack of Chicago—Koko Taylor blues, the piano player at the Redhead, the quick hiss of bus exhaust fumes, robotic announcements on the Brown Line. Every few minutes, a drowsy horse and carriage trotted past, but they moved more slowly now than they did when the sun was still shining.

I rode the elevator to the children's ward, the part of the hospital where little kids are sent after breaking their necks on trampolines or flying out of their car seats during terrible crashes. This was where Mike lived now. No one could say if he'd ever walk again; it could take up to two years, or it could never happen at all. At least he's young and strong, the neurologists say. One of them pulled me aside yesterday and asked, "Do you pray?"

So: this was where Mike lived now, and this was where we listened to our old friend, Saturday night. He had been in the hospital for only four weeks, but sometimes it felt like forty. He lay stiffly in a mechanical bed, looking more like a leading man after losing twenty pounds, but he lost the weight because he was being fed through a tube, and his face was perpetually lit up with a fever that came on when he contracted bladder infections from the catheter. Anyway, he *looked* healthy, and I tried to be grateful. Grateful is what I was learning to be. After all, he was alive, he could breathe on his own, he could speak. They removed the feeding tube and he was eating his favorite pizza for the first time tonight. Lou Malnati's: dripping ropes of cheese and buttery mushrooms. He ate half a slice instead of his usual three, and then he and I lay in a slightly raised, white-sheet hospital bed, looking out of our seventh-floor windows into an inky night sky. Two bodies tangled in the bedsheets, a stark contrast of black on white.

After a while Mike said, "We always wanted to live on the lake, didn't we?"

I thought about the frozen water and wished it would melt already. Then I got out of bed and started pinning up Get Well Soon cards and inspirational clichés on his bulletin boards. I straightened the displays of stuffed animals and cookie bouquets. (No flowers allowed at RIC.) When I looked over to see him watching me, I liked it.

The first time he had wanted to kiss me, several years ago, I sucked on a peppermint and looked at the floor.

"Why don't you spit that out?" he said, smiling.

"Because I'm nervous," I said. "Because I'm freaking the fuck out. I mean, what if I have halitosis? I think I have a fear of kissing. I really do. I think it dates back to the eighth grade—"

"Why don't you spit that out?" he repeated softly, and then he held out his hand.

* * *

After I finished with the bulletin-board additions, I got back into bed and tried to be still. I had always been the type to toss and turn, but stopped myself now because I didn't want to make him any more aware of his body's betrayals. On Saturday nights, I rarely fell asleep. Instead, I kept myself awake, making silly little lists in the dark. When this nightmare was over, would we go to London to see a show or Montego Bay to scuba dive? Also: What would we name our perfectly healthy children? Seamus, Jackson, Molly? When Mike woke on Sunday mornings, he usually had questions to answer. He would press the nurse's button, look at me, and say, "Jackson, Molly, Montego Bay. Now get out of here so I can have my diaper changed."

I sat up in bed and grabbed the half-empty box of pizza from the table over the bed, felt the heat of it still, then placed Mike's hand on the box.

"This is warm," I said.

The therapists had told me that this could help him to remember temperature.

"I still can't feel it," he said. "But if you think about it, that sort of makes me a superhero."

I walked up and down the hallway after that, offering leftover pizza to the nurses and PCTs and parents. Walking is controlled falling, they say at the hospital. Isn't that amazing?

When I got back to our room, I said, "Good dinner?"

"Best pizza I've ever had in my life."

Then I crawled back into bed and pressed the button on the bed's railing to see if there was anything good on TV. We were still learning about Saturday-night programming because we had never really stayed home on the weekends, but it was nice to go to bed early, and Saturdays were the only nights I could sleep over because there wasn't any therapy scheduled on Sunday. During the week, Mike had Play-Doh therapy, where the therapists would put it in his hands and encourage him to squeeze it. They lifted and stretched his legs and arms to see if they might remember how to move. The patients at RIC were so tight that their limbs felt like rubber bands about to snap; the stretching felt like burning, to Mike, because it confused the damaged nerves. During these sessions, his therapists often advised him to go to his special place.

"So where do you go, anyway?" I asked one day. "I mean, what is your special place? Why don't you scream like the others?"

"I pretend I'm in the Matrix," he said.

* * *

The nurses always knocked or laughed loudly to signal their arrival. They came every four hours to turn him, and that's so he wouldn't get bedsores.

"Hello! Good evening, Mr. Thornton!"

Maybe they made noise before entering the room because they didn't want to disturb us. Admittedly, we had been caught making out a few times—the luxury of not having a roommate. When they checked on Mike, that meant changing his diaper, draining his catheter, taking his blood pressure and temperature, giving him his spasm medication and baby aspirin. Their entrances were my cue to leave, and that was for Mike's dignity. We had learned about dignity on one of our first days at the hospital when Shirley, one of the patient care technicians, introduced herself and explained that she would be the one to bathe him tonight.

"I will use a sliding board to transfer you to this bed," she said. "I will wheel you into the shower room and bathe you," she said. "I will make the water the perfect temperature, soap you but not get you too slippery. I will use your shampoo and soap from home so that you can smell the way you like. I will not let you fall."

Shirley went into the shower room to turn on the hissing water, and Mike panicked.

"Tell her I'm not dirty," he said. "Please, Mag. I can't. If I start to slip off, what the hell is she gonna do? She's one hundred pounds soaking wet. I'll fall, I'll get hurt again. Just tell her you'll give me a sponge bath, okay? Promise me. Please. Sweetheart: I'm begging you."

But I didn't tell her any of that. Instead, when she asked me to help her undress him, I did exactly as she said. Mike looked like a statue as he lay pale and naked and perfectly still on the portable bed.

Shirley said again to Mike, "I will not let you fall."

As she wheeled him into the shower room, he glared at me and said, "Go home then. Just get out. What's the point of you being here anyway?"

Then I sat on the edge of his bed, while my guts churned, and chewed at my fingernails. I fantasized about going home and never again worrying about being late to my jobs or this terrible, terrible hospital. I fantasized about taking a bubble bath in our claw-foot tub and drinking a glass of champagne. I had only been able to drink legally for four years, I thought. There were still so many champagnes to discover.

Sometime during the shower, Shirley and Mike started cracking jokes and laughing. When she wheeled him out, all wrapped up in fresh towels and smelling like Irish Spring, he looked up at her and said, "This would be the life of Riley if it weren't for dignity, huh?"

She smiled as she taped up his giant lavender diaper and said, "You ain't never know who's gonna give you a glass of water."

Then she made her exit. I knew she must've been afraid too, with a man his size, but she just moved on to the next room, and I wondered how much they paid her, and I knew it wasn't enough.

"Ernie! Hey baby! You ready for your bath?"

Ernie, the next-door neighbor, was two and a half years old. He had a very high fever one day and suddenly found himself unable to toddle or talk. I always said I would love a baby as brave as Ernie, but I was also afraid now of a baby having a fever, and I was afraid because the doctor had said that we might not be able to have children at all. Not naturally, at least.

It was time to get out of the way so the night nurses could do their work. As I headed out into the hallway in my winter coat, I could hear Mike flirting with the Nigerian women.

"Grace: Is that a new top or something?"

Grace hooted in response. "Okaaaay?"

To the nurses, he was a sick man with a fever who couldn't feel when he'd soiled his diaper. He needed aspirin to thin his badly behaved blood and booties on his size-thirteen feet to keep that bad blood circulating. But to me, he was six foot two. He could ride his bike from Chicago all the way to Highland Park. He could juggle bottles of beer and drink entirely too much of it. He could carry furniture all the way to our second-floor walk-up, run around the stage at The Second City, and make the people laugh all night long. He could make other women fall in love with him every time he did a show.

I walked away from the room and past the lounge where Mike ate lunch every day, where he was currently learning how to hold silverware again with the assistance of a red spongy apparatus. Sometimes I took a cab from my office on his lunch break so he wouldn't feel so lonely—he had always hated eating alone. In the lounge, Ernie's mom and dad were hissing at each other next to a restaurant-sized refrigerator stocked full of pills and syringes. I hung back until Ernie's mother stormed out, which I knew would happen soon.

I waved to her and smiled. "Hi, Jennifer."

She smiled back, weakly. She, who once upon a time had been a real-life punk-rock kid. She, who had lived in Humboldt Park long before it was gentrified. She, who had traveled the world on her own, and built her own garage by hand, and had her baby in a kiddie pool in her living room. She was here now, reduced to this haggard existence. She still wore her lucky Ramones T-shirt, but her jeans were hanging off her now and her face looked sallow and ten years older than it had when I first met her, just four weeks ago.

I looked at Ernie's dad and held up my cigarette pack as an invitation, and he followed me to the sliding glass doors.

"I heard your man broke these today," Ernie's father said.

"First time with the electric wheelchair."

"He always been a bad driver?"

"He's always been kind of a troublemaker."

When the elevator dinged, we squeezed in as quickly as we could, even though minutes would pass before it closed. The elevators were lined with mirrors so wheelchair drivers could navigate in and out with ease. I looked up at my face in the glass ceiling and wondered how much I'd aged. Ernie's father stuck an unlit cigarette in his mouth.

"Haven't had one yet today," he said. "Jennifer really wants me to quit."

"I'm trying too, but it's hard at a time like this."

"You can say that again."

"How's Ernie today?"

"He's good, having his bath now. I read *Good Night Chicago* to him—he likes that one. Trying to convince Jennifer to go home and I'll stay here tonight."

"Yeah."

"She hasn't been home in a week."

"I know."

The elevator doors opened and we headed outside through the back doors to a small area where smoking was allowed. Ernie's father lit my cigarette and we listened to Chicago. Cabs honking, DJs spinning, the shrieking and squealing of happy girls. We smiled at each other sadly as we remembered our old lives. He looked at his feet in his worn gray running shoes; I looked at my scuffed-up Mary Janes. Both of us walked to the hospital from the train station after commuting from our respective jobs. The train let us out at Chicago Avenue every Monday through Friday. "This is Chicago!" the conductor said every time. Yes it is, I thought. Then I would get off and walk past multilevel record and book stores, restaurants owned by clothing designers, and malls made of marble, feeling so alone in the crowd. But now I had Ernie's dad.

"I remember when Ernie was born," he said. "He was ten pounds—can you believe it?—and I said it was because his soul was so giant. Jennifer thought that was poetic." He looked at the ground again.

"Are you guys married?" he asked.

"No. We were living together though, saving up."

"I remember those days." He smiled like a man who'd seen it all.

We breathed our smoke in deeply, and when a group of girls passed, I listened carefully to the clicking of their heels.

"I can't believe you gave him your number!" one of the girls said. "You have a boyfriend!"

"I am so over said boyfriend," the brunette said.

Part of me wanted to go to her and beg her to give her boyfriend a second chance. Was he unfaithful? I wanted to ask. Was he mean? If he was unfaithful, how many times? Maybe it was only once and maybe it was because he didn't know what to do with that first little taste of fame. Maybe he really does love you. Let me ask you a question: What if he can't walk tomorrow? I stared at them too long: camel-colored leather thigh-highs, black-and-white snakeskin boots with square heels, nail-polish-red stilettos with pointy toes. They didn't think about walking; they didn't will it to happen. Controlled falling, I repeated to myself. Maybe if I studied their feet long enough, I could figure out how to make Mike's move too.

Ernie's father said he was going back inside. He squeezed my shoulder and said, "Have a fun date night." The waves of Lake Michigan crashed against the rocks. I heard a fistfight breaking out, maybe a gunshot in the distance. Some kids came to the hospital after being shot in the back or hit in the head too hard. Mike came to the hospital because he felt like a team of football players was standing on the back of his neck. I stamped out my cigarette with my heel.

"Hey Supergirl," my favorite night-shift security guard greeted me. "How was date night?"

"Great," I said. "We had Lou Malnati's for dinner."

He handed me a stand-up comedy DVD, said we might enjoy it.

"You guys like Dave Chappelle? Return it whenever you're done. Take your time. If he's too tired tonight, that's okay."

I found kindness in the strangest places in those days. I found comfort in the lunchtime cab drivers, mostly. In the days before Ubers and Lyfts, I would get into their cars and when they asked about my day, I would tell my story. They always did look pretty heartbroken when I got to the climax. *Thornton! Critical!* Some bummed me cigarettes, some bought me coffee at the drive-through doughnut shop, some offered discounted fare, and some promised prayer. Cab drivers are wonderful people. And I needed to repeat the story—needed it to be new and fresh like it felt—but my family and friends all knew it by heart, and they listened to the dailies.

"He held a pen long enough to do half the crossword puzzle today. No, his toes still haven't moved, but they will. I know they will."

I smiled at my favorite security guard, then I just threw my arms around him. A few minutes later, I waited for the elevator doors to close before crumpling in the corner. As soon as I started to unravel though, I stopped myself, took a deep breath, swiped at my tears, and stood up again. Get up and stand up straight, I said to myself, because you can. After pressing the button for the seventh floor, I fished some lip gloss from my coat pocket and reapplied. Shirley always said it was my obligation to keep on looking good for Mike because *that* would keep him going. So: I smoothed down my hair, and practiced my most winning smile.

Back on the floor, everyone seemed to be sleeping. That's because Sunday was a big day. On Monday, the floor looked like a hurricane. There were old women walking like sailors with sea legs and little boys wheeling around and grabbing the asses of the nurses, gangbangers yelling that they don't want to do no goddamn exercises.

But on Sunday, there were field trips and five-star meals, and family members came from all over the country to push their loved ones out on the town. To the Water Tower movie theater, the American Girl Place, any restaurant they wanted. Yes, everyone was dreaming now of Sunday. The nurses were quiet at their stations.

When I saw the time, I realized I'd been gone too long, so I jogged down the hall to Mike's room, where I found him staring at a blank television screen with headphones covering his ears. He wore the look of senility now, an equal ratio of vacancy and fear. He, the one who told me every night before he fell asleep that we were Super Couple and we would get through this. He was Michael Patrick Thornton, for Christ's sake. Had I forgotten who he was? The psychiatrist offered him antidepressants every night and he turned them down with gusto. "No thanks, I don't like pills." He said this on days when I wanted to grab them and chug them down with bourbon.

When I entered the room, I cleared my throat loudly.

"Oh, no no no," I said.

Mike lifted his eyes, begrudgingly shook the headphones from his ears.

"Not today," I said. "Maybe you can give up tomorrow, but not tonight. Tonight I am gonna kick your ass in Scrabble. You need to work your fingers."

His vacant face came alive again.

"I just realized," he said. "I think I love you more than Lou Malnati's. I could be wrong, but I don't think so."

It was only week four of the rest of our lives.

CHAPTER 8

2002

Something had happened before we moved into the apartment. Something had happened that maybe forced us to move in together. It all started when Mike turned Equity. His first big break came from BJ Jones at Northlight Theatre, who cast him in the Irish play *A Skull in Connemara*, which ended up being a sensational hit, even before Martin McDonagh had written *Three Billboards*. Northlight was a major Equity house that paid their actors well; the subscribers were mostly suburban, many of them Jewish, and the artistic director knew how to balance cruise-ship shows with serious art to keep them all coming back. BJ had directed some of the best plays I'd ever seen.

At about the same time Mike was cast, I left my reporter's life behind because I hated it, I realized, and started to think maybe I should pursue acting more fully. All of the actor biographies said you sacrificed for your art, so I took a job at a massive cylinder factory at North and Elston, where a bunch of my neighbors worked. I would be a liaison between the guys on the floor and the women in the office, which was a good fit for me, I thought. Working a mindless job meant I could free up more space for my art. Initially, Mike agreed, but then I noticed he wasn't as interested in my stories when I came home from work.

Mike started going to Equity rehearsals every day from ten to four while I went to the factory from seven to three, and suddenly, I started to feel far away from him. That's when I signed up for an audition class, rented every French film I could find, went to a play every time there was an industry night, read every book I could find about the actor's craft. I would be proactive, I could get better. Next time I auditioned, I'd get cast in something. I got busy, and Mike did too. He got so busy, he didn't call to say goodnight anymore.

* * *

Pacing my parents' living room on a Thursday night, I waited for the phone to ring. Maybe we could play Scrabble tonight, I thought: Mike always took such pleasure in winning. Or maybe we could rent the Bruce Willis movie I usually said no to. Absence makes the heart grow regretful. I put on a record and checked the time. Eight o'clock, and I could've sworn he'd said rehearsal would be over by six. I shaved my legs and moisturized them, put on a demi bra and plucked my eyebrows. When I finally gave in and called, a bar came alive in the background.

"Hey babe," I said. "Where you at?"

"Chief O'Neill's. Whatcha up to?"

"Why don't I come and meet you?"

"Don't you have to be up early?"

So I hadn't been "fun" for the last few weeks (meaning: irresponsible) but I'd show him I could still be queen of the bar. I was young, could still drink my share and make it to work by seven with bright eyes. An hour later, I walked into Chief O'Neill's, where Mike sat in a booth next to John Gawlik, his friend who had been cast as his brother.

Gawlik had blue-black hair and a Kennedy smile. I was always commenting about how handsome he was, and usually, Mike could take a joke, but I could tell he didn't like it. The woman sitting next to John could've been Meg Ryan's twin, except she was heavier and had visible lines around her eyes. I knew that the only woman in the cast played Mike's grandmother and was seventy-five years old, so this must be the stage manager. I bent over to kiss Mike hello, and he lifted his finger to signal that he needed a minute—he was in the middle of a story. He was actually butchering a wonderful story about William Butler Yeats, and I know because I had called him long-distance from Ireland to tell him the goddamn story.

Once upon a time, I had been awarded a scholarship to study abroad in Ireland. I sent in a portfolio of academic and creative writing, and the powers that be decided I deserved to study with authors, editors, literary managers, and playwrights all over Dublin and Galway. Now I was here, in some wannabe bar, trying to remind my boyfriend of my value.

"Magnolia!" John Gawlik cried. "How's my girl?" He was visibly drunk, so they had been here for a while.

"Maggie," Mike finally said. "I'm so sorry. This is Suzanne Grimes, our stage manager."

"I've heard so much about you," she said.

Suzanne wore her blond hair cut short with a streak of her bangs dyed green. She wore jeans that had probably fit her once, and an Irish cable-knit sweater. She had a beautiful face, despite the lines; her eyes looked like Southwestern jewelry. When she reached for a cigarette, Mike leaned across the table to light it.

"I love the green streak," I said.

"Thanks." Then she put on a terrible Irish accent. "My husband left me, the man himself, and I had a midlife crisis, wouldn't ya know? Dyed my hair green, took up the fags and drink again." She smiled self-deprecatingly, returned to her normal voice and raised her glass. "Slainte." With this, she broke my heart a little. Her husband, an Equity actor, had been cast in a show on Broadway. Soon after, he ran away with a young actress and never came home again.

"We kinda want to beat the shit out of him," Mike said.

"How long have you been doing this?" I asked.

"Since I was eighteen."

"And now she's production manager at Steppenwolf," Mike said.

"You have to tell us stories," I said.

"What do you want?" she asked. "I got it all."

Suzanne told stories while we drank pints of Harp. She told us about the famous actress who got the call just before going onstage that her mother had killed herself. Then she hung up and made her entrance. She told us which ensemble members had found God and who had had to give up drinking. She caressed her pint glass as she searched her memory for more stories that would impress us, and I could see that Mike was riveted. When she excused herself to go to the ladies' room, he followed her with dreamy eyes.

"She's terrific, isn't she?" he said.

"Incredible," I agreed. "What a storyteller."

"I think Johnny should hook up with her," he said, jabbing John in the side.

"Go for it," I said to John. "She's hot."

I played along because jealousy was a turn-off, I knew, and I couldn't compete with her life. I got up unsteadily to leave, and Mike, for the first time ever, didn't ask me to stay.

* * *

A Skull in Connemara opened in March, and Mike asked me to round up a group of friends for the dress rehearsal, so we drove down Lincoln Avenue toward Old Orchard, an outdoor mall that had historically been hard for me to stomach because the rich North Shore teenagers walked around with overstuffed shopping bags from high-end designer stores where I couldn't even afford the socks. Northlight was across the street, and many of the subscribers had dinner at the mall restaurants before or after the show.

Skull was a dark comedy and the actors needed to gauge their laugh lines and pacing, so it was time to add the audience. BJ, the director, knew Mike was the youngest and had friends who couldn't afford full-price tickets. He said we could all come for free. I called everyone from the Gift, then I called Tabitha and Shannon because I knew they'd be impressed, and that it might allow them to forgive me for neglecting them. While they had spent their early twenties barhopping in Wrigleyville and going to concerts and Cubs games, I had spent mine seeing plays and taking acting classes, or drinking with other actors.

"Thornton," I said at the box office, enjoying his last name in my mouth.

The house manager showed us to the theater, where a cluster of photographers fiddled with their cameras, waiting to take publicity shots for the newspaper while BJ paced the aisles.

"Hey gang," he said to us. "Why don't you sit in the third and fourth rows?"

I sat next to Brendan while BJ addressed the photographers.

"I'll let you know what I want," he said to them. "I'll let you know when the good shot's coming."

Then he looked back to us. "You guys are friends of Michael's? You should be proud. He's gonna sell this show. Believe me, I know these things. This kid is very talented. He's gonna make us some dinero."

Then he called up to the booth. "Suze, how they doin' back there? We gonna be ready to go in five?"

Suzanne came swishing down the aisle, wearing her tight jeans, a bandanna on her head, and a practiced look of fatigue on her face.

"Hey Maggie, hi Brendan," she said as she passed.

"How do you know her?" I asked Brendan.

"I've been out with her and Mike a few times," he said.

"Do you like her?"

"Yeah, she's fun."

As I distractedly flipped through my Playbill, Brendan put his hand on my knee and said, "Stop shaking. He'll be great. It's *Mike*." Brendan had a bottle of Jameson waiting under his seat, a congratulatory gift. I had ordered a ridiculously large bouquet to be delivered to Mike's dressing room on opening night, and was starting to regret it. The house lights dimmed. Brendan squeezed my hand and I squeezed back, hoping that he, our mutual friend, an anchor, might be enough to keep me and Mike together.

When the lights snapped up on a cottage in rural Ireland, every detail was perfect. I know because Mike and I had once spent a week traveling the Irish countryside, visiting his family and mine, having tea and biscuits in all their homes. One of our favorite Chicago actors, Si Osborne, was playing the lead, who was rumored to have murdered his wife. Throughout the play, it's hard to tell: Is he grieving the love of his life or nursing his guilt? Just when the room starts to get too uncomfortable, the door flies open and in blows Mike Thornton, wearing a Manchester United jersey and a pair of jeans that don't fit him. There he is. His intelligent face looks so dopey, I can hardly believe it's him. The truth is, I don't entirely recognize him onstage or off lately, and don't know if he's the kind who loves his wife or wants to snuff her out.

"How is all?" he cries out. The audience starts laughing. All he does is enter and say three words, but everyone is hooting.

"Now," BJ whispers to the photographers, and the cameras start clicking.

After the show, I felt a little intimidated by him. He walked straight at me, still wearing his jersey. I thought of college, when I would take the bus to see him in plays in Iowa City. He would always write *For Maggie* in his bios, and when I saw him after, I'd say, "Hey dude" and slap him five. "Can you say something besides 'Hey dude?' " he'd ask, laughing. So this time I said, "Mike Thornton, I have never been more proud."

"Thanks for getting all my kids here," he said.

Brendan handed him the bottle of Jameson and said, "You sonofabitch." He looked at Mike, sadly. "Will you really not be able to act with us anymore?"

"Not until we can pay Equity wages," Mike said.

Twenty people stood around, feeling proud of him, wanting to be near him. He hugged everyone too quickly, and I asked if we shouldn't go for a drink.

"Suzanne's having a party," he said. "You can come if you want to, but that's it."

"Can't you have one drink with us first?" I asked. "With your theater company, with your friends?"

"No," he said. "I can't."

"You're an asshole," I said.

* * *

Four hundred subscribers, theater critics, artistic directors, and minor celebrity actors filled the theater on opening night. I sat in a balcony with Mike's parents, wearing a cocktail dress that I had bought specially for the occasion. The show sounded like a rock concert that night; the theater echoed with laughter. I watched the audience more than I watched Mike: critics slapping their knees as Mike lazily dug a trapdoor grave and stopped every thirty seconds for a smoke break. I saw their skin crawl when he was left alone with the skulls and frightened of them, sensed their fear when he began to smash the skulls, remembering a girl who had broken his heart. It must've been so thrilling up there. I looked back at the booth, but it was too dark to see Suzanne now.

Sitting there in the dark, I thought about husbands and wives, all those wives of powerful men who tolerate their affairs. All those powerful men who say they honor and respect their wives but go around humiliating them. I sat there in the dark. The audience clapped when the first couple actors came out for their bow. They clapped even harder for the next round. Mike jogged out last, smiling and sweating as if he'd just run a marathon, and the audience got to their feet one by one. It looked like fire catching.

Hedy Weiss of the *Chicago Sun-Times* said this about him: "But it's Thornton, a relative newcomer, who steals the show. A bearlike fellow with a boxy head, he captures Mairtin both inside and out. Here's a human punching bag who thinks he's the champ. You can easily see him dying young, choking on his own 'sick.' "

Mike and I drove to Pete Miller's for the opening night reception. BJ had rented out the restaurant, ordered a buffet and open bar with a sweets table. There were billiards tables in the back room and a piano player up front. Mike and I walked in holding hands, but he let go when he saw Suzanne wearing knee-high boots.

"Wow," he said. "You look great."

"I changed," she explained, coyly smiling.

A thin woman with pinched nostrils and sculpted hair rushed over. "Michael Thornton, we need your autograph!"

"Nice to meet you," he said. "Um, this is my girlfriend."

She pulled him away then and I was stuck with Suzanne.

"It'll be like this all night," Suzanne said. "He has to work the board for BJ. These are some of the richest people on the North Shore and without them, the theaters go dark. Go and eat something, honey."

I piled up a plate and went to sit with Mike's parents. His father was an older version of him, thinner with silver hair. His mother had a perfectly creamy Irish complexion and dyed-black hair. They looked around the restaurant; they looked the happiest I'd ever seen them.

"Hey Little Bit," Frankie said with his mouth full. "Whatcha drinkin'? It's open bar, you know."

Frank Thornton, even in his late fifties, still got visibly excited about an open bar.

"I'll take a whiskey," I responded. "What the hell?"

Si Osborne, the veteran actor, came over and joined us. He wasn't getting as much attention for this production, but he didn't seem to mind.

"So Maggie," Si said. "Will I see you next week?"

"What's next week?" I asked.

"Didn't Mikey tell you? We're going away for a night, getting out of town. All of us. Johnny, Suzanne, my wife, myself. Lia and I have a house up in Wisconsin. You'll be able to make it, won't you?"

"Absolutely," I said.

Frankie ordered me another whiskey, and the thing is, I can't handle the stuff. By the end of the night, I found myself sitting next to BJ's wife, laughing, and saying to her, "Your husband's completely full of shit, isn't he? I mean, isn't he? You're so down-to-earth and he's so full of shit!" Not the smartest move. BJ's wife told him what I'd said, of course, and he called Mike the following day to tell him about it.

* * *

I was spinning myself around in a stained old swivel chair in a factory office when the phone rang. I was making fun of a coworker named Jimmy and trying to distract from my opening-night hangover.

"You don't take leftovers from a wedding," I said to Jimmy. "You just don't."

"Oh yeah, Miss College. You know how much food gets wasted at weddings?"

The phone rang and I answered.

"I'll get outta here," Jimmy said with a wink. "Let you and your boyfriend talk dirty."

But there was no talking dirty that day.

"I heard what you said to BJ's wife," Mike said.

". . ."

"What were you thinking, Maggie? This is a big deal for me. I have to be a professional with these people. Jesus Christ! I am furious with you."

And I you, I thought. Then I looked around the dingy office, listened to the country station's favorite song about rain, and cried. It was like my boyfriend had become a crocodile. It was like I had become one too.

* * *

I took a couple days off from the factory. I waited in the Northlight parking lot for Mike, so we could leave as early as possible to make the drive to Si and Lia's. Mike said he always felt a little lonely when he left the theater on Sundays. The parking lot looked so sad and empty, he said, after playing to a packed house all week. Sunday afternoon was his Friday, the day that signaled a short stretch of freedom. I waited in the lot, and wondered if I didn't make him sad too, after that adrenaline-filled weekend. He snuck up behind me and slapped my ass, hard.

"Ready for a road trip?" he asked.

I settled into the passenger's seat and prepared for our journey. Si and his wife, Lia, were already strapped into their mint-green Jeep with their two little girls and their dog, waiting for us to follow. They waved to me through the window. We were to follow them to the Northwoods of Wisconsin, to their log cabin, the one Si had built for them with his bare hands.

We followed Si and Lia, and when the sky went dark, I played sad songs with lyrics that indicated I was suspicious. Mike didn't seem to catch on. He kept his eyes focused on the road, on the green Jeep in front of us with sleeping children and a dog in the back seat. Several hours later, we pulled onto a dirt road and parked in front of a log-cabin house surrounded on all sides by a forest of towering red pines and maples.

"Let me listen to the last line again," I said, but Mike had grown impatient after hearing the same song three times in a row.

"Come on," Mike said. "I don't want to sit in the car all night."

Si got out of the Jeep, scooped both girls up in his arms, and carried them inside. Lia let the dog out of the back and followed her husband. Mike and I followed them, and I was envious of the stability of their life, the routine they knew so well, the vows they had exchanged. Once inside, Si put the girls down in their beds in the basement. Lia turned on the heat, then gave a tour of the house with the log-cabin walls. She pointed out where we would sleep, and where John and Suzanne would sleep, when they got here. She pointed out sterling-silver-framed photos of her wedding day where she looked like a bride figurine placed on top of a cake with shoulder-length blond hair and a simple veil, laughing with squinty eyes directly into the camera. Si looked serious and secretive, as if he'd just stolen a museum treasure. Lia poured rosé and Si started cooking.

"So Maggie," Lia said. "You saw *Faith Healer*?"

"It changed my life," I confessed.

Which was true. Mike and I had gone to see it together when we were still just friends. When I had a boyfriend who didn't like plays, so I went to the theater with Mike. We saw *Faith Healer*, an Irish play by Brian Friel, and Si and Lia played an explosive couple. Mike and I left the theater that night and all I wanted to do was that; I would never again be satisfied if I couldn't. I didn't know yet that I wanted to be Brian Friel, which is to say, the writer.

"Those actors are married," Mike had said at the time. "Maybe we could get married someday."

"Mike Thornton," I had said. "I wouldn't marry you for a million dollars."

"So Maggie," Si said. "Mike says you're interested in writing. There's an excellent writers' retreat nearby. Have you heard of it?"

"Of course I have. I'm considering applying." But it had been years since my writing workshops. My professors had always said I was good, and that I should keep at it, but lately I hadn't made the time. Lately, I had started to doubt myself and all of my abilities.

John Gawlik and Suzanne arrived soon after we did. They had driven up together, even though the romance had never taken off. "Hello?" They poked their heads in the front door, unwound scarves from their necks, dropped their duffel bags on the floor. Si put on a scratchy record and we sat around a scarred wooden table, ate tuna steak with our wine. We drank a lot of wine, and Mike and John did impersonations of BJ.

"Michael," John said, pretending to chew gum. "Mr. Mike! I need a house laugh on that line, buddy!"

Everyone laughed; Lia rocked back and forth with her laughter. She cried, "You guys are so funny! I wish I could be funny." It was amazing to me that this woman who was gorgeous and loved and talented ever wanted anything else.

"You're drunk, Lia," Si said. "Quit flirting. It's unbecoming."

"Shut up, Si. I'm too old for them anyway."

"How old are you?" Suzanne asked. "My age, right?"

"Thirty-eight," Lia said with a sour mouth.

"Wow," I said. "You look fabulous."

"Oh, shut up," Lia said. "You're young. What the hell do you know? How old are you? Sixteen?"

"Go to bed, Lia," Si said.

"Twenty-four," I said softly.

Mike laughed and said, "Hey Lia, I personally thought you were, like, fifty."

She rubbed her temples and laughed politely. John, just like a Kennedy, poured more wine for everyone.

Later that night, I sat in the porch swing, suddenly missing my parents, my neighborhood friends, my ensemble, all the people who knew how to love me. I wished Mike would come out and sit beside me; I wished he had defended me more directly. The trees were so big, I felt smaller than a child. "You're drunk," I thought. "There's no affair. You're paranoid. Go back inside and be charming."

I slipped back into the house where Suzanne snapped photos with a fancy camera.

"A photographer too?" I said.

"You know?" she said. "Whenever I feel nervous, I just kinda hide out behind the lens."

It looked to me like she wanted a lot of pictures of Mike smiling at her.

Cat Stevens came on the stereo and I said, "I *love* Cat Stevens."

"What's your favorite song?" Suzanne asked.

" 'Rubylove,' " I responded.

"Oh sweetheart, that's not him," Suzanne said.

"Yes it is."

"Common mistake, but it's not."

Cat Stevens sang, "Oh love, sweet love . . ." Si extended his arm to Lia and they began to dance. He wrapped her up in his arms, held her as they swayed drunkenly.

"I love you, sweetheart," he said. "I'm jealous, I'm an asshole, I am so in love with you."

"I hate this beard," she said, tugging at it.

Then she pulled him by his beard and kissed him urgently. Soon after, they went to bed.

Which left me, Mike, John, and Suzanne at the table, opening yet another bottle. It was a showdown now. I would stay awake until I knew what was going on. Suzanne put on a CD she had brought along.

"Remember this song?" she asked Mike.

"I like this one," he responded, after hearing only a few notes.

“This is Eva Cassidy,” she said to us, but she looked directly at Mike. “She’s an amazing talent. When she sang at the Green Mill, they limited the ice cube count so everyone could hear her. God, she died too young.” John closed his eyes to listen to the music, but I kept my eyes open.

“I’m going for a cigarette,” I announced.

“I’ll join you,” Suzanne said.

This would be the scene, I thought. This would be it. We sat beside each other on the porch swing.

“I love this house,” I said. “I love Si and Lia’s marriage.”

“You’ll have one like it,” Suzanne said. “If you want it, you can have it too.”

I shrugged.

“You’ll have it too, Suzanne. You’ll have it again. I’m so sorry about your husband.”

“Thank you. You know I think the world of you, Maggie. You are such a bright girl,” she said. “Such a wonderful, wonderful girl.”

“Thank you.”

“You think you and Mike’ll get married?”

“I don’t know. Things are weird right now.”

“Really? How so?”

“Yeah, ever since the show, I don’t know.”

“Sometimes people grow apart.”

The wind rustled up through the trees.

“Well,” I said. “You guys have become friends. I mean, you’re the wise one around here. This is all new to me.”

“You want to know what I think?”

She pretended to hesitate.

“He’s not right for you,” she said. “*You* have so much to offer.”

“Well of course, but he does too.”

Clearly, Suzanne thought I was the college girlfriend he would outgrow, and I was worried about that myself.

“Being out here makes me want to write,” I said, allowing her some time.

“Mike says you’re fantastic.”

“I’m okay.”

“Oh Maggie,” Suzanne said. “I adore you.”

“I adore you as well.”

"This too shall pass," she said with a sad smile.

This woman could not hold her liquor, I thought. I slid my arms inside my sleeves and underneath my shirt.

"Maggie," Suzanne said. "Michael and I have been together."

CHAPTER 9
2003

Mary Ann Thebus, Mike's friend and former acting teacher, came to visit at RIC on a day when we were feeling especially hopeful. After he had been there for about a month, spring came to lift our spirits. On those blue-sky April days, I took him for walks outside because he was finally able to sit upright in his wheelchair without sliding out. At first, when we would buckle him into the chair, he would, most of the time, slip right out. Caitlin, a little girl who had cerebral palsy and whose parents didn't visit very often, looked at him one day and said, "It's okay, Mike. It happens to me too."

But now, I buckled Mike in more easily, and we went outside for short walks, smiling at all of our friends who were impressed with his progress. Sometimes his legs would spasm when we hit a crack in the sidewalk, but the fresh air was good for us, and Caitlin was proud. We were going to get out of the hospital soon, I knew it. We were going to leave this hospital and he was going to walk again. We were going to walk everywhere from now on. To the grocery store, to the library, to the movies. Fuck cars. We were going to walk everywhere, Mike with a limp and me on his arm. And then he was going to walk with me down an aisle just like that. He was going to thank me for sticking by him through it all. That fling he had with Suzanne? That was nothing. We were going to get old and gray together and ask our children, Jackson and Molly, if they understood how lucky they were.

Mary Ann was the grande dame of Chicago theater, perhaps most notable for her role as the mother in *Rudy*, but also one of the most versatile and commanding stage presences and the most sought-after acting coach in the city. Mike and I had both studied with her, and while he was famously one of her pets, she'd had a little more difficulty with me. I had been late to our first private session, in the days before cell phones, and hadn't called ahead to say so.

"You're cute," she said to me that day. "And talented too. I like how you tell Michael what's what. But you think you can get by with your charm, and that's just not possible. You're acting like a damn teenager, and by the way, you won't be this young forever. You'll need to grow up if you want to do something with that talent."

Now Mary Ann sat outside the hospital with us, telling us about the plays she had seen lately, the ones that had really moved her.

"Did you see *The Old Man and the Sea* at Redmoon Theater?" she asked me, knowing I worked there as a day job.

I had seen it, but Mike hadn't—he always thought the "puppet theater" I worked at sounded a little silly, but then Mary Ann and I started recreating the play for him while sitting in a sea of wheelchairs. I described the beautifully carved old man puppet, the wood distressed to make his skin look weathered. Mary Ann explained to Mike that a human child was cast as the little boy who wasn't allowed to fish with the old man anymore, and then her voice broke, and Mike started to cry too, even though he hadn't even seen the show.

"It was based on Hemingway's book," Mary Ann said, "but that wasn't the title, was it?"

"It was called *Salao*," I said. "The worst kind of unlucky."

She looked between me and Mike with her milky-blue eyes. Me: tired and haggard. Mike: in his borrowed electric wheelchair with a neck brace. And I knew what she was thinking: I wasn't a teenager anymore, and Mike was the worst kind of unlucky.

We'd had several visitors that week, even though quite often, Mike didn't want any at all. Tabitha and Shannon barged in with all kinds of presents and said, "Hey, think about *My Left Foot*, okay? Remember Daniel Day-Lewis? Your acting career is not over." Paulie came and said, "I just moved to Chicago, you fucker. Come on. Get up." One morning, we woke to John Gawlik standing at the foot of the bed with a carton of orange juice and a box of coffee—he had dropped by just to wish us a good morning. You have never known intimacy until you've lain with someone in their hospital bed, and you have never known generosity until you've seen life from that perspective. Connolly came after he'd lit a special candle at church. Lynda came, but she also sent decorations for our bulletin board. She wrote a poem about the day she heard the news (oh boy) and drew comic strips about a wheelchair superhero and his sidekick. Our friends who had married early, whose wives had banned them from Friday nights with Mikey, were allowed to visit him in the hospital, and when they did, a kind of heaviness filled the room. My family came. My sister had her fifth-grade students make Get Well Soon cards for Mike, which were funny and sweet. Mike's extended family all took turns—they had always been good at that—and the relatives in Ireland sent holy water meant for healing. The Thorntons and I were there every day. Everyone said, "He looks so handsome."

A new nurse had come to cath Mike during our visit with Mary Ann, but she didn't want to be rude, so she said she'd check on us later. After Mary Ann left, I called the nurse, and while waiting for her to finish, I thought of our apartment and how soon we'd be returning. The nurse filled two urinals and the color seemed to drain from Mike's face. He started to sweat profusely, but he was always sweaty in those days, so I said, "Let's go for a walk. You need some air." We were going to take a walk someday without this wheelchair.

"It's happening again," he said.

"No," I said. "It can't be. Let's go out and get some lunch."

"I don't want to."

"Why?"

"Because my legs shake."

That was true. This had happened several times last weekend. Mike's legs shook so hard when we hit a crack in the sidewalk that I was afraid he'd fly out of his chair.

"Who cares?" I said. "Who fucking cares if your legs shake?"

We were going to forget this all someday. This was all going to be a dream. We were going to take up the whole damn sidewalk with our expensive baby stroller and our big old golden Lab.

"It's happening again," he said, as I wheeled him toward the elevators.

"It's happening again," he said, as he started to suck the air.

"It's happening again," he said.

And he was right. It was.

I rushed him back to his room and called his mother. Paramedics rushed him next door to the emergency room at Northwestern Hospital, and Caitlin stared at us, sympathetically. Everyone on the floor remembered the origin of their injuries, and that's when I suddenly had a feeling that Jackson and Molly were never coming.

* * *

In the ICU at Northwestern, the doctors were the smartest in the city but had terrible bedside manners, and the nurses took forever to come, but there was a Starbucks in the building and Frankie loved the cafeteria food. Poor Frankie, poor Rita, poor Mike. He couldn't move anything below his head, again. I didn't leave Northwestern after that—didn't even go to work anymore. I was staying right there with Mike, because I was convinced of it: He was going to die and abandon me this time, leave me alone with all the people who didn't know how to love me.

In the intensive care unit of Northwestern, Mike and I watched *Always*. Or, I watched it sitting in a chair beside his bed while he drifted in and out of consciousness, an oxygen tube under his nose. It's an eighties movie he'd wanted me to see because I'm crazy about John Goodman. We watched the terrible scene where Holly Hunter has one last dance with the ghost of her dead boyfriend so she can move on and fall in love with someone else. I sat at the foot of Mike's bed and cried all over myself. "I don't want to date anyone else," I said out loud. "I don't want to love anyone else." He looked at me sympathetically and then drifted away again.

Mike whispered sweet and scary things to me during the brief moments he was awake. ("I love you so much." "Give my books to Connolly and Brendan. "You're perfect like a ninja.") But he didn't whisper to be romantic. He whispered because this stroke had stolen his voice. The neurological team had a variety of leads and theories. If it was Devic's syndrome, he could go blind any day. If it was indeed a stroke, they may keep happening. The team consulted with the Mayo Clinic but no one there had any answers either. Frankie and Mrs. Thornton started investigating their families' history of stroke; I think they were tempted to blame each other.

On the seventh night after the second stroke, I slept lightly on a cot across the room. I would've slept closer, but the nurses needed a path to get to Mike. They came in at various times throughout the night to take his vitals and sponge him down. He was so sweaty then; he never stopped sweating. I had a recurring dream where I was Holly Hunter in *Always*, and my boyfriend had died, and I had to start over with someone new. I also had nightmares about amputees and skeletons, so when I woke to a tapping, I didn't immediately know if it was a dream or rain on the window. I looked up, and it was Mike, looking at me with big, alert eyes, tapping the pulse ox clipped to his finger, the metal chip that measured his heartbeat, on the railing on the side of his bed. I scrambled off the cot.

I screamed, "Are you . . . ? You're moving your fucking finger!"

A smile split his face.

Come on back, I thought. Come on back to me now, *Salao*.

But instead I said to him, "You look like E.T., phone home," and we broke out laughing in the middle of the night.

CHAPTER 10

2002

The swing completely stopped rocking and I looked at Suzanne. I had suspected it, of course, but had no idea how visceral the confirmation would feel. Don't say any more, I thought. Tell me everything, I thought.

"He loves me, Maggie," Suzanne said. "He said so. We've fallen in love, I think. I'm so sorry to be the one to tell you, but I think you deserve to know."

I flew into the house, forgetting there were children sleeping, a married couple making love, forgetting it was two in the morning. Mike sat with John on the leather couch in front of the fire, and I looked at him from a distance.

"I'm leaving you now," I said. "John will take me to the train in the morning. Right, John?"

"Whatever you want," John said. "Whatever you need."

I ran up the stairs, crying now, involuntarily, too loudly. It all sounded very ugly, and unfortunately, this was not a dramatic performance. I slammed the door and couldn't have stopped the tears if I had wanted to. John, Si, and Lia all knew. BJ knew. Everyone in the cast and crew. The word was traveling around Chicago right now. Did Brendan know, did anyone from the Gift? Why had they not told me? I stood and paced the room, then started to pack my suitcase.

Goddamn you, Mike Thornton, I thought. Everyone in high school hated your guts and I said, "I think he's funny." I wanted nothing to do with you but then you wanted to be my boyfriend and you pursued me for years, wrote all those poems about my yellow glow, my aura, how I was created on God's best day. I taught you how to charm people, how to come out of your bedroom and stop being afraid of them. And you learned quickly. I didn't even know real people followed their dreams and then you started talking about art and changing things. We could dream big too, you said. You promised me a life I had never dreamt of. I took buses to cornfields to visit you in college, fell in love with every single one of your friends and family members. I watched football with the men and listened to the women, learned everything I could about Brecht and Grotowski. I cried for you when you didn't get cast, saw all of your shittiest shows. That one where you were cast as a giant insect? I never told your secrets. I made love to you for the first time in Ireland in a thunderstorm; you were reading James Joyce in bed. Yes, she said. *Yes, yes, yes, yes, yes.* Please deny it, Mike. Tell me it's not true. Tell me you're not tired of me, you *can't* be tired of me. You're the only one I've ever loved. I'll get better, and you'll miss it. I'll have the children with or without you. I know she's new, I know she's exciting, but I can still make you laugh, I can still make your jaw drop. Who the *fuck* do you think you are? Oh my God, I could not breathe.

"Maggie," Mike said through the bedroom door. "Come and sit with me."

I followed him like a robot. We sat in front of the fireplace and I didn't look at him this time. Suzanne and John had disappeared.

"It was one night," he said.

"Tell me," I said. "I've heard her story. I want yours."

"She drove me home. I was too drunk."

"You deliberately got too drunk."

I wanted to imagine every detail because maybe that would make me not love him.

"Maybe so," he admitted and he looked so sorry, his eyes shining with tears, but how can you trust an actor?

"And?" I said.

"I don't want to again."

"Not good enough," I said.

"I prayed to my grandfather," he whimpered. "I prayed you wouldn't leave me."

"Quit with the Irish bullshit."

"I should've told you." He broke down. "But I needed to do this, to know. I needed to have the affair. Now I know better. Now I do. I want to marry you," he said.

". . ."

"She looks ugly when she yawns," he said, wiping at his eyes.

"I'm still leaving you," I said.

I said it because I wouldn't respect myself if I didn't. Then I walked back up the stairs, got into bed, and disappeared into sleep. The next morning, I woke to my boyfriend lying on the plank flooring beside me like a dog. I woke to the sounds of breakfast being made, bacon sizzling, and voices saying, "God, I drank too much last night." I woke to the voice of the woman that Mike had been dreaming of for months, this woman who had replaced me in his thoughts, this woman who was old enough to know better.

* * *

While I did leave him, I can't remember for exactly how long. It could've been weeks or months; I don't know. I do know that he worked hard to win me back, and that I once walked out of a restaurant in the middle of dinner because I still couldn't look at his face without feeling unbearable rage. I do know that I found gifts she had sent through the mail: theater postcards, plays in paperback, homemade CDs. Here's hoping I tore out all the pages—here's hoping I smashed all the music. I discovered the affair in March of 2002, just a year before the stroke. And six months after the discovery, I did what any twenty-four-year-old idiot in love would do: I packed up all of my things and moved in with him.

CHAPTER 11

2003

By the time *Six Characters in Search of an Author* opened, Mike was back at RIC, so we had to get a day pass to see it. When he moved back to RIC, he returned to the pediatrics floor but he now had a roommate named Tommy, a retired city worker from the South Side, a Black man in his seventies, hands the size of boxing gloves. Tommy's grandsons lived with him because their mother had passed away. They came every Sunday to see him, closed the curtain that divided us, and sometimes complained when Granddaddy wouldn't get his lazy butt out of the bed and play with them. He laughed until they left, then he lay in bed and sighed a lot until Mike asked him what was wrong. Shirley, the showering nurse, always seemed to come right in the middle of things. She was the same age as Tommy, had grown up in the same middle-class Black neighborhood.

"Hey Mr. . . . Mr. . . . Mr. Man!" Shirley yelled, because she could never remember his name. "You ready for your shower?"

"No, I am not ready for a shower," Tommy said. "I am conversing with my friend."

"Suit yourself, Mr. Man," Shirley said. Then, underneath her breath: "You old crabcake."

As soon as Shirley left the room, Tommy would say to Mike, "That woman is so arrogant!"

Tommy and Mike spent several nights lying in their beds, looking out the windows, unable to get up and go to each other, knowing the other was crying, but never saying a word. In the afternoons, after long therapy sessions, Frankie, Mike's father, would bring Tommy chocolates and Tommy would eat them by the handful, until Shirley informed us he was diabetic ("Oh, no no no. Mr. Man has the 'betes.") and then Tommy resented her even more.

One night, Mike and I said goodbye to Tommy and Shirley. Our first time away from the hospital was to see the opening night performance of the Gift Theatre's *Six Characters in Search of an Author*. We signed all kinds of release forms. On opening night, the nurses told me to take my time getting ready and they would take care of Mike. I put on a red dress and heels, and when I showed up, he was wearing jeans for the first time in a long time. I knew how difficult that must've been because dressing a grown man without his being able to assist is harder than you think. Mike and I made a big show of kissing each other and complimenting each other so the nurses could take our pictures, so they'd know they had helped with something important.

Mike's parents met us at the valet because I didn't own a car at the time, and I would've been too scared to drive with him anyway. We used a smooth wooden board to slide Mike into the passenger's seat, where he slouched a little, then we buckled him in, and Mrs. Thornton and I sat in the back together. When we arrived at Raven Theatre in Rogers Park, Mike asked his parents to leave and told them I would take it from there, though secretly I wished they would stay.

In Rogers Park at the time, there were many theaters, which made sense, because it was truly the most diverse neighborhood in the city, right on the lake, an urban oasis. I had always said it was where I would live if I didn't already have a place, because it was the attic of Chicago, where all of the people who didn't easily belong had a home. It was home to Loyola University, so there were students and faculty, but also ultra-liberals living alongside pockets of old money, a park with a mini zoo, and a pond full of sunbathing turtles. In high school, we spent so many weekends watching *The Rocky Horror Picture Show* at its one-screen movie house and hanging out at Don's Coffee Club, which hosted proms for eccentrics of all ages. Raven Theatre was a mainstay in Rogers Park. I pushed Mike's wheelchair through the suddenly narrow doors and tried to navigate nonchalantly through the lobby where people whispered as we passed.

"It's Mike Thornton, you remember. The one from Northlight. I read about it in the paper."

"But he's so young! What happened to him?"

"A stroke. Can you believe it?" As if the stroke had made him deaf.

"Mag!" Mike gritted his teeth. "You just knocked me into the concession stand!"

"Fasten your seatbelt," I growled.

Always a clumsy girl, always a terrible driver. Wheelchair attendant was not a good fit for me. And the irony? That was Mike's first job. He had pushed the elderly and disabled through O'Hare Airport as a teenage boy. He and his friends bet money on who could pop the best wheelie, who could get from one end of the concourse to the other the fastest. He remembered himself and his buddies racing through the food court while old men and women swore at him in one hundred different languages.

After everyone had been seated, the house manager led us to the wheelchair-accessible row, which means we sat on the stage, faces burning with embarrassment. Our first time away from the safety of the hospital felt like an excruciating performance and we had a full audience watching us sweat underneath the stage lights. During the preshow, Mike looked at me and whispered, "I think it's happening again."

"It's not happening," I said. "Focus on the show now. Get out of your head."

He took measured breaths, and I held his knee.

"Deep breaths," I said. "Okay?"

It all sounded like acting advice, to me, and like I was unconvincingly reading from a script. Here's an acting exercise: Pretend you haven't had two strokes. Pretend your body *hasn't* betrayed you. I mean: What if it *was* happening again? Then I would be responsible? I didn't feel at all prepared for that. Needless to say, I was grateful when the show began and we were able to disappear into an Italian play from the 1920s and avoid a full-blown panic attack.

Six Characters was certainly not the Gift's best work. Many of the performances felt stilted; Mike and I couldn't help but think of the way he would've played the Director, and the adaptation drew attention to itself. In a way, it was flattering that the company was struggling in our absence, but also unsettling, because we couldn't lose momentum now. When the curtain call came, I clapped my goddamn hands off. It didn't matter if they had bombed or not, it had to have been nerve-wracking to perform for their beloved artistic director. Admittedly, what I remember more than the climax of the play is that that was the first night I had to cath Mike. After we both clapped a little too generously at the curtain call, we waited for the crowd to thin.

"Now?" I asked.

"Yes," Mike said. "Can we wait for a few minutes though? I don't want anyone to know."

After waiting for the theater to be completely empty, we stole away into the wheelchair-accessible stall of the men's bathroom with the house manager's permission, and now it was my turn to perform. Jazz hands! Bob Fosse: Showtime! I tried to conjure the lesson the nurses had given me, tried to recall the way they positioned their hands and remember their words of caution and encouragement. Unzip the jeans. No underwear now, for convenience and ease. Insert tube into the tip of the penis, feed it through, slowly, patiently. It was the sexual organ, the one I had spent five years learning, so this felt like betrayal, but I needed to be good at this.

"Are you scared?" Mike asked.

"Not at all," I said.

Are you scared? The same thing he asked me in the moment before we first made love, in the small garden house in Dublin. His mother's wealthy cousin gave it to us for all the nights we spent in the city. I stripped off my clothes and lay beneath him, trembling in the drafty house, with the fear that he might not love me forever. "Are you scared?" he asked, and I whispered, "No, I'm ready." I never asked if he was scared in the bathroom stall because I already knew the answer. My hands stayed perfectly still, and my sweat soaked right through my dress.

We went out with the cast after, sat around a table in the beer garden of Weeds, always one of our favorite places. Mike sat sullenly as our actor friends complained about roles they hadn't been cast in, scripts they would've died to work on, everyone nonverbally agreeing that "normalcy" would be best. Brendan had been cast as an understudy in *The Violet Hour* at Steppenwolf and even had a few guaranteed performances. Connolly told Mike that their agent had been asking after him. Connolly said that he had felt embarrassed the week before, because just before hanging up with the agent, he accidentally said I love you. Which made us all laugh really hard. Except Mike. He looked at me and rolled his eyes, and said, "Why is this important?" He took two hours to drink his Miller Lite, and I remembered days when I had to drag him out of the bars. I wanted those days back now. Drink faster, I thought. Go faster. Get better faster, please. I feel my spirit vanishing, I feel myself changing shape. Sergio, the big Puerto Rican owner of Weeds, pulled me aside after I paid our bill, as I watched out the door for Mike's parents.

"It's okay if you wish he would die sometimes," Sergio said. "He feels that way too."

* * *

Mike's parents came at eleven o'clock, yawning. We were yawning too. And then we did our dance. Frankie pulled up the car a couple feet from the curb. I pushed the wheelchair between the curb and the car door, flicked up the armrest, clicked the footrests out from under Mike's gym shoes, placed them gently on the ground. Frankie wedged a smooth slab of wood underneath Mike and pulled him at a slight angle while Mrs. Thornton and I pushed.

"Swivel your hips, Mike," I said. "The way the therapists taught you."

I directed him now, the way he'd always directed me, in the bedroom, in the theater. Firmly, with tenderness. He was in the passenger's seat now and safe. His father buckled his seatbelt; his mother pulled the slide board from underneath him. Mike looked around to make sure no one had seen our private dance. I ripped the cushion seat off the wheelchair, tossed it in the trunk while Mrs. Thornton folded up the chair and did the same. Frankie asked Mike how the play was. Mrs. Thornton and I sat beside each other in the back seat and watched Chicago go by. Alexander's, where Mike and I ate fluffy omelettes on Sundays; Mary Ann's apartment, where we went for monologue coaching; the Griffin, where I'd blown my audition. All the places we went to on our own, all the things we hadn't noticed.

Frankie headed back to the Rehabilitation Institute of Chicago, making sure he drove the speed limit.

He dropped us off at the front doors of RIC, then I took Mike up in the elevator. The hospital was quiet and still, and we felt safe again. Mike's room was dark already and Tommy snored softly in his bed, but Shirley was awake, sitting in a corner, drinking coffee, waiting to undress Mike and put him into bed.

"How was the jazz show, Michael?" she whispered.

Mike looked at me and winked.

"Best jazz show I ever saw," he said.

Shirley tucked us in, gave me the secret shoulder squeeze she always did, and then Mike and I slept hard through the night. In the morning, I awoke to a sensation of warmth and wetness underneath me. Mike had wet the bed—*on his own*—and we knew that he was healing. The world was full of possibility and hope again, and we couldn't wait to tell the doctors. We laughed and high-fived each other, over and over, and the sun shot in bursts through the windows.

CHAPTER 12

2002

Before the hospital became our home, we had briefly lived together in a light-filled apartment in Jefferson Park. We moved there in November 2002, just months before the stroke. I had left the factory and had to work two new jobs to make my share of the rent. Redmoon was a nationally regarded theater, heavily influenced by the spectacle theaters of Europe, and the Art Institute was one of the oldest and largest art museums in the country. I was part of the administrative staff at both places, and hoped that being around the artists and curators would teach me something about art. Redmoon's office was like a beautiful little museum in a Scandinavian city, and I always loved being there, but the artists themselves seemed to have disdain for traditional theater types, or people like me. I didn't mind. I was happy to spend my days promoting them, and secretly learning how to do publicity for the Gift.

Mike had a chunk of money left over from a national commercial, but also took a job at a corner bar in Andersonville where he watched *Jeopardy* on weekdays and served rotgut whiskey to the regulars. During the day, I was a publicist and he was a beer slinger, and at night, together, we were artists. Brendan and Connolly helped us carry our boxes up the narrow, winding stairs, all my cardboard boxes full of nothing. Precious Moments figurines, college textbooks, and prom dresses. They carried the boxes up to the second floor of a Chicago bungalow, with hardwood floors and light slanting into the sunroom.

We bought bookcases and lamps from IKEA, and Connolly gave us an entertainment center too big for our little TV. We scored a white couch from a thrift store, assorted dishes and glassware from married cousins who were upgrading. I framed photographs of us and made up the bed with flannel sheets. Jefferson Park was the farthest from downtown I had ever lived—most actor types called it the suburbs—but I knew I could adjust, and the rent made it worthwhile. Mike's parents approved, probably because they lived just a few blocks away. My father refused to step foot inside the place, and didn't like my mother and sisters to either, even though Mike had asked his permission to live with me. The problem is: Mike asked this question the same day I told my father I'd been cast in another play.

"How are you gonna live?" my father asked. "Have you ever thought about that?"

". . ."

"You have a college degree and you wanna be an actor?"

His wife had walked down the aisle at twenty-two, a veil trailing behind her, her mother's wedding gown.

"You don't have a pot to piss in," my father said.

"What would you like me to do?" I asked.

He would've liked me to take a job that paid well, one with benefits, that would give me a sense of security.

"I worked my whole life to make you comfortable," he said. "Vacations, restaurants, new shoes every year. You'll have none of that."

"I don't give a shit about that," I said.

"You don't give a shit?" he said. "For a smart girl, you're pretty stupid."

"And what should I do? Be like you?"

"My dream was to make money, Mag. That's all. I wanted more for you."

"But I'm happy," I said, too eager for his approval.

And the fact is: He's not been unhappy. He has loved his wife and daughters, his furloughs, salary, and benefits.

"Happy don't pay the bills," my father said.

That's when my mother entered the room and said, "Al: Why do you insist on crushing her dreams?"

"Because she's so fucking bright, that's why."

My father's high opinion of me feels like too much; it always fills me with shame.

* * *

"I have every intention of proposing," Mike said to my father, who pretended to look for something in his wallet.

"I love your daughter, Al. I want to live with her."

"You're both adults, Mike," my father said. "What can I say?"

"He said yes," Mike told me, smiling.

"No, he didn't," I said.

It's not that my father is a social conservative. He believes strongly in women's rights—"I'm not a girl. How the hell is it my decision?" But he did not believe in me living with Mike Thornton at the age of twenty-four. Maybe he knew about the affair; maybe he knew what came next; maybe he knew all kinds of things I didn't.

* * *

Mike and I got into his Toyota Corolla, the one his parents had bought for him, and as we drove, I envied the way he could so easily spout his artist philosophy because he didn't need to worry about money or their approval.

"He'll come around," Mike said.

"It's not like your parents," I said.

And yet, it wasn't so different.

"Our parents just aren't like us," he said. "They just don't have big dreams."

"See, don't do that!" I said. "They *do* have big dreams—they're just different. They dream of more money and bigger houses. They dream your dreams for you."

"All I'm saying is that if you're an artist, you have to divorce yourself from all that. You can't worry about what *anyone* thinks. Even me."

* * *

We moved into the apartment shortly before we started rehearsals for *County Fair*, my first leading role with the Gift, and Mike was directing. The Thorntons gave us a pack of grocery-store gift cards for a housewarming present because we had never fully realized the expense of food. Imagine a couple of twentysomethings pushing a shopping cart together, looking totally unqualified. Me looking for the best sales, and Mike saying, "This is so depressing. We can't even afford frozen pizza. I thought going Equity was supposed to make our lives better." But later that week, we found ourselves in our kitchen on an especially sunny Saturday afternoon, mixing up a homemade pasta sauce and dancing to Bob Dylan in the kitchen.

"My gypsy bride," he said to me. "You are so much better than wine."

Soon enough though, I started to doubt that. After Mike's initial string of successes, he had done a show at Next Theatre in Evanston that wasn't received as well, and he still seemed to be reeling from the reviews:

> Chris Jones, *Chicago Tribune*—"With the help of [director Kate] Buckley's typically snappy transitions, Gregory and Thornton do their best to make [*Cherry Docs*] work. They have a few powerful moments of connection, but, in the final analysis, neither performance rings true . . . Thornton's a good and honest actor, but he feels unrehearsed and unsure of how to get inside his character's twisted brain."
>
> Hedy Weiss, *Chicago Sun-Times*—"[The character] Michael's 180-degree turnaround is something considerably short of believable, and while Thornton easily humanizes the guy, neither he nor the playwright is entirely convincing. Redemption is a far more anguished, complicated and perhaps incomplete process than what is shown here. And in some cases, it may be an impossible one."

After *Cherry Docs*, his agent continued to send him out on auditions: commercials, plays, and television. He was forever getting called back for TV roles but never landing the job—he'd had two callbacks for a sitcom with Joan Cusack but didn't make the final cut. He didn't have anything else lined up, and actors are dangerous beasts when they don't have anything else, especially twenty-three-year-old actors who don't know that they'll have to become accustomed to such things. Mike had decided to direct *County Fair* to distract himself, but every day, it drove him crazy that he wasn't onstage himself.

* * *

He got laid off from his bartending job. The owners couldn't afford to keep the bar open, so now he had no job and no intention of getting a new one, which means he started drinking more regularly. His parents felt sorry for him and secretly started paying his half of the rent, and when I found out, I went ballistic.

"I'm working two jobs and transferring money from my childhood savings account!" I cried. "And your mommy and daddy are footing the bill? Grow. Up. Michael!"

* * *

The Art Institute lions were decorated beautifully that year with Christmas wreaths and bows, and Michigan Avenue was bustling with shoppers and tourists, but I was busy writing thank-you letters to donors for end-of-year gifts and sending out invitations for the annual holiday party, ordering tea and finger sandwiches, which I wouldn't be allowed to eat. If I was working too much at the museum, I was working even harder at Redmoon. They were famous for their secular winter pageant, full of giant puppets and banjo music. In addition to courting the critics and delegating to the photographers and videographers, I also took tickets and directed traffic in the parking lot, even when the temperature had dipped below zero. Mike never made it to see the show—he was too busy, he said—but my parents came one night, and when I saw them in the audience, I had to keep myself from running to them and begging them to let me come home. I was homesick for the warmth and chaos of their house during those holiday months, our first ones in the apartment. One night, I told Mike it just didn't feel like Christmas. No music, no decorations, no money. I was too tired to watch movies after work, too broke to buy presents, and we never could get warm enough in our drafty apartment. Also, I hadn't yet found my way into my role in *County Fair*, and didn't have much time to do anything about it.

Mike called one day and said he'd be picking me up from work.

"Leave early," he said. "You deserve it."

At three o'clock in the afternoon, I looked out the window just as he came tripping out of his car, holding up a bouquet of roses, while all the girls at Redmoon Theater looked out the window, and I could feel them envying me. There was no work-from-home option then, so this felt like an unspeakable luxury. Mike and I listened to Christmas songs on the car radio, and when we arrived at our apartment, the front door was decorated with metallic gold wrapping paper and a red velvet bow. I pushed open the door to see a Douglas fir decorated with metallic ball ornaments just like a vintage department-store Christmas tree. Nat King Cole crooned about silver bells, Mike pulled me in close and kissed me, and I dissolved through my thick winter coat.

* * *

My father came to pick me up from my apartment on Christmas Day, and I asked him to come inside as I stood in the snow shivering in a cocktail dress.

"Please, Dad," I said. "It's decorated so pretty."

". . ."

"Can you at least come in and see the tree?" I asked.

My father looked straight ahead at the blizzard as if he could see something in the distance I couldn't.

"Get in the car," he said.

* * *

Mike would direct me, he promised, as the sixteen-year-old ingénue in *County Fair*. And he did. But whenever I wasn't called for rehearsal, Mike would go out after and end up at the four-o'clock bars. He would tiptoe up the stairs, through the apartment, and climb into bed with me. The following day, his voice would be hoarse from dehydration but he would still say such insightful things, so I wouldn't tell, I *couldn't* tell, the others. How after the cast abandoned him, usually around eleven or twelve, he started dialing everyone in his contacts, begging them to meet him at the late-night bar. Actors he had performed with, his cousins, bartenders he'd gotten to know.

In rehearsal, I heard him say to Lynda, "Repeat that line for me, will you, dear? Let's work on that one, okay? Right now, it's confusing to my ear." Something in me would go weak for him, the way he stood up and went to his actors, the way he spoke to them so gently. Lynda would nail her monologue, and Mike would say, "Now we're cookin' with gas." I would forget about the night before.

Alex Main played my mother in the show and became a company member by the end of it. She was exactly what we needed at the time, a killer actress in her forties and a patient den mother. She had wispy, honey-colored hair and a doll's face, wore a uniform of a long, baggy sweater, yoga pants, and wooden clogs. We rehearsed the first scene of the play, a scene between me and my mother. She and my father were divorcing, my brother was dead, and it was time for the county fair.

"Keep it simple," Mike said. "I just want you to talk to each other."

You have no idea how hard it is to just talk to each other sometimes, so Mike dug into his bag and pulled out a light bulb, tossed it to me, and I stiffened.

"What's your first line?" Mike asked me.

"I don't want to go to the fair."

"And yours, Alex?" he asked.

"We have to," she said.

"Okay, go," Mike said.

Alex smiled at me, patiently.

"I don't want to go to the fair," I said, and then quickly tossed the bulb.

Alex caught it, gently.

"Hey Mag?" Mike said. "Try throwing it *on* the line, sweetheart."

Alex and I played catch with a light bulb for an hour, said our lines to each other until they sounded natural. Nothing, in the end, was broken.

* * *

We all just loved being together in those days, when we didn't have any other real responsibilities. No children, no mortgages, no pets. A quote in a Lost Generation biography sheds some light on that time. A friend of F. Scott and Zelda Fitzgerald said, "But it was not the parties that made our life then . . . It was the great affection between everybody. You loved your friends and wanted to see them every day . . . It was like a great fair, and everybody was so young." Sometimes Mike made rules that if anyone mentioned Grotowski or Stanislavski, he would throw rocks at their heads, but most of the time, we couldn't help it. When we didn't talk shop, we told stories about ourselves. Lynda's nephew had been born and she showed us new pictures every day. Connolly told us about his spectacular dating adventures: "It went well. She was wearin' a miniskirt." And then we told him the 1980s called and wanted their terminology back.

"Mike," I asked one night. "Can I have next Friday off?"

"No."

"Really? Why not?"

"Because I said so, and I'm the director."

"It's my birthday. Can I please miss rehearsal just this once?"

"No, you can't. You're just not good enough yet."

* * *

At rehearsal on my twenty-fifth birthday, Alex confided in me. "Birthdays are hard," she said. "Thirty was so hard for me. Ask my husband."

"I'm having a hard time with twenty-five."

"But if you have a hard time now, maybe thirty'll be a breeze."

"Twenty-five just feels so inexplicably sad."

* * *

Mike and I walked from rehearsal to our apartment later that night. We trudged through the snow and ice. I had struggled in rehearsal, not able to forget what he'd said. *You're just not good enough yet.* I was struggling even now. But when he opened our apartment door, still wrapped in gold paper, everyone jumped up from behind couches and out of closets and yelled, "Surprise!" Mike pressed a button on the stereo and our favorite love-for-life anthem came blaring from the speakers.

The entire cast of *County Fair* had come—Alex, my mother, and Brendan, my brother. The actor who played my father and the one who played my boyfriend, Will, who had written the play, and all of the designers who had made it come to life. My little sisters were there with their fiancés, and Shannon and Tabitha, my high school girlfriends, were there, putting the birthday candles in a cake and telling everyone to shut the hell up. Brendan was wearing his infamous wizard hat and Connolly had brought me a beautifully wrapped present even though I knew he couldn't afford it. My cousins, the landlords, had made us a tray of Jell-O shots. Everyone was still wearing nineties clothes, flannels and overalls and V-neck sweaters. It was like a great fair, and it was my twenty-fifth birthday.

"Happy birthday, *principessa*," Mike said.

He put his arm around me and we sang as loudly as we could about making the best of what's around. By midnight, we were all saying we loved each other and dancing on the couches. When I woke the next morning, there were sleeping bodies all over my apartment, and I smiled and made them coffee.

* * *

We moved from the rehearsal warehouse to the National Pastime Theater in Uptown, and Mike found the Bar on Buena. Checkered floors, an old-fashioned jukebox, young Middle Eastern owners, Mediterranean menu. Wooden booths that we all squeezed into together after the show to remember the audience responses. Once we started the run, Mike would go to the bar and be whiskey-drunk by intermission. Meanwhile, I put on headphones and listened to songs that helped me to imagine that Brendan, who played my brother, was really gone forever. After the show, we sometimes chatted with the audience members, who shared the moments that had touched them: "I was in 4-H, too! I got out of Alton, Illinois, as fast as I could." People who had been raised in small towns in Ohio and Indiana: "I got out as fast as I could." They had come to Chicago, the closest big city, and this show allowed them to miss their homes, to grapple with their identities, and parents who did their best. They remembered their own brothers and boyfriends dying in car crashes and farm accidents.

After a number of good reviews, I felt brave enough to invite my coworkers, and the following week, at both my jobs, I enjoyed a certain kind of attention. I was no longer just the girl who planned parties for rich folks and wrote press releases about who gave which donations, though those jobs are certainly important.

I continued to go to work and Mike continued to drink like it was his job. He thinks his drinking in those last weeks had something to do with a clock ticking inside him, and I can't completely dismiss it. Was it happening even then? When he came home from the four-o'clock bars, ate fast food in the front room, turned up the television too loud, came to bed beside me, whispered that he loved me, and kissed me before he started snoring?

One morning, as I was dressing for an important meeting at the Art Institute, I heard him vomiting in our bathroom.

I banged on the bathroom door and yelled, "You think you're James Joyce? Think again!"

Later, as I stood in our bedroom doorway in a nineties business suit, he sat on the hardwood floor in gray briefs, looking pathetic. I turned on a song about leaving and then I cranked the volume as loud as it would go.

A few months later, the apartment was no longer our home. Our real home had become the hospital, where everyone was like us.

CHAPTER 13

2003

After the opening of *Six Characters*, Mike knew he had to get back to his company. He suspected they were struggling without him, and truth be told, they sort of were. He started reading plays and *PerformInk* again. In the early aughts, we all still heavily depended on *PerformInk*. You could order a paper subscription and have it delivered to your home, or find a physical copy at Act One, the drama bookshop. We read for local theater news and artist profiles, but we also needed it for audition notices. Every week, Mike would read *PI*, then dictate a list of plays he needed to read. After his eight-hour day of therapy and dinner, I pulled out his bedside table, set up a clipboard on wheels, and banded a script to it. Turning the pages was good occupational therapy, but when he got frustrated, we would assist. Weeks flew by and Mike hadn't found a single thing he liked. The problem was: After living in a children's hospital ward, nothing seemed important enough.

Paulie called and said he had seen a play called *Language of Angels* in San Francisco and there was one copy in the city, at the DePaul University Library downtown. I snuck out of the Art Institute where I worked under Christa Thurman, the curator of textiles, who was brilliant and German and yelled at me about something almost every day I saw her. Every time I entered or exited the museum, I tried to memorize a new painting or sculpture to describe to Mike. *Time*

Transfixed was his favorite these days—the locomotive train shooting out of a fireplace. We also had a soft spot for the Cornell boxes, and van Gogh and Gauguin, their work side-by-side. Today I would tell him that Chagall's *America Windows* made me believe in God. My favorite pane was the one dedicated to literature—the darker, muddier one.

I walked down Jackson to the library, past bookstores and corporate bakeries. I entered the library and felt an overwhelming feeling of sadness, as I always did, for all the books I would never have time to read. Then I made my way up to the top floor so I could look down on the Loop's lunch scene. Spring had come and the women wore floppy sun hats now. The businessmen loosened their ties and stood on the bridge, contemplating the river.

Language of Angels was waiting for me at the reserve desk. The title sounded hokey, but I had promised Paul I would take a look, at least at the first few pages. I found a a heavy oak table near a floor-to-ceiling window where I could spread out my things. My purse, my backpack, my paper-bag lunch. I took in the cabs honking below and salsa music from Daley Plaza, the farmers' market and Picasso-inspired sculptures. In a way, I wanted to spend my break just looking out the window, but then I opened up the script. In the preshow, there is whispering. The stage direction reads: "Darkness. A cave. A velvet darkness, dense and complete."

The play centered around a group of teenagers in Appalachia, a group of kids who liked to drink beer and get high, until one night, they heard their friend screaming, and then: She disappeared. Decades later, they are all still haunted. For an instant, I'm aware that I'm in a library with other human beings, then I read on and forget. Not only do I forget I'm in a library, I forget about the hospital where I spend most of my life. I devoured *Language of Angels*, scrounged around in my purse for change, and illegally photocopied every page. After coming back almost an hour late from lunch, Mrs. Thurman yelled at me in her thick German accent about my faltering work ethic, but I was far away in a cave in North Carolina where a fifteen-year-old girl, who'd had an inner light, had been murdered.

I took a cab to RIC after work, didn't have the patience for all the stops on the train. (In my thirties, I was still paying off credit cards because of the way I lived beyond my means back then. If I was depressed, a massage. If Mike was depressed, an extravagant dinner date and an unpaid day off of work.) I jumped into the elevator, jogged down the hall to his room, and outside it, saw the day nurse carrying a urinal full of blood. My heart went plunging through me.

"Is that Mike's?" I asked.

She nodded. Another urinary tract infection from the last days of the catheter, another astronomically high fever. No therapy until he was better, the nurse said. No appetite to speak of. I walked in and looked at him, propped up in bed listening to Tom Waits on his headphones. Tom Waits singing "There's a Place for Us." Talk about suicide music. Missing therapy for a few days meant no progress, and no progress meant going home and giving up. Mike was constantly anxious, constantly competing for a bed. I pulled out the bedside table and banded the photocopied script to the clipboard.

"Read this," I said. "Tonight."

Mike's fever broke the next day, and he announced auditions for the Gift Theatre's *Language of Angels*, Midwest premiere, at the Rehab Institute of Chicago.

* * *

While actors were preparing their monologues and audition sides, we had other things to take care of. First, we had to conquer the toilet. Mike was terrified of this new assignment, afraid of falling off. A near-death experience stirs up incredible anxiety, after all. There were kids on the floor who had been on feeding tubes so long, they were afraid to put anything in their mouths. They were afraid to brush their teeth. I told Mike I would sit with him if that would make him feel better, so we sat together in his private bathroom and talked about *Language of Angels*. Sometimes we played board games. I would sit on the floor and he would tell me where to move his chess pieces or his trivia pie and then one day, he wasn't afraid anymore.

* * *

I can't imagine what actors thought when they saw the audition notice in *PerformInk*: *Auditions to be held at the Rehab Institute of Chicago*. I can't imagine what they must've felt. But huge crowds of actors came and lined up outside the presentation room on the fifteenth floor, which was usually reserved for seminars on spinal-cord research. Now it was a place for a different kind of imagination, a place to audition for Mike Thornton, who had been respected in the theater community before this, and now he had become legendary, for better or for worse.

* * *

In the days leading up to auditions, Mike's therapists and his mother told him he'd better have a part for me. His mother sat at the foot of his bed, rubbing lotion into his feet. "After all she's done for you," she said, as if I wasn't there.

"I honestly don't see a part for her," he responded.

"But of course you're welcome to audition and prove me wrong," he said to me.

"Oh, don't worry, asshole, I will."

He laughed, and I really didn't mind that he wouldn't compromise, that I knew he wouldn't cast me if I bombed. I didn't want to worry about feeling like I'd been given something I didn't deserve.

On the first day of auditions, I took the train to the hospital from work. At the entrance, I said hello to my friends, outpatients waiting in wheelchairs for their rides, inpatients smoking cigarettes with their twisted hands. Corey, who was exactly my age (drunk driving), showed me that he could cross his legs now, which was cause for hugging and outward celebration, but also, secret envy that Mike couldn't do that yet.

As I crossed the lobby to the elevator bank, I made sure to look up at the banner, my favorite, the stenciled tree and the quote that calmed me back then. From the Book of Job—*However, there is hope for a tree: If it is cut down, it will sprout again. And its new shoots will not fail.* I took the elevator up to the conference room where actors lined the hallway: beautiful women with perfectly toned bodies and flawless skin, who were insecure anyway. Men with messenger bags and pant legs rolled up, leaning on their bikes. Some were actors I recognized, but most I had never seen before. I pulled the sides from my backpack so I could read for Allison and Danielle, the dead girl's best friends.

This audition was different from the others. The stakes were higher because Mike couldn't act now, or maybe ever again. He had made significant progress, though progress happens in the tiniest increments these days. He was almost ready to try a sit-to-stand, but still wearing a binder around his belly for breath support, and his one arm still hadn't moved. He couldn't push himself in a wheelchair or laugh out loud, so I had to do well, not just for myself, but for him. My ego was no longer a factor: There were code blues and children dying all around us.

When I walked into the room, Mike sat in the back, buckled into his wheelchair. He may have looked like a tragedy to those who didn't know him, but to me, he looked powerful for the first time in a long time, with a pencil tucked behind his ear, ready to get to work. No matter that I could see his diaper bulging through the midsection of his athletic pants, no matter that his arms looked thinner now when they poked out of a T-shirt. No matter that his one arm stuck to his side and wouldn't let go. He had a vision for this production. He had already put in a phone call to Victory Gardens and they had agreed to give us their studio space for six weeks. He looked alive again.

"How was work?" he asked.

"Sucked," I said.

He smiled.

"Try the Allison monologue for me," he said. "You're not old enough to play Danielle."

I was twenty-five years old and he was twenty-four.

I positioned myself cross-legged on a chair as if I were sitting in the passenger seat of a big old truck, telling my story to a stranger who might whisk me out of town. Mary Ann Thebus, the acting coach, had once said that only crazy people can really imagine another character listening when they give a monologue. But I swear, that day, I saw a truck driver listening to me and I mustered up all my charm for him. Why? So he would drive me away from RIC forever? No. On that day, I enjoyed very much the role of Mike's girlfriend, the one who had stuck around. Corey's girlfriend had left, everyone's girlfriends had left, and I was staying right here.

I gave my monologue to the truck driver, told him all about my boyfriend, and how I had to get out of town. I had memorized the monologue, worked harder than I ever had. The Appalachian accent came naturally, and my throat caught when I said, "Did I tell you that I loved him?"

"Great," Mike said. He uncapped his pen with his teeth, pressed the pen awkwardly into his palm, made a note in his pad. "Now start it drunk, Mag, high as a kite. You just met this guy at a roadhouse bar. He thinks he stands a chance. Trust me on this one. Okay?"

I took a minute, switched to soft focus, switched right into drunk. Started the monologue laughing, pretending like I didn't give a shit about said boyfriend, so that when I admitted I loved him, it surprised even me.

"You took the note," Mike said, impressed. He thought for a minute. "I'll have Lynda come in and read with you."

Lynda read for Danielle and I for Allison. In the play, we waited tables together, got drunk after work in the parking lot. She got drunk in a different way though, not in a giddy way like me; she had a well of sadness. And that was me and Lynda at the bar any night of the week. She had grown up tough, had lived through pain that I was just now learning. We looked at each other and smiled, ready for a hot date. We told stories about our dead girlfriend to strangers and to each other. There are few things I love more than being onstage with Lynda Newton. She's so good you can't help but rise to the occasion.

Mike cast Lynda as Danielle and me as Allison. Danielle was the more challenging role, but I didn't fully get it then. I still had hope in those days that Mike would make a full recovery and soon, that he would win an Academy Award and thank me for sticking by him, that we'd have houses on both coasts. I really did believe this. I think believing this was a way to be happy, and it kept me from making big wishes for myself that might take me somewhere else. I listened outside the room while Lynda read a scene with a string of male actors, one better than the next, but her last line always killed me. I wished I could deliver it like she did, like she had been put on this earth to say it.

The stranger asks Danielle, "How long you been sad, girl?"

Danielle says, "Feels like a lifetime."

Soon enough, I'd know the feeling.

* * *

Mike and I lay in bed after the auditions. He got sore from sitting too long in the wheelchair, so we lay in bed a lot.

"I really didn't think I'd be able to cast you," he said. "You excited for VG?"

Victory Gardens had just won the regional Tony; they were known nationally for producing dynamic and inclusive new plays. This meant the critics would come—it meant high visibility and full houses. But most importantly, I loved the play. For a moment, everything felt exactly as it should, everything felt normal. I slipped my hand under the covers and tried for normal. I watched Mike's eyelids flutter, listened to him say my name. I mounted him, as quietly as I could, so as not to wake Tommy, who was snoring over the television. Mike and I knew just how to be quiet; we had had years of practice with college roommates and the years in his parents' basement. But we gave up, at a certain point, because we didn't want to ruin a good day. I put on my shirt again, looked out the window so I didn't have to look at him, felt my eyes sting with tears and pushed his hand away, too hard, when he tried again. Maybe it was only me who couldn't stand it any longer. Couldn't stand feeling like my twenty-five-year-old body was not enough to bring his back to life.

"Call the newspapers," Mike said, refusing to wallow. "We need publicity for this show."

CHAPTER 14

2003

The newspaper writers wrote about Mike's girlfriend, Maggie, and how she was his rock. They wrote about how we lived together in the Jefferson Park neighborhood before the stroke and how we had been saving up for a red couch from IKEA. There were two distinct goals while Mike was at RIC and they were written on his bulletin board so he could see them every day:

1. Get back to the theater.
2. Get back to the apartment.

The physical therapists, occupational therapists, speech therapists, doctors, nurses, other patients, and their families: the population of our new life. Tara, Mike's physical therapist, stretched his legs until he cried, shocked them with electrodes in the hopes that they might move. Becky, his occupational therapist, cast his arms in the hope that that would straighten them. Laura, his speech therapist, sat with him for several hours while he ran out of breath delivering monologues that he had once upon a time used to impress me. He recited a sonnet at the Newberry Library once, for a monologue competition, which he won, and he dedicated it to me. *My mistress's eyes are nothing like the sun* . . . I didn't mind that he was half in love with his therapists—my eyes were nothing like the sun.

Tara, the physical therapist, was Mike's favorite. I often noticed him looking down her shirt as she knelt at his feet. I'm sure she noticed too. She was good at her job and did all the things for him I couldn't—I loved her for that, too. After the second stroke, the recovery was longer and harder. Tara suggested, at the three-month mark, that Mike try the electric wheelchair, but he said absolutely not because the electric wheelchair meant he wouldn't be able to return to our apartment.

"Speaking of, when are we going to discuss the living situation?" she asked.

After that, Mike refused to work with her for a week. I went in to see her in her office, where she was filling out paperwork and looking uncharacteristically haggard.

"I'm sorry he's being an asshole," I said. "I know you're trying to do what's best."

"Thank you," she said. "Please help me. He listens to you, Maggie. Please convince him to at least try. It'll make things so much easier."

"I'll talk to him," I said.

She pushed the bulky, black power chair into his room, and I sat in it and waited for him to get back from an occupational therapy session. When he saw me and the chair together, he started throwing things as best he could.

"Goddamn it!" he yelled. "You too? Is no one fucking listening to me?"

He thought it was the easy way out. He was afraid it would make him lazy. He knew it was an admission of defeat.

Mike's parents drove me home later that night and said, "Maggie, you should pay off your credit cards. Please don't pay rent anymore. You're hardly ever there."

* * *

Tabitha and Shannon stayed after I scared the others off.

After half a bottle of red wine, I was suffering an irreversible attack of self-pity where I couldn't scrub the hospital images from my mind. The inpatients of the hospital joined me at the kitchen table, as they often did. They surrounded me in their walkers and wheelchairs as I swam in Spanish wine and loneliness. I divulged graphic details of the hospital visits to prove to my friends that I was entitled to this self-pity, and Tabitha and Shannon never disputed it. It had been a few months since the stroke, and that's when tragedy seems to lose its novelty for those who aren't directly involved, but even months in, Tabitha and Shannon sat at my kitchen table and looked at my face. We sat at the table for hours, and I reminded them that Mike and I had eaten here so many times together. We had eaten fruit and scrambled eggs for breakfast, ramen when we felt lazy. We had eaten birthday cake and Christmas pies. Shannon refilled my empty wine glass.

"My sister gave these to us as a housewarming present," I slurred.

They tried to convince me to come to their place because they didn't like me in the apartment alone. I told them I couldn't because Mike's parents were picking me up in the morning, as they always did. I didn't have a car of my own, and I had to be there when he woke.

"Why?" Shannon asked.

"Because he looks so sad otherwise and it makes me want to kill myself."

She pulled tortilla chips from the pantry and a jar of salsa from the fridge, knowing this would entice me to eat. She said she was going grocery shopping tomorrow—could she get me anything? "No," I said, "I'm fine."

"Do they have good food there?" Tabitha asked. "At the hospital?"

"I always eat half of Mike's."

"Then why are you so skinny?"

The phone rang and I grabbed it. I hoped it was Mike, hoped it wasn't Mike, hoped it wasn't bad news in the middle of the night.

"Hello," I said.

"Hey sexy."

"Mike."

"Your tits look amazing tonight."

"You sound weird."

"Who's Mike?" he asked.

"You're scaring me," I said.

"I'm gonna lick those tits like no one's ever licked 'em."

"Who *is* this?"

"You know who it is."

I started screaming and swearing, and Tabitha wrangled the landline phone from my hands.

"Stop," she said. "Hang up the phone. It's a pervert."

But I didn't want to let it go. I wanted to trace this call, find this man and claw his eyes out, squeeze my hands around his throat, make him cry and apologize for this nasty trick he's played on me. I wouldn't let Tabitha take the phone. I swatted her away, screamed into the phone that I would find him, I would kill him, he has picked the wrong girl this time.

"I love when you're angry," he said.

Then I handed the phone to my friend and she hung it up. The refrigerator hum grew loud and angry.

We sat at the table and looked around the room, my very first kitchen. The refrigerator door was adorned with classic movie magnets. *A Streetcar Named Desire*, *An Affair to Remember*. An electric bill that I had yet to pay pinned up with poetry magnets that spelled out some nonsensical message. I wanted to call Mike, but the room phones didn't ring after ten. Patients couldn't be disturbed.

"Do you want me to call the nurse's station?" Shannon asked. "Say it's an emergency?"

"No," I said. "He needs to sleep."

I dumped the remainder of my wine into the sink.

"Who was that?" I asked with my head in my hands.

"I don't know," Shannon said. "It was a very bad person. Okay?"

And I needed to be spoken to like that, like a baby. I needed an explanation.

After my friends had left and I had locked the doors and windows, I went to my bedroom closet and looked at Mike's shirts and jeans, waiting so patiently for him to come home. I got into bed and before turning off the light, ran my hand over his wallet on the nightstand. He had had it with him the night he went to the emergency room, but then I had taken it home and it had been here now for ninety days. "He'll be back," I told myself, screwing my eyes shut. He's just out late again.

* * *

Tara asked if I could leave work a little early the following Friday, so I did. Mike and I sat in a conference room on one of the higher floors with a team of the best doctors and therapists in the country and, also, his parents. Outside, the city of Chicago was golden with late afternoon sunlight, the most beautiful city in the world to us, especially from this height. We watched children playing in the park below us, tourists leaving the contemporary art museum and heading for their hotels, commuters rushing to the train, ready to start their weekends. Tara started the meeting by saying that a power wheelchair was her official recommendation because Mike's left arm wasn't showing signs of improvement.

"Absolutely not," Mike said. "I can't get back to the apartment with that thing. We don't have an elevator."

"It doesn't mean you guys can't live together, Mike. Maybe you can just find a different place without stairs. That's all."

That's all. You try finding a safe and affordable apartment in the city, let alone a safe and affordable apartment without stairs.

Dr. Todd Kuiken explained very clinically that they were going to discharge Michael and needed to know where he would go.

"So you've stopped believing in me," Mike said.

"We absolutely believe in you, and we'll still see you for outpatient therapy a few times a week. But you can go home and sleep in your own bed now. Don't you want that?"

I assume that Mike, like me, felt terrified at this prospect. We didn't have anywhere to go, and who could be with him while I was at work? How much would outpatient therapy cost and who would get him there? What if something happened in the middle of the night? How could we ever live again without the comfort of nurses?

"But Tommy's walking now," Mike said. "And that little girl who broke her neck on the trampoline? She's walking too. I had a second stroke, remember. Doesn't that buy me extra time?"

He was right, but their recoveries had happened within the first few months, and we were past that point now. Kuiken said he would try to get Mike into a cutting-edge neurological study as soon as possible. He gave us a booklet that would help us with the transition back into the world and the rekindling of our sex life. The booklet said that making love was about warmth and tenderness, and not just genitals. Then it got more helpful.

"You can still have a wonderful life together," Kuiken said. "It'll just be different."

I hated the sound of "different."

"Mike," Tara said, too sweetly. "You didn't want to direct your play here, did you?"

But he did. How could we ever readjust to our old life of designers and actors and directors? How could we live among people who weren't like us? I pushed Mike back to his room while his parents went out to pick up dinner. It felt like coming home from a funeral in the middle of the day. I helped him slide into bed and then crawled in beside him. We didn't turn on the television or listen to his headphones together, just looked up at the ceiling.

After a while, he said, as if he'd been rehearsing it: "Well, I guess I'm not makin' it back up those stairs, huh?"

He swallowed and then continued in a strangled voice, "You'd better get rid of the apartment. I know you can't afford it on your own."

He sat there, stone-faced crying, and then I couldn't help it either. He said he had never heard such desperate sadness in me—said I sounded like a tea kettle at its boiling point. I thought of the new couple who would move into the apartment after us, and I hated them already. Maybe the new girl would wait for her boyfriend's footsteps late at night. Maybe they would put a rug under the bed so the landlords couldn't hear their squeaking bed, their lovemaking and laughing. Maybe the girl would be afraid when her boyfriend came home drunk that he would wake the landlords. But I was the passenger in the car outside that apartment when he said, "I can't go in there." I needed to hear his footsteps bounding up the stairs. I needed him to yell and throw things like he had last week. It looked like the light had been kicked out somewhere deep inside him.

* * *

When I walked into my apartment for the last time, there was an eerie feeling that someone had been there. The TV and electronics were there, and our milk-jar bank was full, but something was definitely missing. When I finally opened the closet door in our bedroom, all of Mike's clothes were gone. Every tie, every sweater, his checkered shirts on their hangers, his jeans and winter hats. I looked at the nightstand, and his wallet wasn't there. I called my mother and burst out screaming and crying. Our apartment was the last of my privacy, a place where I could go to change my clothes and take a shower and a few deep breaths. It was the solace sandwiched between days in an office and nights in a hospital room.

It wasn't that Mrs. Thornton had taken his clothes back to her house, to wash them and find space for them, but I couldn't believe she had asked for a key to our apartment without telling me. I couldn't believe that she had come while I was at work, not even warning me that our apartment would be half empty when I got home from the hospital that night. I couldn't believe she had ended this chapter of my life before I even knew it was over, and worst of all, I couldn't bring myself to believe it was over. It had been my first apartment. A place of shouting and Christmas miracles and play readings and surprise parties and coffee and hangovers and life. And now it was half empty.

At the hospital, with Mike, I couldn't stop. I paced around the room while he lay in his bed and kept his voice even.

"She took the extra sheets! She took your *wallet*!" I cried.

"She's trying to be helpful, Maggie."

"Then why didn't she ask me? Tell her to stay out of our apartment. Tell her to give me back the keys."

"I won't do that."

"Why not?! Stick up for me!"

It had been so hard for all of us. Mike had just turned twenty-four, and had just moved out of her house before moving in with me, so none of us were ever sure who was in charge. Mike had asked me to stay and his mother to leave when the nurses came to check for bedsores. The staff had trained me to cath him and administer suppositories, even though she likely would've been better at it. Naturally, his mother wanted to monitor her son's care as closely as possible, but Mike sometimes acted as if she wasn't there, and I admit that I rolled my eyes when she asked me to rub holy oil onto his legs at night. Clearly, I didn't yet understand the cruelty of motherhood.

"Stick up for me!" I cried.

"What am I supposed to do?" Mike asked. "She's my primary caretaker."

I think he knew, even then, that she was the one who had to stay, not me.

* * *

I never went back to the apartment after that. Our parents moved us out, little by little, piled all of our things into the garage where Frankie used to drink. Our friends from the Gift had helped us move in just six months prior. I had brought my girlish things to the apartment, and they stayed there after I left.

CHAPTER 15

2001

The Thorntons' garage had once been a place to change into your swimsuit, a place to hide from the rain on a summer day. There used to be a big hi-fi stereo, a fridge stocked only with booze. The garage had always belonged to Frankie. After Mike's good reviews for his very first Chicago show, his parents had taken us to Noodles to celebrate, the restaurant down the block where blue-haired old ladies drank old-fashioned cocktails with their husbands, and lounge lizards sang Frank Sinatra. The menu advertised "angle hair pasta" and "fettachini alfrado," five dollars for a big wooden bowl. Mike's parents drove home from Noodles, but Mike and I walked, and I scolded him all the way.

"You yawned all through dinner," I said. "They're excited for you. They want to hear about your successes. They want to hear about your life."

We walked past the parking lot of the 7-Eleven where Polish and Mexican teenagers sat on top of their Mustangs and drank supersized cans of beer. We walked past the postwar bungalows and sprinklers in the dark; we walked in perfect sync. Mike looked up at the sky and found a few stars, pointed them out to me.

"Stars," he said in his contemplative voice.

"Weird," I responded. "We usually don't see them around here."

An airplane flew noisily over our heads as we took in barbecue smells, said, "Hi, how are ya?" in soft voices to young families sitting on their cement porches, eating Popsicles.

"I'm proud of you," I said, lowering my voice. "But don't be an asshole to your parents."

". . ."

"Do you like that woman who plays your wife?"

It seemed that the taller he walked, the more courage I lost. I wasn't yet able to distinguish between someone else's strength and my own weakness, didn't know yet how I could be strong too, or that I could be even stronger. Mike and I cut down an alley where the garages were lit and bushes grew out over the fences. We walked down the alley to the Thorntons' backyard, which was bigger than their house. The chlorinated blue of the swimming pool shimmered in the dark. We rounded the pool and came to the open garage where Frankie sat in a patio chair next to an oversized stereo speaker. His collection of one hundred hats hung from the ceiling rafters. Chicago Police Department hats with checkered bands, baseball caps from various winning teams, a mesh hat that read *Women love me. Fish fear me.* Ceramic watermelons and bottles of rum lined the shelves. Brightly colored Hula-Hoops and white roller skates hung from the hooks on the wall.

Frankie had changed into a pair of swimming trunks and a T-shirt, slapped a fisherman's hat onto his head. Mrs. Thornton had gone inside to watch her soap operas while Frank held a can of Miller Lite in a beer cozy, and looked to be conducting a symphony of his own. The music of Peter, Paul, and Mary drifted from the speakers, and I couldn't believe that this cop who intimidated men half his age could sing such a tender lullaby.

"I used to sing this to you when you were a baby, Mikey," he said.

Mike looked sad at first, but then he smiled.

"Let's have a nightcap," Mike said. He clapped his hands together. "It's a gorgeous night, what the hell? Mag, can I interest you in a nightcap?"

Frankie's eyes shot open. He rushed to the garage refrigerator and pulled out two bottles of Heineken.

"Only the fancy ones for my babies," he said. "I love you guys. You know that."

He loved us because we were good friends to each other and to him, and I think he loved me because I understood him in a way that many of Mike's actor friends just couldn't. We pulled out a couple of patio chairs, watched him slur his way through the rest of "Lemon Tree," and in the static between songs, I squeezed his hand and said, "That was a good one, Franco."

At midnight, Mrs. Thornton peeked her head out the side door and said, "Frank, turn the music down. We have neighbors." He turned the music down until her head disappeared and then he turned it back up. The neighbors liked him too much to complain.

Mike and I went inside after the nightcap, but Frankie stayed in the garage. We slipped in through the side door and snuck down to the basement, which is where we slept in those early days when he first came home from college. He had plastered the mirror above his dresser with photographs of us. The two of us dancing at family weddings, screaming at each other onstage in San Antonio, posing with relatives in Ireland. His acting mantras hung on the ceiling so we could read them before we fell asleep. *Stand still—you are enough. Always find the red rock. The actor makes a total gift of himself.* His bookshelves were lined with plays and poetry, and he had actually read all of them. Outside of his bedroom, the washer and dryer chugged all night with his mother's laundry, and the barroom sometimes exploded with the laughter of his father and his cop friends who drank there after they got off midnights.

But on the night of "Lemon Tree," Mike grabbed under my skirt and pulled at my bra straps as I walked ahead of him in the dark. We made our way blindly past the washing machine, into his room that smelled of fabric softener. We fell onto his bed—forget the covers, leave the lights—peeled off our own clothes, quickly now, and then he was on top of me, smelling like citronella candles.

"Promise you won't ever let me sing in the garage by myself," he said. His face looked like his baby picture, the one where he looked so nervous. We made love to a mix of garage-song lullabies, in a bed that was getting too small for us.

"I promise you," I said.

CHAPTER 16

2003

The week before Mike was scheduled to be released, we organized a home visit, which means Frankie, Rita, and I drove to their house in Jefferson Park and waited for Mike to come with Tara and Becky in a customized van. When I walked into the Thorntons' ranch house, everything was just as I remembered. A small kitchen with a mustard-yellow refrigerator, fully stocked. In the living room, a scrunched-velour couch, embroidered with orange and green flowers, and a hutch filled with Belleek china. The high school poem Mike had written for his dying grandfather framed and hanging on the wall. Everywhere else, photos of the sprawling Irish family. The children at milestone stages, the women at varying weights, the men at dizzying levels of drunkenness. Mike as a nervous baby, Mike as a chubby boy with a crewcut, Mike as a skinny teenager with acne. There were even a couple of me, tan and glowing with my arms around my boyfriend's neck. One was taken at a wedding where Mrs. Thornton had commented on the inappropriate length of my dress.

Now here we were, and I felt so sorry for her. She put on her reading glasses, showed me the medical bills and the application she'd filled out for the handicapped parking placard. She confided that Emma, the old Italian woman across the street, had been nosier than ever lately. We peeked out the front window, only to see Emma doing the same, waiting for Mike to arrive. The child she had watched grow up, the child she had yelled at to get off of her lawn. Mrs. Thornton and I laughed, and Emma closed her curtains.

"I cleaned out the guest bedroom for him," Mrs. Thornton said. "I just hope the wheelchair fits through the door. And Mag, you stay here as often as you like."

The van pulled up in the side drive and Frank helped Tara and Becky lift the wheelchair over the cement step, through the side door. I held the door open as widely as I could, and made myself as small as possible. Mike looked uncomfortable in his chair and growled under his breath. Mrs. Thornton hurried to put out a lunch spread, all of Mike's favorites. Frankie said, "I'll fire up the grill. Burger, hot dog?" It hurt my feelings when Becky and Tara confessed that they were vegetarians because he wasn't prepared for that. Tara and Becky left Mike in the kitchen with me while they began a house tour with Mrs. Thornton. They measured doorways, drew quick and efficient diagrams of the bathroom. The house had always been cozy, but with the addition of a wheelchair and the subtraction of the basement, it became somewhat claustrophobic.

"Good to be back?" I asked.

"No. I want our apartment."

"Me too," I said. "Me too."

I took a can of iced tea from the fridge and opened it for him because he didn't have the fine motor skills to do it himself.

Tara and Becky returned with Mrs. Thornton, who was an incredible improviser and undeniably competent. We would transfer Mike to his grandmother's old wheelchair to get him in the bathroom for a shower. She would station a portable commode in his bedroom for instances when he couldn't make it in time. Frankie's buddies would be over the next day to help him build a ramp up to the front door, and the disability checks would start arriving any day now. Mike would be assigned to David and Katie, the outpatient therapists, and everything would be done by the time he moved home next week, his mother promised.

We would live next door to his parents' bedroom, the one we listened to at night. His mother would say the rosary over and over until Frankie said, "Rita, get some sleep now, honey." Sometimes we heard his mother crying, sometimes we heard his father crying. Always, Mike said to me, "Turn on some music or something. I can't stand it." Always he looked at me and said, "This is temporary. Remember that. I am *not* disabled."

CHAPTER 17

2003

We slowly became accustomed to a life outside the hospital, and the world of the theater became our home again. Mike and I woke up with the birds now while our friends slept their lives away. Mike spent a few hours in the bathroom every morning and used the time to map out *Language of Angels* rehearsals, make outlines for design meetings. How should he light Paul? What costume might I wear? What kind of waitress was she anyway? Would Victory Gardens allow spray paint on the walls to give the effect of the cave? And what about the song the girls sang in the script? He listened to every version.

I got ready in the basement where we used to sleep—memorized my lines down there, broke scenes into beats, called the newspapers and pitched our story. We were still often late to rehearsal, because it took Mike so long to be done in the bathroom and get dressed, even with my help.

We held rehearsals at a friend's garage in Jefferson Park, partially to save money. Most of the actors lived closer to downtown, but they took trains and buses to make it easier on Mike. We opened the garage door for ventilation and rehearsed all summer long. Mike did table work with us, showing us maps of North Carolina, photographs of caves, asking us clarifying questions about our relationships with one another, to make sure we were all telling the same story. Paulie's ugly little Boston terrier sat in the garage and breathed noisily while we rehearsed. John Gawlik ran around, shooting at me with his prop gun. During rehearsal and after, we all took turns pushing Mike out to the car, packing up his briefcase, opening his water and snacks.

* * *

About five months after the strokes, Mike stood. It went like this: David, his outpatient physical therapist, tied a gait belt around his waist, then he rocked back and forth as he counted. "One, two, three!" He had been trying this for several weeks, and usually, the rocking would lead to Mike moving an inch off of his chair, maybe two. But one day, the rocking worked and he made it all the way up. When he got to his feet, his legs spasmed and shook, then calmed down, and he stood, six foot two. I had forgotten how tall he was.

"Babe," I said.

He looked down at me and smiled, then fell back into his chair with a thud.

At the five-month mark, we were well into rehearsal for *Language of Angels*. Mark Brown, a columnist from the *Sun-Times*, showed up at the garage one night, and we all felt like our lives were beginning. This is how he described it: "A summer breeze had cut the temperature inside the garage from stifling to merely stuffy. A box fan hummed on a floor partially covered with thin gray carpet. A window air conditioner had been installed but abandoned as useless . . . A lawn mower and leaf blower were shoved to the side with the paint cans and used tires. They weren't props." We hoped that everyone in Chicago might read the feature-length article and come to see our show. Mark Brown's article was entitled "A Greater Appreciation of Life, Less Fear of Death." He ran a photograph of Mike sitting in his wheelchair, smiling and wearing Converse All Stars. He made the big announcement: "At therapy the other day, Thornton stood for a minute and a half." In a way, that sounds prettier, doesn't it? And in a way, more vulgar. One sentence can't convey the beauty of that moment, or the horror of how far we had to go.

At the six-month mark, Mike and I would sit with his parents in the kitchen for breakfast and in the middle of it, while we were doing crossword puzzles or reading the newspaper or memorizing our scripts, he'd scream, "Get the urinal!" One day, I raced for the blue plastic container, and got it to him just as he was fiddling with his waistband. But with the unpredictability of his hands, he didn't quite make it and urine started shooting all over the kitchen like a crazy fountain. We all laughed at the slapstick comedy of it, and I was so proud of us for learning to laugh together this way, but then Mike started to cry. That terrible moment where laughter turns into crying.

Mark Brown's article began with a quote from Mike: "The last thing I want about my story coming out is the triumph of the human spirit." Mike also was quoted as saying, "I know it sounds ridiculous but I really wouldn't exchange the experience for anything." He put on a show for the newspaper reporters and his actors, but I got the real Mike Thornton. That was something I had previously been proud of, but now it was beginning to make me angry. *Wouldn't exchange it for anything?* Mark Brown did his research and interviewed Chicago directors about Mike's talent and promise. Sheldon was quoted as saying, "He has charisma on stage. You just always want to watch what he's doing." BJ said Mike was a born performer, and he was confident in Mike's eventual return to the stage. Mark Brown reported that "[the directors] base some of their faith on Thornton's support group, which includes his chums, his parents, and his girlfriend, Maggie." BJ said it was "so Chicago," the way "they take care of their own." We puzzled over that quote at the time. What else was there to do, but take care of your own? His mother said he didn't laugh when I wasn't there. What else was there to do?

* * *

We spent the hottest weeks in August in the studio theater at Victory Gardens, such a change from the residential garage in Jefferson Park. We were blocks from the lake now, had air conditioning that worked, a box-office staff, and a state-of-the-art sound booth. Outside, the Lincoln Park Trixies paraded from bar to bar, looking for a doctor or a banker to save them. Inside, Mike sat in his chair and we spread out in the theater for notes while Connolly, the one who had driven Mike to the emergency room, spray-painted the walls with our character names. *Billy loves Allison. Seth loves Celie. Remember me forever and ever.* The sound designer sat in the booth, fiddling with the sound cues, voices echoing in caves. The lighting designer sat on the floor with a headlamp and a lantern, trying them with different bulbs. Mike was in a shitty mood.

"Paul," he said. "You 'sore' it?" (Letting him know that his New York accent did not belong in this show about Appalachia.)

"Lynda, you went up on your lines. Again." (In a totally monotone voice, reading from his notebook.)

"Yikes," I said, trying to be funny. "Somebody ate a bitch burger today."

"Maggie, this isn't theater camp. We're gonna have the most visibility we've ever had and you're acting like it's theater camp. Your monologue is not there yet, by the way."

Then it was time to open and we weren't fooling around anymore.

We all went to our day jobs, as usual, with gnawing feelings in our stomachs, looked at our scripts for the first time in weeks because we were now in total panic mode. We arrived at the theater earlier than we had to, tried to eat and couldn't. Someone most certainly said something motivational, though I've no idea what that might have been. I do know that Lynda had posted Dolly Parton lyrics all over the dressing room mirrors and plugged in a coffeemaker so we didn't have to buy it. We retired to our corners of the small dressing room and listened to the audience. Subscribers and critics, artistic directors and agents and members of the Jeff Award committee, local family and friends. Then we tried to forget they were there as we listened to the sounds of the preshow. The cave that we all imagined we had been in together more than a decade ago. The sounds of our own scared voices in the dark.

Paulie, looking shell-shocked, stood eerily still in a cave inside Victory Gardens Theater, wearing a down vest and a miner's helmet clamped down over his curls. His headlamp was the only light in the theater at first, the walls graffitied with scribblings of lost love. *Billy Loves Allison. Seth Loves Celie. Remember me forever and ever . . .* The space was inundated with sound cues: echoes of laughter, young girls calling out to their boyfriends, hurried footsteps, squeals of delight. A small girl's silhouette appeared in a shadow and she began to sing, in a weak, unsteady voice. "What'll I do when you are far away and I am feeling blue?" It sounded like one of the girls in the cave couldn't find her boyfriend. She called out to him, timidly at first, but soon screaming. The shadow continued to sing. "What'll I do with just a photograph to tell my troubles to? What'll I do?" The voices cut out abruptly, the shadow ran away, and the play began. Paulie turned on his light, searched every face in the audience. Then he said softly, almost inaudibly, "This is how it went, this is what I remember . . ."

Lynda and Brendan, my best friend and my boyfriend in the play, had a knock-down, drag-out fight about the way he treated me, and I left the scene, got the hell away from these drunken hillbillies. I listened to them scream at each other until Lynda came storming offstage and punched her hand into a brick wall. Then I went on for my truck-driver monologue. I sat in a bucket seat, looked out into a sea of blackness, and started laughing, nervously, in the company of strangers. I began to tell the story of leaving my boyfriend. I came offstage, feeling a little stunned. Lynda and John had their scene at the end, where he comes to her, trying to figure out if she knows he was the one who killed her friend all those years ago, and now he's the sheriff of our town. It's a menacing scene—they are really good. John leaves the trailer, Lynda puts on a pot of tea, and the ghost of her best friend appears in the doorway to join her. The audience audibly, collectively gasped, and the play was over. At the end, when we took our bows, it was hard to think there was anything better than this.

The next few mornings, I woke up before Mike, snuck to 7-Eleven, and picked up a newspaper and quickly scanned it for our review, so that if I got a negative mention, I could feel sorry for myself before he woke up. But the day it was printed, a full-page review with a color photo, that wasn't necessary. We had been highly recommended by Hedy Weiss, the most influential critic in Chicago at the time. She called Lynda a powerhouse, said Paul's performance was lyrical, said the last scene between Lynda and John "crackled with Pinteresque danger."

"*Language of Angels* has been vividly directed by Michael Patrick Thornton, who no doubt drew on his own recent brush with mortality this past winter . . . Whatever the source of his inspiration, he has elicited first-rate performances from his actors, including Maggie Andersen as Allison, Danielle's naive, fast-talking youthful pal, and Brendan Donaldson as the melancholy Billy." She also wrote, "The past lives. It can haunt us. It can keep guilt alive . . . The past can speak to us in strange, if strangely recognizable tongues that deserve to be heard."

We opened in August of 2003 and ran for several weeks, then we extended. I did a monologue five nights a week about the guilt I felt over running away from my boyfriend, even though it was ultimately the best thing for me. I did the monologue so many times that I started to feel like the kids in the caves were us and like some older version of me was telling the story of our failed relationship to an audience full of strangers.

CHAPTER 18

2003

In 2003, the Chicago Cubs were in the playoffs. Mike bought me a paper-thin Cubs T-shirt and requested that I wear it whenever we watched games, or every day if I wanted. Whenever I wasn't at the theater, I watched the games on TV with Mike. We watched our home team win and lose, win and lose again. We cheered and booed from his parents' living room, felt the air go out of us when they made careless errors. It was the year of hoping an underdog could win.

Imagine a high school gymnasium, the sort of state-of-the art gym built for a college prep school known for its academics *and* sports teams. This is where Mike went to high school, although he never had much use for the gym. His most distinct memory is a pep rally he emceed in his sophomore year. He spent several nights reading joke books and tips on how to write a roast; he wrote and rewrote a script to take him through the hour-long pep rally, intended to celebrate the sports team's victories. This was the high school his father and uncles had attended. They played baseball and basketball there, and this was his way of paying some tribute to them, trying to fit into their tradition. He got up on the stage, full of confidence. He stepped up to the microphone, introduced himself, tried out his first joke ("A shamrock walks into a bar . . .") and a few football players in the front row started a chant with smirks on their faces. "Lo-ser. Lo-ser." The chant spread like wildfire, a sea of adolescent boys soon screaming and stomping their feet until a blush rose up Mike's neck, and the teachers decided to pull him off the stage. This story makes me want to find those boys, who are men now, and punch them in their faces.

Ten years later, Mike stood on a stage in that same gymnasium on a walker. A benefit, raising money for his medical expenses. One thousand and some people filled the space. Our extended families, every friend we had ever known, our parents' friends, alumni of the high school, local actors and directors, neighborhood folks who had read about Mike in the newspaper. Mike's mother and aunts catered the benefit with homemade pasta and beef sandwiches. His father, uncles, and cousins tended bar at long collapsible tables. Pretty actresses worked the room, hawking raffle tickets and talking up the silent auction. Many of the partygoers had to sit in the balcony because the gym was so crowded. I suppose Chicago does take care of its own. I suppose Chicago is a bit like A. J. Liebling called it, a big-city facade with the soul of a hick town.

I had written the plea letter, per Mrs. Thornton's request, and tried to conjure images that would evoke compassion. "Michael had been saving for a couch, a red one from IKEA." His mother and aunts edited out my best lines, I thought, before we sent the invitation. I didn't complain, but clearly, I had started to care about the quality of my writing again.

Halfway through the fundraiser, Mike stood shakily at a podium and read a speech that he had written, thanking everyone for coming, commending everyone on their generosity. Murmurs went through the crowd. "He's so handsome, isn't he?" And that was not charity. He really had become even more handsome, one of those men who gets better with age. When he spoke, everyone listened, and I was reminded of how he should always be on a stage, though that would prove more challenging now.

In the speech, Mike thanked Rita and Frank, his parents, for being "in the trenches" with him. He thanked my parents, Laura and Alan, for raising a daughter who was his best friend and the love of his life, some sort of angel. He said we'd been dating for five years now and he couldn't wait to spend the rest of his life with me. I found out later that everyone thought he was going to propose to me that night, but I just stood in the audience and bit my fingernails down, swallowing over and over. My father found me in the crowd just to hug me. The joke in my family is that my father only hugs us on Christmas, so this was unusual, and sad.

The fundraiser was a success, raised over $100,000. Mike said the money would eventually help us to start a life together, put a down payment on a house, but I thought it should be earmarked for continuing doctor's visits, outpatient therapy, and workout equipment, a supplement to the meager disability checks and Frankie's pension from the police department.

* * *

Mike called me some sort of angel in the speech. But *was* I? God no.

* * *

One day, all the Redmoon Theater bosses left early and a coworker told me she was skipping out to meet some friends at a Wrigleyville beer garden; she tried to entice me to come along. "You look so feckin' pale," she said in her best Irish accent. "A pint would do ya good." It was an unseasonably warm September day, the Cubs were on a winning streak, I had made all my press calls for the week, written all the media releases. Why should the devil get all the good tunes? I didn't call Mike and tell him, and didn't have a cell phone at the time, so he couldn't reach me if he tried. Certainly, I'd have a couple beers and then head to his parents' house, be home in time for dinner, as I always was, now that *Language of Angels* had ended. I had a bed at my parents' house, but almost every night, I stayed with Mike.

My work friend and I walked to the beer garden, and when we arrived, there were several men from Philadelphia waiting for us. They sat around a picnic table with several pitchers of beer. They wore polos and cargo shorts, were on vacation, away from their wives and girlfriends and jobs, had wads of cash to spend. My friend introduced me as "a Chicago girl" and it was intoxicating just to be around men who didn't know my circumstances. I had a beer and it was like heaven; it was one of those days where everyone looks beautiful. I had a few more, then decided to play tour guide, took the men on an impromptu Wrigleyville pub crawl. In one bar, I asked for the manager, Joe DeRosa, a friend of mine from high school. He wasn't working that evening, but the bartender called him, told him I was there, and then picked up our tab. The men were impressed, and drunk. They started doing impersonations of my accent. "Ay bartender, tell Joey Dee to hook me up. It's me, Maaagie. Don't you know who I am?" But that only encouraged me to impersonate their accents, and talk trash about their team. They offered me their extra ticket to the game, and I took it.

A night game at Wrigley is a romantic thing to a girl who grew up two miles away. It's childhood and possibility, the first time you get to stay out late, feel the magic of the night. At the park, the Philly guys bought us anything we wanted. Hot dogs, pretzels, peanuts. At some point, I did call Mike from someone's cell phone and tell him I was at the game, but I'd leave early, before the seventh-inning stretch, I promised. I wouldn't make it for dinner, but maybe we could have a nightcap in the yard. I pretended not to notice the disappointment in his voice. Fuck him, I thought. I stay with him every night. I *deserve* this, I'm *sad*.

I had nicknames for all the Philly guys. Ray Liotta, Five-Foot-Two, Tubby the Tuba. Their faces are all fuzzy to me now, but what is not so fuzzy is that I went down to the concourse to smoke a cigarette with one of the few single ones. I rambled about the first game my father had taken me to, how some drunk in the bleachers had spilled a beer on my head and my dad went bullshit crazy.

"I always loved to keep score," I said. "Still do."

"Who was your favorite player back then?" he asked.

"Ryne Sandberg," I said.

"Ryno," he said, smiling.

"I hear he coaches the minor leagues now."

"I want to kiss you," the man said, looking helpless.

I tucked my chin and laughed, nervously. We went back to our seats, and on the way, I avoided looking at the handicapped section, where Mike and I had sat just a few weeks before. Old-timer Cubs fans sitting in wheelchairs, children with bald heads and cancerous brain tumors, women and men whose legs had been blown off by landmines.

I took a cab to Mike's house, long after the game was over, still dreaming of kissing the man I didn't know, still empowered by my accidental sexuality. But also, my stomach churned with anxiety. "Sober up," I thought. "Get ready for an argument."

The cab driver pulled up in front of the ranch house and said, "A ramp? Somebody is in a wheelchair? Your grandma?"

I ran up the ramp, so much easier when I wasn't pushing, and flew in the front door, propped open because of the weather. Mike waited beside the door with his back to me, and I decided to take the affectionately drunk attack.

"I'm sorry, baby," I said, playing up my drunkenness, hugging him around his neck. "I had fun though. I wish you could've come and met us." This was the era when he refused to take the free disability cabs, or a ride from anyone other than his parents.

"I'm glad you're safe," he said without looking at me.

"I brought you a program," I said. "Did you watch?"

"I'm furious with you," he said.

He watched the television and ignored me.

A clean house after a wasted day of drinking is so sobering, inflicts such guilt and pain.

Frankie came in from the kitchen.

"How you doin', Little Bit? Good game?"

"I think I'm ready to go to bed," Mike called to his mother, instead of asking me.

I sat there on the couch, smelling of sun and hot dogs and beer. Mrs. Thornton came in and started pushing Mike toward his room, always a challenge on carpet.

"Michael," she said, just loud enough so I could hear. "Don't be unreasonable. She's twenty-five years old; she's done a lot for you. She deserves a night out once in a while."

I sat there alone on the couch.

Frankie explained in a whisper. "He's been waiting by the door for you since six."

"I know," I said. "I'm sorry. I guess I lost track of time."

I had completely lost track of time. I mean: How old was I now? What were my goals and my dreams? Who had I wanted to be by the age of twenty-five?

In bed, we lay far apart from each other. Mike's happiness depended too much on me now, which is what he had once resented me for. I thought of the statistics I had read about caretakers and their compromised life spans. I knew I had made Mike feel sad and embarrassed in front of his parents, the way he had felt at that pep rally in high school. When the silence became unbearable, I whispered, "Sometimes I just want to kill myself." When the affectionate drunk didn't work, I switched to a different approach. But as Mary Ann Thebus had once taught us, it was all inside, just waiting for the actor to open the appropriate window.

CHAPTER 19

2004

Mike made the announcement that he would be focusing on therapy for a while, so the next season would be put on hold. When he made this announcement in 2003, a few of our company members quit. To me, it felt like a betrayal, but Mike said it was okay. He had to focus on his recovery now and couldn't afford to be distracted.

We hung out in the Thorntons' backyard on the Fourth of July. Paulie came, and so did my sisters and Mike's new therapists. Paulie swam around in the pool in his cut-off jean shorts. Connolly came after a Cubs game and thoughtfully brought Mike a souvenir bat. Mike tried to swing it for a photo op, but had a little trouble, and that's when I sensed his grief taking over. Frankie grilled burgers for us and told stories about how all the men in the family loved when my sisters and I came over and swam in our bikinis. Paulie and Connolly laughed, but Mike didn't. When he asked me to come inside and help him change at some point, I said, "Hey, it's a beautiful night. Remember 'Nightswimming'? Remember when we used to listen to it on repeat and swim in the pool at night when we were first falling in love? We were so young then. We were so foolish."

He smiled.

"And how much longer do you think Paul's gonna wear those jean shorts? He's gotta get out of the seventies."

He laughed.

Later, I sat in his lap when it was time for the fireworks, which were always biggest in a cop neighborhood, and kissed him while the night sky exploded just above our heads.

Wedding season came around again and I went to all of them alone because Mike had understandably become sort of agoraphobic, but I reported back to him on all the gossip. I didn't tell him how at one, everyone kept on telling me we would get married too someday, that we could win one of those contests and get our whole wedding paid for, that we were supposed to have been first, that it was a tragedy, what had happened.

"I heard he was roofied at the Heritage Center," someone said.

"No, it was food poisoning from Taco Bell."

They were all crying and carrying on, and I comforted them, but then I got so sad realizing it was my story they were telling, I left before the cake was cut. Shannon and Tabitha put me in a cab, took the driver's picture, and told him they'd cut off his balls if I didn't make it home. I started to nod off in the back seat. The driver asked me where he should take me, and I remember saying, "I don't know" and feeling so disoriented.

"What do you mean you don't know?" the cab driver asked. "Where do you live?"

Fall came and the wind tore the leaves off the trees. Mike was doing the Lokomat study a few times a week with his new therapists, which he and I called "the Robot." I would come and watch once a week, and David would play our favorite songs. He would buckle Mike into a harness and then "an electromechanical gait orthosis" would help him to walk on a treadmill. I would stand there and watch him joke with the therapists and the neurologists, throw around all the fancy scientific terms he had learned in his deliberately pretentious voice.

"Mag, this is an electromechanical gait orthosis. Basically, it's trying to help me remember how to walk."

We would listen to "Smoke Gets in Your Eyes," and once Mike got going, David would whisper, "Go ahead." That was our favorite part. I'd get up on the treadmill, facing Mike, and he would, with a little effort, get his arms around my waist.

"This is how we'll dance at our wedding," he said, smiling. "My God, are you a midget."

We dressed up for Halloween as Mantacore, the Siberian tiger, and Siegfried, his trainer. It was Mike's ridiculous idea. In real life, the poor trainer had had a stroke after being attacked by the tiger, but Mike didn't want to be the trainer; he wanted to be the tiger. He had to find some kind of wicked humor in his situation, and I was happy to help. I went to Joann Fabrics and bought sequins for my jumpsuit and fur for Mike's coat. My mother helped me make the costume, and Mike and I laughed hysterically as he smeared fake blood on my neck with his good hand, painted his own face white with black stripes. We hung a tail from the back of his wheelchair.

Christmas Eve came and I went to my family party alone because Mike said he just couldn't do it. There were very few places he liked to go in those days; he hated his wheelchair being carried up and down the stairs of old apartments, and preferred to hang out with his therapists and other actors, the people who made him feel like himself. His therapists had witnessed his progress, and in acting circles, he was still king. I felt lonely as my aunt played "The Twelve Days of Christmas" on the piano and my sisters and their fiancés drank eggnog and sang along. It was the first time in years that Mike hadn't been there with me, and I wondered if he would ever come again. After dinner, I went to the Thorntons' house. Mike and I weren't able to make it down to the basement where the real party happened, so we stayed in the kitchen upstairs and had dessert alone. He gave me black leather pants for a present, which I never would've bought myself, but I did like trying them on, and it was good for both of us that I feel as sexy as possible. Costumes made everything better.

On New Year's Eve, Mike and I hosted our own party because we had missed quite a few that year (see: stairs) and wanted to ring in 2004 with friends. To be fair, Frank and Rita were perfectly happy to have a night to themselves. We bid on a handicapped-accessible hotel suite on Michigan Avenue, which means wider doors and an accessible bathroom. I knew because we had rented accessible hotel rooms near the airport a few times. Mike usually rented those in response to my complaints about living with his parents.

"How much longer?" I would ask, and the next weekend, we'd have a hotel room.

Mrs. Thornton and I went downtown early with the commode, the walker, and a few bottles of champagne. Mike and I checked in later that afternoon and delighted in the room. Pocket doors, puddle curtains on the windows, a view of the Magnificent Mile and the white lights in the trees. Later that evening, in the middle of a card game, Mike looked at me and whispered, "I can't breathe." This was becoming normal and usually happened when we stayed in a hotel. I think he was afraid, in those early days, of being too far from home. Also, the last time we stayed in an airport hotel had been especially awful. I had brought along the lingerie. He lay in the bed, I unzipped his pants and ran off to change. He watched soft porn, just like the binder from RIC told us. When I returned, he looked at me like he was really going to enjoy this. He turned off the TV, pulled me close to him and, after some kissing, looked at me with that same panicked face and started to gasp for air. I couldn't even cry—my guts were wrenched with sobbing.

When our friends asked how our sex life was, or even if they didn't, Mike would say, "Amazing. Mag totally got it up the other day."

I would nod and smile, complicit in the lie, and say, "I'm a special snowflake."

We excused ourselves from the New Year's party and I helped Mike into the bedroom, closed the pocket doors. Tabitha turned up the music, which was thoughtful. Mike and I whispered to each other. His stomach was upset, he said. I let him have his privacy, then I awkwardly entertained our guests in the other room until he called for me. This is the kind of thing many couples have to go through, I know, but usually it's after years of marriage, after the children and grandchildren, after gray hair and vacations, after longer lives. I just had to grow up a little faster, and didn't feel prepared. When Mike returned to the party, an hour later, he made a joke of it all.

"Well, that was awkward," he said too loudly. "But I feel much better now. Who wants to play some dice?"

That night, Tabitha asked me to be her maid of honor. She and her best guy were getting married, at the age of twenty-six, and Mike and I were such an inspiration. She couldn't think of anyone better to be her best lady.

* * *

Sometime in the spring, Mike took his first steps. We credited it to the Lokomat. With the assistance of electrodes that David taped to his legs, he was able to take a strong step with his right foot and then drag the left behind. He took the electrodes and practiced at home, for me and his parents who cheered him on.

"I'm like the Little Engine That Could," he said.

Carpet was difficult, so we tied plastic bags onto his feet to make the left foot slide more easily. The sidewalk also proved to be a challenge because of the inconvenience of cracks, but Mike never stopped trying. He usually got tired after a few steps, but that was good enough for all of us. He usually got scared if the wind kicked up, but David, his therapist, always said, "He *will* fall, eventually." Mrs. Thornton didn't like the sound of that.

"Not on my watch," she said.

"Mother," David said with a gentle smile. "He will fall."

Mike would be reading or watching movies and I'd get annoyed that he wasn't doing more. This was the year devoted to therapy, after all. But he got so sore after a two-hour workout, he would sleep twelve hours after a good session. Even David said that every other day was probably best; his body needed time to recuperate.

I often encouraged him to try again, while his parents were more cautious. Whenever they went out to run errands, we conducted our own therapy sessions. I studied the physical therapy diagrams and stretched his arm up and out to the side while he lay in bed and ground his teeth. I couldn't do this when his mother was home because she'd appear in the doorway like she had ESP or something and say, "Stop now, Mag. I think you're hurting him." One day, we decided to tie the plastic bag on his foot and try a few steps, even though he'd walked the day before. I suggested it and he went along with it, albeit a little reluctantly. Look what he could do when he rehearsed a role long enough—I knew he'd get the hang of this, no problem. So: He rocked and stood. Mission accomplished. Then he took a step with his good leg and dragged the weaker one behind it.

"Again," I said. And probably promised a sexual favor too.

He did it again, beautifully.

"One more time," I said. "You can do it. I love you."

He leaned into the step and then his good leg started shaking.

"Get the wheelchair," he said.

"Don't be afraid," I said.

"Goddamn it, get the wheelchair."

Just like that, he was down, lying twisted on the floor, red-faced and angry at first, but then he must've seen my face go white. *Not on my watch.*

"Okay," he said calmly. "Bruiser. Listen to me. Bruiser? Calm down now. Listen to me."

He directed me on exactly how to help him into a sitting position, and eventually, I had him propped him against the elevated mat. When he slumped over a little, I'd straighten him back up. We sat there and waited for what seemed like an eternity, scared kids waiting to get busted for the wild party they had thrown while their parents were out of town. When Mrs. Thornton did come home, she walked into the living room, saw her son slumped on the floor, and screamed. I stopped trying so hard after that. I didn't trust myself anymore, and I don't think Mike trusted me anymore either.

* * *

Not long after, the doctors at the Rehab Institute of Chicago called in "the family" for a meeting. Mike, his parents, me. Again, we sat in a conference room on one of the higher floors. I thought maybe they would congratulate us on Mike's walking, but also worried that maybe the insurance had run out or that we had to change therapists. Maybe we had become too close with David and Katie. After all, they had taken us to a riverboat casino to celebrate Mike's first steps because it felt like such a lucky day. They had come to the big party I had thrown last month for his twenty-fifth birthday, and they had stayed the latest. I smiled when they entered the room, but felt nervous when they wouldn't make eye contact.

Dr. Kuiken started with the big announcement: They would be discontinuing outpatient therapy altogether. Then he turned it over to David, who explained that Mike had hit a plateau and the recovery might very well continue, just in smaller increments and more slowly. Katie encouraged him to continue whatever he had been working on at home. He had surpassed the one-year mark, she said, which indicated the end of progress. Katie and David both looked sheepish, and Mike looked at the floor.

"I don't care what you say," Mrs. Thornton said. "I pray to God and to my father and mother, and I know my son will make a full recovery."

Frankie seemed totally bewildered. "But he just took his first steps. Doesn't that mean anything?"

Mike shook his head and clenched his jaw, and then I made it worse.

"How can we work on him at home?" I cried out. "What are *we* supposed to do? I don't have a PhD in physical therapy. I don't know what to do, I don't know how you do what you do. Katie, David, *please*."

Nobody said a word.

"Are you kidding me? Are you fucking kidding me?"

The room buzzed with silence.

"Help us!" I cried. "Please help us!" Then I stormed out of the room.

I went downstairs, took a few minutes to pull myself together with all the rest of the desperate families, and when I met Mike and his parents at the valet, I forced a laugh and said, "God, I'm sorry. I have such a bad temper. I really have to work on that." Mike's parents looked defeated, and he just looked angry.

"I'm so sorry," I said to Mike. "Let's rent a funny movie or something. I mean, fuck them, right? They don't know who you are. Fuck them."

CHAPTER 20

2004

I continued to write whenever I could. On trains and buses, in the morning, at night, when Mike was sleeping and when I should've been. About a year after the stroke, I started surfing the internet at work, trying to find cheap ways to get to all the places I had always wanted to see. Berlin, Rio de Janeiro, Hong Kong, Saint Petersburg, Prague. This kind of daydreaming staved off the depression.

My day job at Redmoon Theater was slowly driving me crazy because I realized, during my time there, that it was the writer I wanted to be, not the actor. I was sick of working so hard as their publicist and not doing anything with my own creativity. I was writing mostly confessional poetry, which wasn't very good, but it did make me feel better sometimes. I knew I needed concentrated time if I wanted to improve, so I decided to apply to the Prague Summer Program, a creative writing program in the Czech Republic that offered scholarships based on portfolios and letters of recommendation. I hadn't been in school in years, so I didn't have professors I could ask for letters. I read all of my poems, picked the strongest ten, ordered them and reordered them obsessively. Then I started to work on my statement of purpose: Why did I want to study in Prague?

Franz Kafka and Milan Kundera were both Czech and happened to be two of my favorite writers, for *The Metamorphosis* and *The Unbearable Lightness of Being.* But also: My maternal great-grandmother,

Johanna, had been born and raised there. She came to the States as a teenager with her husband and her baby. They settled, eventually, in Chicago, where her husband and child died in the influenza pandemic soon after they arrived. Men from the health office came to their flat and burned all of her furniture and belongings, and she wandered the streets, homeless. I made my grandmother tell her mother-in-law's story to me, over and over again. Johanna remarried and had more children, eventually. She met a baker, had two sons with him, and made a new life. She *lived*, and that was a story I needed to hear. I wanted to see her childhood home, wanted to be near her somehow.

The Prague Summer Program hired award-winning writers to teach creative writing workshops. I found their books at the public library, read them one by one, and found myself imploding with excitement, imagining myself far away. Learning a little Czech, studying history and literature, meeting students from all over the world. I wanted to get away, wanted a break, wanted to be alone, and I had never wanted that. After growing up in an apartment crammed with five people, I didn't even know how to be alone, but suddenly I knew I had to learn.

Mike and I lay in bed and I told him about the program. His small bedroom was our only privacy now. Our home was the house of a semi-retired couple in their fifties, not a couple in their twenties, but we filled the bedroom with our things and locked the door. We had our own television, a few of our favorite posters, a bamboo plant, and a bookcase. I showed Mike the brochures I had sent for, told him how the former president of the Czech Republic was a celebrated playwright, then I asked him to write the recommendation. He was an artistic director, after all. His name signified prestige; it looked good on paper.

"Will you write it?" I asked.

"Of course," he responded.

"And what if I get in?"

"It's only six weeks," he said. "Anyway, do you really think I expect you to change my diapers your whole life?"

He sounded like a bad actor when he said this, and I still don't know what he expected. In our minds, it was all still a fantasy. Prague Castle looked like a fairy tale to me, one that made me believe in happy endings. Mike typed a beautiful letter for me with one finger, then he asked, slightly embarrassed, "Honey? Where is Prague?"

"In the Czech Republic," I said.

"Okay. Cool. Thanks for not laughing at me."

* * *

I was accepted into the program with a scholarship, which made me feel like myself again, like the person Mike had fallen in love with a long time ago. I would leave for Prague on the third of July, stay in a Czech dormitory, just a few train stops from Charles University, where my classes would be held. I would take a six-week leave of absence from my job and have a place when I returned.

* * *

Sometime in the spring, I started hearing songs differently. I'd find myself turning up the car radio without even realizing it. I used to be so judgmental of friends who didn't visit enough, friends who didn't visit at all, but one day, I heard "Babe I'm Gonna Leave You" by Led Zeppelin, and started to panic. Once the song had ended, I told myself that Prague would be a much-needed break and I would return, refreshed and ready to tackle anything.

* * *

Before I went away, I did one last show, back when we still rented from an old speakeasy in Uptown called the National Pastime. The same place we had done *County Fair*, the last show before Mike got sick, the last show before our world turned upside down. Will, our co-artistic director who lived across the country now, had written the script and it probably wasn't quite ready for production, probably needed a couple more drafts. I told Mike I thought so and he said, "Mag, take off your writer hat if you want to do the show. Put it back on when you go to Prague next month. For now, you're an actor. Nothing else. Get out of your head. I only need your heart." It's true that I was feeling more like a writer than an actor lately, that something was shifting in me.

A Young Man in Pieces was about the quarter-life crisis because there didn't seem to be enough plays written about twentysomethings at the time. I'm sure there's good reason for that, but it did make our season planning more challenging, when few of us looked old enough to have our own children or aging parents. None of us looked old enough to have "real problems," though I'd argue we all had our share. Brendan played the central character, a trust-fund boy who finds himself alone in a big city. His parents find themselves in a loveless marriage, his brother seems to have lost his soul, and then there was me. I played the role of his trust-fund cousin, the only one in the world he trusted. She, Molly, had a corporate job, even though she didn't need it, and she was forever trying to rebel against her conservative family. She predictably hated her father, self-medicated, and slept with strangers, and her cousin was the only person in the world she truly loved. She was nothing like me, and that's how I came to love her.

On a weekday afternoon in 2004, I sat in a street-level beauty salon on Montrose Avenue, a storefront smaller than my bedroom where Mexican boys get their hair braided and telenovelas play all day and the haircuts cost seven dollars. I asked Mimi to cut my hair into chunky layers and dye it fluorescent pink. She feared we were encountering a language barrier and started pulling out magazines to make sure she understood me. Mimi knew I'd had the same bob cut since childhood, so she didn't believe that I was asking her to strip my hair of its natural color. However, I was convinced this would help me to understand Molly in a physical way, which I was still struggling with in tech week. Molly, despite all of her efforts not to, still moved with the elegance of money, the grace I'd been born without. I'd been manicuring my fingernails so my hands might handle things more eloquently, and the costume designer had scored me a pair of designer jeans and killer heels: things I had never worn before this production, and guess what? Designer jeans really do take off five pounds. These things would help, I thought, but I still needed to try on the rebellion, needed to feel how far she would go in an attempt to be someone else. So: There I was, trying to convince Mimi to transform me into a character. Three hours later, I looked into the mirror, hated what I saw, and headed to the National Pastime for the first day of tech.

Half a block from the theater, I got off the bus. The National Pastime was located on Broadway, in the middle of a row of storefronts that have matching awnings now. African hair-braiding shops,

Pakistani-owned convenience stores that sell drug paraphernalia along with milk and cigarettes, Cambodian-owned boutiques that sell wigs and kimonos and fancy bobby pins. A pizzeria, a liquor store, and a little Thai joint with fifty flavors of bubble tea. I got off the bus and saw Mike first, sitting in his wheelchair, surrounded by actors and designers. A woman with indie-darling bangs was putting on an impromptu puppet show in the street. Her name was Lauren, and she played Brendan's love interest in the play. We had all fallen in love with her giant eyes and her offbeat humor, but suspected Brendan was in a little deeper, especially when he joined in on the puppet show. Everyone shoveled takeout into their mouths and watched and laughed, but when they saw me, everything seemed to stop.

Brendan said, "Holy shit, Maggie!"

Lauren said, "Oh boy, I love it."

Mike said, "I don't even recognize you."

Something in his face looked afraid and maybe even resentful. *I don't even recognize you.* Everyone grew awkward and silent as they did in those days when every detail of our relationship seemed to take on extra weight. But then, someone opened the door, I pushed him inside, and we got to work. Mike took his seat out in the audience, looked at the set with the designer.

"I like the big open space," he said. "We do need a couple of paintings on the wall though, don't we?"

Karen Meyer, the hearing-impaired journalist from WLS, came in with a television camera crew to interview Mike. He stood awkwardly in his walker and waxed eloquent about his craft. Everyone we knew tuned into that five-minute clip on the evening news.

"I can't believe I had to have a stroke to get on TV," Mike said, rolling his eyes.

We, the actors, hung our costumes on the dressing room rack, tacked up a sheet with light and sound cues for each scene. The creepy guy who worked in the National Pastime office smoked reefer and listened to Derek and the Dominos every night we were there. At some point, I had to ask him to turn it down, then I asked him to teach me how to roll a joint because I had to do it for the show and I was really bad at it. Then I just sat there and listened to "Bell Bottom Blues." I thought of Mike as he continued his interview. The thing about him is: He's a magician. He has this ability to make a Monday afternoon into a Saturday night, an apartment into an art gallery, an average-looking girl into a princess. He has the ability to take an underdeveloped script and make it work.

"Maggie," he said at an early rehearsal. "She's almost thirty years old and still all she wants is that Cinderella dress. Her nanny took her to Boca and the Keys, but she only wanted Disney World, with her father. She's a *little girl*." This is how he created the magic, and then we transferred it to an old speakeasy, full of ghosts. On opening night, I tried to conjure all the notes I had gotten, the argument we had had during the rehearsal process.

"Mag, I need you bigger. Start again."

I took a few steps back and reentered.

"*Mag*, I need you bigger, I said. Start again."

I took a few steps back and reentered.

Before I said a word: "Bigger."

"This is as big as I get! FUCK!"

Brendan, my cousin in the play, my scene partner on that day, waited for the storm to pass.

"That's not her!" Mike cried. "Molly's not afraid of looking foolish. She's not afraid of anything!"

But I was so afraid. Afraid of looking foolish, afraid of Mike's going places without me. Afraid he'd have an accident or a panic attack or fall down when I wasn't there. He had taken to standing up in his walker, which was good, but he was still so wobbly. I was afraid of being a terrible actor, that I'd never get good enough, that I'd embarrass us both, that I was wasting my life. And that's why I needed to go away and worry only for myself. Mike motioned for me to come closer to him.

I bent over and he whispered, "I know you can get there." But he said it as if he was tired of saying it, as if it was taking a good amount of effort.

It's true. I had nothing to lose. I was leaving for Prague in six weeks. Even if I got an unflattering review, it would be forgotten by the time I returned, so why not go for it? I had certainly gotten through harder things. Mike still has this ability to strike me down with perspective. If I'm anxious, he simply says, "Take a deep breath, dear. There are children dying all around us." And because we witnessed this together, it always makes an impact.

On opening night, I sashayed up the backstage steps to the second-floor doorway in my designer jeans and high heels. I lit my fat fake joint and breathed in deeply. I listened to my cousins' conversation about this couch, the family room couch, all the memories of this silly couch. I pushed open the door and entered, high as a kite. Lazy eyes, pot smoke coursing through my body, ready to kill them all with my wit. I swayed in the doorway and said in a voice, so different than my own, "I hate couches . . . Couches blow." The audience broke into laughter.

The audience laughed at me, but they felt for Brendan, this poor little rich boy, and his Waspy mother in the midst of a nervous breakdown. They watched us all try to laugh at ourselves. Brendan fell in love with Lauren over the course of the play, and he inhabited the world so honestly that we all saw them falling in love offstage, a little more each day. Their onstage kisses would last too long. Lauren would go to the bar after the show and stay out late, even if she had to work in the morning, just so she could drive Brendan home. I don't know how everyone else felt, but I was jealous when they walked home from the theater sometimes, when they rode their bikes around the city together, when they went out dancing one night. I was jealous, and I hated that about myself.

In act 2, I found my cousin in a depressive state, unwilling to leave his apartment, and I always felt such urgency with that scene. It was the way I felt with Mike on nights when he got sad. I need to make this better—how can I make this better? I went to my cousin, tried to convince him to smoke with me, have a drink with me, take a Chicago vacation with me. Light bulb! We'll fall in love with our city again. That was the moment where Mike wanted me bigger, but this was about me and Brendan now. I studied my cousin, and he looked inconsolable. I knew that his mother was unwell and that he was lonely for a woman like he'd never been before. All I had to do was make him laugh. Forget that there were one hundred strangers watching us, strangers who might write nasty things about us in the newspaper. This was about me and Brendan, and this scene needed some life. I started singing to him, "Come on, baby, don't you want to go?" In a big voice like a blues woman: "Come on!" He looked surprised. I started crawling all over him, messing with his hair. "Back to that same old place, sweet home Chicago!" He looked at me for a minute, impressed, I think. I started dancing around the room, playing an imaginary saxophone, pleading with him, pushing my little bag of weed toward him. Have fun with me! He broke out laughing, and I would know if he was faking.

He put on his coat and said, "Let's go."

The audience laughed, the energy changed, and I felt like I never needed to accomplish anything else. I would think of "Sweet Home Chicago" when my plane took off. I would think of this song and wonder why I was leaving my home, which was Chicago and the theater.

Most reviews criticized the playwright, unfortunately, but all of them championed the ensemble and Mike's direction of us. Rick Reed wrote of Mike's "fine craftsmanship," his ability to keep things going at a "sprightly pace." Reed described Molly as "tough and funny." Hedy Weiss wrote of my "wonderful turn." It was a wonderful turn, if I do say so myself.

I miss that window of life sometimes. Ten people with the same goal, striving for excellence, just wanting to tell the same story and entertain an audience, make them feel a little more deeply before going home to the same old. I miss Lauren and Brendan holding hands before their final entrance, adults behaving like children without the assistance of booze, and Mike's laughing from the audience. The she-finally-got-it laughing. That knowing laughter that kept us all going. The Pied Piper and all of his followers, the constancy of the creation, and the immediacy of feedback. The theater, and the strange things that happen when you're living under that spell.

On opening night, three of the actresses wept during preshow because they had broken up with their boyfriends. Three women on the same night. Lauren wore eyeshadow and Brendan wore a tie. At the party, at the bar across the street, after Lauren had cried with the other girls, she announced that she and Brendan were a couple. She had broken up with her boyfriend so that she could be with Brendan. I sat in Mike's lap at the party. At some point, he bit down on the fingerless gloves that helped him get traction when he pushed his chair. He pulled them over his hands with his teeth, then wheeled toward the jukebox and took a five-dollar bill from his shirt pocket.

"Whatever you want," he said, as he handed me the money for the jukebox.

"Was it a Gift show?" I asked.

A Gift show signified our highest standards.

"It was a Gift show," he said. "No Billy Joel, okay?"

I didn't play Billy Joel even though I loved him. Instead, I played songs for Mike—old songs and new songs, ballads that would make him sing. I played Derek and the Dominos, and it sounded so good on that jukebox.

"Mag," Mike said, forcing a chuckle. "Are you gonna break up with me?"

"No," I said. "Why would you even ask me that?"

What kind of woman would do that?

Shortly before midnight, Mike's parents came to pick us up. After getting Mike into bed, I pulled the wet seat cover from the wheelchair and scrubbed it with soap and hot water. I took it outside in the backyard, laid it flat in the grass to dry, and wondered who would do this when I left.

I am grateful for the theater because it gave us an escape, if only for a few hours. It gave us power during that period where existing day to day was sometimes challenging. It gave us the pain of others when we had become so self-absorbed.

* * *

The Thorntons hosted a going-away party for me in their yard on a perfect summer night. Everyone from the Gift came and Frankie manned the grill. My friends filled the garage refrigerator with Czech beer and spirits, which was so thoughtful of them, but I didn't drink that night. I wanted to see and remember everything clearly, so I watched my friends get shitfaced on Pilsner Urquell and pear brandy. They went swimming in the dark, built a fire in the pit, and John Gawlik rambled on about the history of oppression in Central Europe. I sat next to Mike and tugged on his ear, then I whispered, "*Muy guapo,*" over and over again.

He laughed and blushed and swatted at me. "Stop it, Mag! Knock it off."

Connolly looked over at us, shook his big head, smiling, and said, "You guys make me sick."

CHAPTER 21

2004

Limping through O'Hare Airport, I thought of the old adage "The show must go on." It was those damn thrift-store heels that I wore in *A Young Man in Pieces*, I think, but anyway, my toenail had turned black and I was leaving the country in a matter of days, so I had it removed by a doctor. The pain was hideous and I felt like such a wimp because of everything Mike had to endure on a daily basis. O'Hare Airport, Mike's former place of employment, looked now like an inconsiderate place to me, because I could only see it through the lens of disability. What if Mike were with me and we were running late? He couldn't sprint through the concourse with me, as we had done so many times before. On our way to New York, San Francisco, Dublin: I think we were late every time. Once we got on the plane, would his wheelchair even fit in the aisle? Could they pull up a seat to make room for it? He still had trouble shifting from one seat to another—getting from the wheelchair to the shower seat was slow and terrifying every time. He could stand in his walker, then swivel and sit, but what if he needed to be changed during the flight? Eight hours was a pretty long time. I took some deep breaths, and the anxiety melted into sadness.

I passed the bookstore where Mike always stopped to buy overpriced magazines and books before a flight, then the food court where he always stopped to buy overpriced concessions. This is how he travels. He believes that money and diet are no longer real things to consider when traveling. He sees every trip as an adventure, and now I was going on one without him.

We had gotten into our first real fight in a European city. First, he had been annoyed because my suitcase was heavy and I expected him to carry it.

"That would be the gentlemanly thing to do," I had said.

He had rolled his eyes and said, "The practical thing to do would be to buy one of those little suitcases on wheels. Then you could be independent."

How true, I thought, as I wheeled my new suitcase through the international concourses.

But the real fight had happened when we missed our bus to Dungarvan, where my father's aunts and uncles lived. We had spent the entire week prior with Mike's family—we'd gone all the way from Dublin to Monaghan, had biscuits and tea in their homes. I asked for one night in Waterford so I could meet the family I'd never known. We burst into the station after oversleeping, the two of us running madly. *The two of us running madly.* We saw the bus pull away and I felt all the air go out of me. The next one didn't leave until the following day, and we were scheduled to fly back home.

Mike looked at me and said, "Sorry, Bruiser. Maybe next year, huh?"

"Next year? What the fuck do you mean, next year?"

Everyone in the station stopped to stare.

"I just spent a week with your family. We are going to see mine."

"Keep your voice down," Mike said. "You're a mental case. This is not my fault."

Then I stomped away childishly with my old-fashioned suitcase, and he didn't follow. I walked through the city, fuming with anger, and he stayed at the station, stubbornly, and waited for me to return, which I did, but two hours later. We made it to Dungarvan after finding a train that got us close enough. It was a good thing, too, because my father's cousins had prepared a steak dinner for us and their triplet boys had really been looking forward to meeting the Yanks.

We played with the triplets after dinner. Aunt Nancy called Mike the map of Ireland and said, with some dismay, that I looked like a Spaniard, like my mother. On the train back to Dublin, Mike admitted that he was glad we made the trip, but that he had never so badly wanted to pull those heavy Irish coins out of his pocket and whip them at my head. We kissed all the way back to the city.

* * *

I waited for the plane to take off without a pile of Mike's books and magazines in front of me, without his empty sack of McDonald's beside me. I pulled my composition book from my carry-on and had no idea what to write, until the plane took off. The plane climbed higher and higher until Chicago became a geometric pattern of rooftops, a child's miniature playland, and then my ears popped and I felt relief. I wrote in my journal: "Maybe I will never go back again." I thought of a favorite line of Louise Glück's poetry and made it my own: "Death cannot hurt me like you have hurt me, sweet life."

* * *

When I got off the plane in Prague, the airport wasn't much different from any small Midwestern airport, except that many of the employees were smoking cigarettes. I went to my baggage carousel and waited—too long, I thought. At the customer-service desk, I waited for someone who spoke English, and eventually an agent explained that my bags had been lost. Maybe they were in Amsterdam, she said. Might be two or three days until they found them, she said. Was there somewhere she could reach me? I searched my carry-on for my itinerary, but found only a paperback book, a toothbrush and toothpaste, some chewing gum, a change of underwear, and a letter from Mike.

> please be smart around strangers, esp. when travelling . . . we americans are not very well liked these days. what a profoundly sad sentence to type.
>
> and remember: it's a great/overwhelming feeling to feel like you're behind and have to catch up. intimidation is a wonderful friend, if perceived properly. i'm sure you are already rising to & above the occasion.

please send me anything you're working on. i won't give any feedback if you don't want any.

i feel like we're a team—each half of us getting better on different sides of the world; one half improving physically, the other artistically and intellectually. the walking yesterday felt very good when it was good, very frustrating when it was bad, but i am totally dedicated to making a full recovery, can't wait to start working out with tara tomorrow & to get on the mat this afternoon. maybe so many people give up b/c they can't find anything to fight for.

i'm fighting for our future.

please try to call once in a while, but i won't expect to hear your voice every day. jeez, leave me alone, would you?

it's very weird writing to you right now. i don't know why. i might be trying too hard to not sound needy. in fact, i'm sure that's what it is.

i love you endlessly & timelessly & can't wait to see what this experience does to your beautiful heart.

love,
michael

When I realized I had packed my itinerary in my suitcase, I felt a surge of panic. I told the Czech woman I would call her later that day, took her business card, and hurried to a pay phone where I called the Thorntons on my credit card. My parents didn't yet have internet at home, which was the thing I thought might help.

The phone rang and I looked down at myself. Mike had always told me to dress professionally for flights; you never knew if you might get upgraded to first class, you never knew who you might meet. But here I was, in baggy corduroys, my neon-pink hair pulled into a half-ponytail. I hadn't slept, wasn't wearing makeup, didn't have any deodorant. I was a mess, with no idea where to go. My classes were being held at Charles University, I knew, but the dorms were somewhere else. The phone rang several times. It was one in the morning in Chicago on Independence Day, and now, on my big independence mission, I was calling Mike in the middle of the night.

Mrs. Thornton finally answered the phone and seemed disoriented, but eventually woke Mike for me.

"Are you okay?" he asked.

He was in bed, so his mother searched the Prague Summer Program website for me, and couldn't find what I needed.

"Hold on, try something else," Mike said to his mother.

"No, just forget it," I said. "I'll figure it out."

How did I think I was going to figure it out?

"Did you have a good time at your party?" he asked.

"I did, babe. I love you so much."

* * *

I got into a black cab and said to the driver, "*Dobrý den. Mluvíte anglicky?*"

"No. Czech only."

"College? Dormitory?"

He smelled like cologne and I smelled like fear.

We drove toward the city. Everywhere I looked, I saw graffiti and Communist architecture. Small, dilapidated houses with Spanish roofs and old women hobbling down crumbling roads. The cab driver took me to three dormitories on the way to the city center. At every single one, I had to ask several students before one spoke English. I would explain my situation, then they would tell me there was no American program here. "You don't know where you're going?"

Finally, we pulled up in front of Masarykova Kolej, which had a sign in front that advertised the Prague Summer Program, sponsored by Western Michigan University. By then, I owed the cab driver a good deal of money, and I gave him a generous tip. When I smiled weakly and said, "*Děkuji*," he looked like he wanted to strangle me.

The foyer was Grecian, and looked more like a hotel than a dormitory. The man at the front desk wasn't fond of Americans and the vending machine carried cans of Czech beer. I checked in with an administrative assistant who gave me my room number and a packet of papers. The first faculty reading would be tonight after a cocktail reception, she said. She gave me public transportation directions and told me to beware of pickpockets on the train. I told her I'd lost my luggage, then walked up a winding, concrete staircase to my room. Maybe if I washed my face, I would feel better. I was beginning to feel lighter. My small room had a bed and some bookshelves, a desk at a transom window, with a balcony overlooking a courtyard. I would share a bathroom and a kitchen with two other women.

There was a goulash tavern on the corner, a metro station a block away, a convenience store that had anything we needed, and a laundromat with expensive washing machines. Plenty of Herna bars (meaning: open twenty-four hours, thick cigarette smoke and slot machines), one upscale restaurant, specializing in duck and cognac. A park where expats and hobos played guitars and drank absinthe all night long. I couldn't wait for my luggage to arrive.

* * *

Mikey,

My first class was unreal. You would be so in love with my professor, Gail Wronsky. Knows everything about poetry. I'm totally intimidated. My class is full of MFA candidates and professors. I was so afraid I'd end up with all the undergrads writing about last night's frat party but I lucked out with a Native American professor who lives on a horse ranch in Eastern Ohio and a professor from New York whose parents were radical Communists. This university used to be a holding place for Jews. Everything is like a maze that you can't find your way out of.

We covered so much in three hours. Started with poems we liked. I brought Sharon Olds, of course. We had a good discussion about her. Gail doesn't like her but that's okay. Gail is fascinated that I'm an actor.

I had a fried cheese in a Czech pub for lunch.

Now I'm in the computer lab doing homework because I have that already. Need a nap pretty soon. Gorgeous weather today. I miss you. Hope you have another good walking day. I am so proud of you for not being frozen on the ladder of your life.

My fave new poet is Larry Levis. He has blown my mind wide open. I'll bring him home for you, okay?

Love, love, love, love, crazy love.

* * *

When my luggage did arrive a few days later, I unpacked my beige bras and practical underwear, and settled in. I wrote Mike's parents a postcard thanking them for the party, but never got around to sending it. I never got around to reading most of the books I brought to read.

I did see the poet Marvin Bell read, at the Ypsilon Theatre, in the middle of the city, in a neighborhood of fashion boutiques, wine bars, and posh restaurants on the water. I went with Eliza, one of my suite mates, who skipped class most of the time. She made the effort for Marvin Bell, and before the reading, we sat in the theater bar and drank frosty mugs of beer while studying the play advertisements on the walls, and the art deco Mucha women. When Marvin Bell read "To Dorothy," in that gorgeous theater, I cried silently in the balcony.

You are not beautiful, exactly.
You are beautiful, inexactly.

I thought only of Mike, slouched in his wheelchair, laughing and exposing his crooked tooth, his eyes sparkling. I was so far away from him now, and knew he would love this as much as I did. Marvin Bell has the most endearing Jersey accent; he looked out at his wife, who was age appropriate, old and gray, like him. (That was unusual in this faculty, to have an age-appropriate wife.) Dorothy smiled like a child, even though I was certain she had heard him read this poem hundreds of times. Marvin Bell said forcefully that all things lost are not equal, and then he took a deep breath before the ending lines: "If I lost you, / I'd have to ask the grass to let me sleep." And then I was pressing my lips together, trying to strangle the sadness rising up in my throat.

"Are you okay?" Eliza asked me.

I nodded my head vigorously.

Why was I crying? Because I had always wanted to grow old with Mike and knew that might not happen now? Because I was so grateful that he *was* alive, that he hadn't left me after all? Because I needed him in a way that was being articulated so beautifully? Marvin Bell's poems left me, most of the time, stunned into silence.

The next morning, I woke up and went downstairs to the cafeteria where I had some bakery bread and a coffee. I reread the submissions for my poetry workshop, looked up words and references I didn't know, prepared notes for discussion. I wrote marginalia and endnotes, and chose each word carefully. Then I rode the metro to Staroměstská and smiled when the sexy prerecorded voice announced my stop. When I walked into the Karolinum of Charles University, I thought, Now *this* is what college is supposed to look like. I visited with some colleagues in the hallway, remembered how much fun we'd all had the night before, after the Ypsilon reading. I had met plenty of young writers, who had read all of my favorite books. When nine o'clock struck, we went to class.

Our professor, Gail Wronsky, began by reciting one of Marvin Bell's poems from memory with her eyes closed, feeling every line break and image. Her hair was dyed black on one side and white on the other—she wore heavy eye makeup and feathery earrings, and her jeans just a little too tight. When she opened her eyes, she said, "So, what did you think?" Some of us had liked Bell's "Dead Man" poems more than others, but disagreeing wasn't enough, and Gail challenged us to articulate our descriptions more clearly. Her husband, also a writer, slipped in and handed her a paper cup of coffee.

"I love you so much," she said to him.

"Couldn't find a coffee shop this morning," she explained to the class. "And I probably had too much to drink last night."

Then it was back to literature with a seriousness I admired. She wrote complicated motherhood poems and odes to Dolly Parton. In her marriage poems, she and her husband were skeleton bones, and she sprinkled in Spanish words and phrases. She had created a life out of words and her imagination, and it seemed too good to be true. I knew she was the woman I wanted to be, and when I saw my future self in that classroom, it was like fireworks shooting off inside me.

After class, I went for a long walk through the city, climbed a hill, and found a neighborhood with brightly colored doors on houses, a restaurant with garden seating, and a little one-screen movie house. I saw a Czech movie with subtitles—*Štěstí*. The title loosely translates as *Almost Happiness*, and I knew I had to commit the phrase to memory. *Štěstí*: almost happiness. I went home to work on my class assignments, then I had goulash at the tavern on the corner with a playwriting professor and his wife. We talked about plays and Chicago, and that was the first time that day I thought about Mike. For the past several years—six years and six months, to be exact—he had been the first thought of every morning.

CHAPTER 22

2004

A wealthy actress who worked with us once told me that she loved me dearly, but couldn't wait to see me after I had done some traveling. This made me defensive, in the way of young know-it-alls, so I reminded her that I'd spent a semester in Ireland as an undergrad.

"Maggie," she'd said. "You need to get out of Chicago. That's all I'm saying."

She loathed her parents and cheated on her husband. Did I have to share her circumstances? Did I have to suffer to be taken seriously?

My time in Prague helped me to see what she'd been getting at though. Being an artist, especially a writer, does require a certain amount of self-knowledge, and that knowledge has to be cultivated through distances of time and space, and through periods of reflection. Suffering isn't necessary, but it also probably helps.

* * *

My foot started to throb about a week into the trip. I wasn't staying off my feet as much as I'd been told, taking several-mile walks every day. That was for Mike. That was the only way I could stop feeling the injustice of it all, the often-unbearable anger. There were very few elevators in Prague, and Mike's wheelchair would've been a nightmare on those cobblestone hills; the only physically disabled woman in the program had had to leave because she was having such a hard time. I went to a Canadian doctor who told me again to stay off my feet. "I'll just take another Advil," I said, and limped back to my dorm.

* * *

baby,

i cried when i read your beautiful e-mail. i'm thanking jesus for technology right now.

medically, i'm a bit of a mess, with my toe infected and swollen right now, but intellectually, i'm satiated.

just had a lecture about the inferiority complex of czechs. similar to irish in that way. the professor said that after the fall of communism, it's difficult to persuade people to read literature when they have never seen baywatch or read a harlequin or seen die hard. they want to do all of those things before sitting down and reading david foster wallace. this is why they wear bart simpson t-shirts, one guy said. he indicates freedom to them.

i have a lot of revisions to do before my workshop tomorrow, but please call me anytime. i should be in my room tonight after ten p.m. and up until at least twelve. i love to hear your voice.

there's a line in a poem that reminded me of us and made me cry. "if the sky should fall, we shall have clouds for supper." (one of my workshop friends wrote that! isn't it good?)

went to the charles bridge last night. it really is heaven. i need to take you there. had drinks and dessert with my roommate last night, & i see my poetry prof read tonight so that should be fun.

i promise, i'm being careful. did i tell you about the george bush nesting dolls they sell here?

i love your face off.

it's okay if you feel needy. it's only love.

dreaming of you and believing in you,

maggie emlyn

* * *

fascinating about bart simpson = freedom. that's so sad & endearing. i tried you a few times today (your night) around 10:45PM and 12:45AM, but didn't get you.

had a good long workout yesterday & read a great book, THE SORROWS OF EMPIRE by chalmers johnson. going to take a shower now & do a light workout before tara comes. very panicky last night but i think it was a big breakthru in recovery on the horizon. had a dream last night of the walking putting itself together & being perfect, walking around a penthouse apartment holding sheldon's hand!

i started writing a bit last night. a collection of short fiction called THE INVENTION OF MONSTERS, inspired by the dali painting of similar name. it's divided into chapters, one character per chapter, and they all share RIC in common.

I've edited out his detailed descriptions of each chapter.

My professor had asked us to read an anthology of Kafka's short stories and then write a poem, mixing the Czech author's words with our own. I read the book in spurts and kept a running list of the lines that stuck with me. The first one would have to be, " 'Yes I'm tired,' I said and sat down on a boulder near the spring." Looking out my window, I wondered where my great-grandmother had lived. "Ancient traditions that recommended the place." Thought of all my friends who were getting married and felt so happy for them, my oldest and dearest friends, but even that couldn't eclipse my sorrow. Perhaps it only heightened the feeling. "Married people among them who were expecting children." But no, I thought, no. Forget the children. This is your time to write. You're in Prague, goddamn it.

The pace of the writing picked up then. "Some people came to me and asked me to build a city for them." "I ought to be in a place where all kinds of people meet." "That's why I am here, I'm collecting advocates!" It's good I'm here, I told myself. Stop feeling guilty. This is where you belong; this is who you're supposed to be. "I do not have to go back again, the cell is burst open, I move, I feel my body." And that line finally felt like relief, like a tremendous weight had been lifted. But in the end, it always came back to Mike: "Receive him in the name of the city."

When I submitted the poem to workshop, Gail said, "I like this, Maggie. It's so weird. I have no idea what it means, but I *like* it!" While I never told my workshop about Mike, I did email the assignment to him.

> mag,
>
> WAY surprised/intrigued/and admittedly confused (stanza III) by your epic. only a first read, though. what is most apparent is the sense of urgency and the repetition of certain lines/ mantras elevates the entire piece to a wonderful level of folk. let me keep reading it: it's TOTALLY DIFFERENT and exciting. it's the first thing you've written (sadly?) whose voice is overwhelmingly woman as opposed to fascinated girl. the tone seems to shift toward the end of that transition. Also the line "I do not have to go back again, the cell is burst open, I move, I feel my body." makes me sad, if i'm interpreting it correctly.

And, of course, he *was* interpreting it correctly. The transition from fascinated girl to woman was something we both had wanted, but we hadn't suspected how painful it would be. After reading that email, I wandered around the Kafka Museum, where the looped klezmer music sounded elegiac. Mike was acknowledging the first time I had expressed a temptation to leave the relationship, and then he decided to ignore it and hope for the best, which made it sound like the klezmer music was swelling just for us.

> in other news, good workout yesterday, as i said.
>
> when you get a chance, respond a bit more to my last e-mail. and your letter hasn't arrived yet. i get so excited when the mail comes, but not yet.
>
> well, time for the little dog to go crawl around his mat and do some steps and march in place. the little dog also hasn't shaved since you left, so he looks more like a little lion.
>
> i love you very much.

Later that night, I went to the student union, which I affectionately called Fraggle Rock. There was always a mix of pink-haired Americans and Czechs hanging around, wearing striped shirts and funky glasses. I went there one night with my roommate, who knew a lot of people in the program because she went out drinking in the morning instead of going to class or doing homework. She brought me to a table of men.

"These guys are kinda old," she said, "but they like to party."

When I sat down and looked across the table, the craziest thing happened: an electrical charge shot through me. I had never experienced this kind of attraction. It was more like that unbelievable thing I saw in movies. The man I was looking at wasn't even handsome. He wore his gray hair closely shaved and had a mouth full of crooked teeth. He had faded tattoos up and down his arms and legs, pretty green eyes, and he made me feel alive again.

"Hey," I said.

We all started telling stories about where we were from. He, Rory, was a graduate student in Michigan, a teaching assistant in the Prague program. His parents were trust-fund kids, some of the richest kids in Southern California, who essentially gave it all up to be wandering hippies.

"Cool," someone said.

"Not cool," he said. "We lived in a hippie commune in Hawaii for a while when I was a kid. It had to be shut down for hazardous waste disposal. No one knew what the hell they were doing."

"Where did you go to college?" I asked at some point.

"San Francisco."

"I was there once. Love that city."

(Mike and I had gone there to visit Paulie before he moved to Chicago. We did wine country and saw plays and live jazz, and hiked in Muir Woods. Stop thinking of Mike already, I told myself. Who's Mike?)

Rory told me he couldn't handle the rules at the dorms so he lived in an apartment with a couple of strangers who became close friends. One of the roommates came out as trans while they were all living together. The memories seemed to keep coming, and truth be told, I was enthralled. He had so many stories, so much life. It was like the play *Othello*, where Desdemona's father accuses him of manipulating his daughter with witchcraft, but it was really the stories that seduced her.

"And then one night, I came home from class and he was dead on the living room floor. It was the first time I'd ever seen a dead person." Then he looked disoriented. "I don't know why I'm telling you this," he said. "I haven't thought of it since I left San Francisco."

"I'm really sorry," I said. "That's terrible."

"But I don't know why I told you."

* * *

I hung out with the writers closer to my age too. We found lunch specials all over the city—chic little Mediterranean restaurants and Chinese dives. We drank absinthe together one night. We watched Barack Obama address the Democratic National Convention on television in a bar and everyone was impressed then that I was from Chicago. We went to every single reading. Gail Wronsky read a breathtaking elegy for Larry Levis and I understood then that the best writing tells the hard truths. In the poem, she describes a scene in which Levis, the brilliant poet and her former mentor, snorts cocaine from a woman's kneecap after shaving her legs and hits an artery on accident. In the poem, she says that like the bleeding, he could not be stopped. In the poem, she eventually admits that she was the woman bleeding. Listening to that poem in the Ypsilon Theatre taught me important things about metaphor and diction. She could tell the truth about him, and it only revealed the fullness of her appreciation, but she had to tell the ugly truths about herself in order to be trusted.

Every night, I watched the director of the program sit in the front row with his young daughters—the little one usually fell asleep by the end—and I dreamed that that's how my kids could grow up. The TAs read too, and the night Rory read, I told my new friends I thought he was talented. They teased me and said, "Come on, dude. He's old. And he's such a snob, isn't he?" I tortured myself with hesitation, read Kafka and Levis and Gail Wronsky, and filled my marbled notebooks.

* * *

We visited Prague Castle and Saint Vitus, all of the cathedrals. I lit candles for Mike in every one. We went to a sex-toy museum and I thought about him there too, thought of coming to bed in an old T-shirt and cotton briefs, Mike saying I reminded him of Janet from *Three's Company*. I thought of his face when I came to bed in nothing but white lace and then I ached for him until I saw him framed in a hospital bed and me on top. Just as quickly as he had entered, I pushed him from my mind. I did not want to think about painful things, and I did not tell my new friends about the painful things. I did not want to be pitied or interesting because of something awful.

When I saw Rory at Fraggle Rock again, he was checking himself in a mirror.

"You can take the boy out of California, but not the California out of the boy," I teased.

He quickly got defensive and said, "Not everyone from California is image-conscious. How would you like it if I said all people from Chicago were criminals?"

So he couldn't take a joke, but I stayed because I wanted to hear about his novel about a gringo in a third-world country and alcoholics who had abandoned their families. I wanted to hear his thoughts about the readings. He always seemed more critical, but then again, I thought maybe he knew something I didn't. He'd been around a while. A redhead student of his came over and started flirting with him pretty obviously, and I thought that was probably best, so I went up to my room and brushed my teeth, feeling lonely and, quite frankly, relieved. Then I locked the door because it was the perfect time of night to sit at my window and listen to my headphones, the CD that Mike had made me. But then: a knock on the door. What the fuck did my roommate want now? But when I opened it, Rory was standing there, panting.

"I ran all the way up," he said.

"But the redhead . . ."

"No no no. I needed to see you. I need you to be mine."

And he was not an actor.

The phone started ringing and didn't stop. Somewhere in the world, a boy called and his girlfriend didn't answer. She knew it was her boyfriend and didn't pick up. He would later ask her why, but she didn't tell him the truth, which was: She didn't answer because this man was in her room and she wanted him to stay. He said she was smart and sexy, and those were things she wanted to feel. She didn't say that she'd dreamt of having sex with the man. She dreamt of having sex with him in the old-fashioned way. She didn't want the kind that she and her boyfriend had now, the new substitute for sex, which lately made her sad. Her boyfriend saying, "I think I just came." Her saying, "No you didn't." She, always positioned on top now, and she, the only one getting off. She hated that part the most. She wondered if he would try with another woman. Maybe a woman who didn't know the previous version of him wouldn't feel so sad. The girlfriend didn't say any of this because she was ashamed. The girlfriend didn't say any of this because the new substitute for sex was *almost* enough.

Štěstí: almost happiness.

* * *

Rory leaned in to kiss me and I stopped him.

"Is this about that boyfriend back home?" he asked.

How did you know, I wanted to ask, but instead I just nodded.

"We'll talk about that later," he said.

Then he looked at my window and said, "You have a balcony? How'd you get so lucky?"

We climbed over my desk and out the window, huddled close together on a small balcony in creamy moonlight. Then I stood suddenly, turned my back to the moon, and started to tell him about my theater in Chicago. They were rehearsing right now for a show called *The Pavilion* about a high school reunion, and it would be the first opening night I'd miss. Paulie and Lynda were playing an estranged couple and that was going to be interesting because they used to date each other. Art imitates life and all that. But then I realized I was telling him about my life with Mike. What was my life *without* Mike?

I told him about the neighborhood I'd grown up in—it had been rough for a while, but now was getting pretty gentrified and I had mixed feelings about that. My grandmother, who had lived in the apartment above us—she had always wanted to go to Europe—asked me to go with her when I was in high school but I was too busy with my friends to go on a vacation with my grandmother. It was one of my biggest regrets, not taking that trip with her.

"Is she dead now?" Rory asked.

"No, but blind and practically deaf," I said.

I told him about my mother who was a wonderful writer but had never really done anything with it, and my father who always mowed the lawn in swimming trunks and dress shoes for some reason.

Rory said, "I want to meet them all. I want every single one at our wedding."

I told him how I'd written obituaries for a suburban newspaper, but I was done with that now. I wasn't going to grow old and wonder about the talents I'd neglected or the trips I'd never taken. I wasn't meant to change diapers for the rest of my life and I didn't have to take anyone's advice. I did not have to be a practical writer. I did not have to be an actor either. I didn't want to be directed anymore, and I refused to be the one whose stories were less important. I was writing my own obituary now: The time had come. I told Rory about the Derek Walcott poem I'd read in Gail's class, and tried to recite it from memory.

The time will come
when, with elation,
you will greet yourself arriving
at your own door, . . .

The scary thing, I said to Rory, is how happy I am being alone. I climbed back into my dorm room, found the Walcott poem, and read the whole damn thing, while standing on my desk.

> . . . Give back your heart
> to itself, to the stranger who has loved you
> all your life, . . .

"Ladies and gentlemen," I said, "Derek Walcott."

I told Rory I loved reading and writing and traveling, and I think that was good for him because he'd been doing those things so long he had forgotten he loved them. He kissed the top of my head and tucked me into bed that night, probably sensing that I was too tender for anything else. Then I drifted off to sleep, determined to save the only life I knew I could. And I signed my email to Mike the next day *Maggie Emlyn Thornton*, which would never be my name.

CHAPTER 23

2004

One of my favorite lectures was entitled *Heimat*, which is a German word, for which there is no exact English translation. The closest English translation would be "home" or "homeland," but that doesn't exactly work. *Heimat* is meant to denote the relationship of a human being toward a certain social spatial unit and usually carries positive connotations.

> honey butt,
>
> it was SO great to talk & laugh with you tonite—i could have talked to you all night, laying on my stomach, twiddling my ankles in the air girl-talk style! that sucked that your phone card cut out on you just as you were telling me how unbelievably sexy i am.
>
> i love you so much, mags, and we'll make anything work if you decide to grad school it. i called your mom today—we're gonna grab dinner next week.
>
> goodnight you tough, beautiful, hot, sexy, talented, brainy bitch. god, i kept thinking tonight how badly i wanted you

next to me playing upwards, watching you look all serious making mad combinations in your mind, a pen getting dizzy as you flip it in your left hand.

again, so proud of you, and let's decide when to talk next.

by the way, that weird fuck is still winning on jeopardy!!!

I LOVE YOU!

God, you make me so happy. do you know that? as you always said in our apartment, "it's nice to be in love, isn't it?"

yes, it is. oh yes oh yes oh yes it is.

Heimat is a German concept, but you can find similar concepts in Russian and Czech cultures. Essentially, one is bound to their *heimat* by their birth and childhood, but also, their language, their earliest experiences, their acquired affinities. It's a trinity of descendance, community, and tradition, and deeply affects an individual's identity.

MAGGIE!

Very happy to hear from you. basically, working out and reading have kept me company. had a nice gettogether Saturday in the garage, making ice-picks for everybody. tara came and hung out for a while—it was interesting to see how respectful people were to her, almost like a silent "we know what you're doing for mike, & we love you for it."

i felt great upright today, was able to lift my leg nice & high. 1 yr, 6 months. at the end of this nightmare, the time we've "lost" will seem like a dream.

Very excited about the novel i'm going to write: AIN'T NEVER KNOW WHO GONNA GIVE YOU A GLASS OF

WATER WHEN: A Creative Non-fiction Autobiographical Tale. I'm seriously debating getting "iListen," Apple's dictation program (i talk, it types) only b/c i have so many ideas that one finger can't keep up with.

how do i feel about marrying a poet? well, you've always been a poet. you just needed this fellowship for validation, i think. and validation, don't get me wrong, is an essential thing for everyone. that's why they call it "validation." maybe that's why you've never been able to really finish anything "long-form"—that at your writing/creative core, poetry is your medium: condensed beauty—just like you.

please let me know what you're reading: i'd love to read some stuff so we can talk about it & you can teach me.

so proud of you.

poet-actress mom & actor-director-writer dad. and i swear to god, the fucking kid will probably read Cliffs notes & be a baseball star.

girls names: Kasey, Ryan. thoughts?

please promise me this experience won't make me unsympathetic to others' problems.

again, send me what you're writing.

yours,
michael

The German professor, as he tried to explain *heimat* to a group made up largely of Americans, said that "home" or "homeland" in English typically translates to a physical or geographic space while with many Central Europeans, physical and geographic spaces hold less power. So: It's a feeling, really. Without your *heimat*, it feels like an appendage is missing.

subject: come home to your kids!

dear mags,

basically the tone is because i miss you incredibly, far more than you miss me, i'm sure, and i really need to just speak with you on the telephone.

it makes me feel dumb that i'm always the one calling b/c then i think that i'm being too needy, but i don't think it's needy to want to talk to you once a week. it's this horrible guy-trap i'm in: i want to be cool & give you all the space in the world during this incredible opportunity which you so aptly deserve, but on the other hand, i want to be able to be honest about my feelings without annoying you or angering you or appearing, yes, weak & needy.

the love in your e-mails is so apparent, but basically, i'll just put this out there honestly: i didn't think it was possible to miss someone this much. i really miss my best friend. and whereas you have new people/ideas/teachers/places to keep you busy and interested during this time apart, i do not.

i just miss you a lot & need to talk to you as soon as possible, okay? so maybe we can just start setting a time once a week or something. that would quiet my catastrophizing mind.

i feel a lot better after all that writing. give a call. i love you.

Heimat, according to theorists, was a reaction to the onset of modernity, and the loss of intimate community. We listened to the Czech national anthem in the lecture hall: "Where is my homeland? Where is my home?" The Czech Jews sang it as they went off to concentration camps, in their language, which was their *domov*, their only true home.

i'm off to bed, you bronze-bodied beauty.

have a wonderful day, i love you.

And while I struggled to keep up with the German professor and forget all the emails from Mike that were making me feel dizzy, Rory passed me a note like we were in elementary school that said, *I am so into you,* decorated with little music notes. It was then I knew I had to tell him. It wouldn't be fair not to. In retrospect, I should've known that Mike was my *heimat,* or a part of it at least: He and I shared a dual citizenship to the world belonging to Chicago artists and the world belonging to its working classes. Some choose one identity over the other, but we were proud to claim both, and I couldn't really connect with someone who didn't understand that. But I had mistakes to make.

When I did start to tell Rory, we sat in my dorm room, on my bed, after class, while the sun was still shining, and I couldn't look at him. I told it in real time. My boyfriend. My first great love. Our theater. The affair. I lost myself somewhere along the way. *Thornton! Critical!* Spinal stroke. Another spinal stroke. *Thornton! Critical!* And he, this older man, just looked at my face, while the sun was going down, and said sympathetically, "Oh, honey." What else was there to say? It was then that we kissed.

We met for lunch after school sometimes, paddled down the Vltava River once, looked at old theater posters in the Mucha Museum under the bridge. He made us picnic dinners, bought Moravian wine and Swiss chocolate, put wildflowers in the wine bottle once we'd emptied it. After all of the ugliness and grit, I realized, I had been dying for beauty.

My friend Shannon came to visit me in Prague around this time. She had been to see Mike and said he missed me terribly. This made me want her to leave, so I told her I was going on a weekend trip, and she could have my bed while I was gone but then would have to find a place of her own. Rory and I took bus trips to Karlovy Vary and Telč, gorgeous little towns in the country where everything shut down by nine o'clock. We listened to classical music in the town squares, which was the only kind of music that could convey the depths of my grief and the elation I felt when I thought I was outrunning it. All of the Czech composers were writing about the same thing, weren't they? I do not want death to come, and thank God I'm alive.

When Monday came, there was a symposium on Kundera, a sensitive subject with the Czechs. He was their most internationally known writer, but he had also fled the country during the Soviet regime—he couldn't stand the oppression. He left, he said, to be worthy of a life of his own, and his family members were punished for his choices. He escaped to France where he lived until his death, and never returned home, even after the fall of the Berlin Wall and the Velvet Revolution. Some of the Czech lecturers described him as a traitor to his country, but I knew better: I knew he was guilty and suffering, no matter what he said. I came back to my room after the Kundera symposium and Shannon said, "What are you doing with that guy? Mike wants to marry you."

"Mind your own business," I said. "You don't know what it's like. Just leave me alone, Shannon. Fuck. And anyway, I am not married. It would be different if I were."

The Czechs were incensed when Kundera published *Ignorance* in French in the year 2000 because this time he had completely abandoned his *domov*, his language, spoken by so few. But I read the book. In it, he writes about Czech expats who, by the novel's end, decide not to return to Prague, even though it will always be the most beautiful city in the world to them. I knew Rory was France and Mike was Prague, and I did not want to go home again. Even so, reading my email responses to Mike years later made me feel like all the good I'd ever done had been erased.

> baby,
>
> i'm in an internet cafe with shannon, feeling oddly homesick, i think. maybe. i don't know what i feel. the program is over soon and i'm beginning to feel freaked out about that. today we had some b-fast at an expat cafe and now we're going to go on an adventure. possibly an architecture tour or the jewish cemetery.
>
> we're having fun. i'll buy a phone card today and call you. my oldest friend becky is getting married today. wow, huh? i wonder who i'll marry . . .
>
> i love you so much.

* * *

honey child,

stood perfectly on my own from chair to walker today. my legs work. they push. i stand. i love you & am going to bed.

huge progress tonite.

slowly. slowly . . . already the pain has set in.

* * *

My last days in Prague were bittersweet. I had workshopped several pieces in my prose workshop, a series called "Chicago El Stories." My classmates responded well to them—my professor, too. I attended lectures about publishing underground during Communism and they did wonders for my work ethic. I knew I'd better stop feeling sorry for myself and get writing—I had the luxury of freedom, the world was enormous, and time was ticking away. Shannon went home, Rory went home, and I stayed on a little while longer.

One morning, I took a city bus to a public swimming pool where I was the only prude wearing both pieces of my bikini. Saw a black-light show based on the Beatles: *All You Need Is Love.* And then I ended the evening with a Czech pianist who said, "I am going to play classical music for you, okay?" and then played "Imagine" by John Lennon. Anyone who says the Beatles are overrated should go to the Czech Republic.

Slouching over his white piano, twenty-six and skinny with little thumbprints under my eyes, I willed myself to imagine a future.

* * *

When I got home, six weeks later, Mike met me at the airport. O'Hare and the Northwest Side of Chicago looked totally ugly and uninteresting after Telč and Karlovy Vary. I took the long walk through customs. Outside the airport, in the oppressive heat, Mike's father pushed him over to me; he was holding a bouquet of flowers in his good hand and had Welcome Home mylar balloons tied to the back of his chair.

"I did it myself," he said. "Good PT, you know?"

His hair was wet and slicked, and he was sunburned on one half of his body. (That's what happens to him in the sun now.) When I crouched down to hug and kiss him, I did it like a ghost.

"Honey," he said, full of emotion. "God, I missed you so much."

I realized, in that moment, I had stopped believing that he was going to get better, and that we belonged to each other. Mike Thornton didn't look like mine anymore that day. He didn't look the way he had the night of the going-away party when I whispered, "*Muy guapo,*" in his ear over and over again. He looked different now, somehow, even though he hadn't changed a bit. It was like I had grown new skin, and the new skin had new nerve endings. It was like I was a stranger, and one I did not wish to know.

CHAPTER 24

2004

Mike and I would often tell our friends that our life was melodramatic and we liked it that way. He wrote that "we want to drink like kings, fuck like minks, kiss like vacuums, believe in The One, know God, write The Novel, and be The Actor. We are the proud, humble, arrogant stars of our own play."

So: I have to write this like a play. I cannot miss my cue. This is the hardest part to write.

THE DEATHS OF TEENAGERS

MAGGIE and MICHAEL sit in a Jefferson Park backyard, two bottles of wine from the Czech Republic on the patio table between them—one red, one white. MICHAEL knows how MAGGIE hates to be indoors on summer nights, knows that his bad reactions to the sun have kept them cooped up too many times while the city outside seemed to taunt them. They sit dangerously close to RITA and FRANKIE's (his parents') open bedroom window.

MAGGIE

There was a man there.

RITA (O.S.)

I knew it.

FRANKIE (O.S.)

Shh. Honey, ssh. Let them have privacy. Please.

MAGGIE

He took care of me, I guess. I felt like I needed someone to take care of me.

MICHAEL

I understand that. (As if his soul is one thousand years old.) But I try to take care of you. I mean, I pay for your cabs 'cause I can't drive you to work anymore. I know how to hug you after a bad audition. I always know how to make you feel better. I write you poems and long letters with one finger. (BEAT) How did he take care of you?

MAGGIE

I don't know. He bandaged up my toe one day. It was infected and I couldn't look. I really couldn't. You know how stuff like that makes me nauseous. He un-bandaged it and re-bandaged it and didn't seem grossed out. (BEAT) Do you really want to know?

MICHAEL

No.

MAGGIE

Let's have some more wine, okay? I love this—this is Moravian. How have things been here?

MICHAEL

The Pavilion is really good. Gawlik did a great job directing. Trying to think about next season. I think *The Glass Menagerie* is next. We've done some new stuff. Now it's time for the classics. Keep thinking about Tom and Laura, for some reason. What about Mary Ann Thebus for Amanda? Did I tell you who's taking her class now?

MAGGIE (Over MICHAEL, to AUDIENCE)

And when he starts to tell me all the gossip I used to thrive on about who is dating who and which shows got which reviews, I couldn't be less interested. I'm missing a Central European city across the world, where no one knows any of these people, where their lives don't seem to exist. Where my happiness is not contingent on the next role or the director who might discover me.

MICHAEL

Maybe the playwright will come in to see *Pavilion*. He's pretty famous now, but maybe. You know he wrote *Six Feet Under*, right? Maybe we'll pick up a couple Jeff Awards. Who knows?

MAGGIE

But I'm also missing Michael already, and thinking of the women who will come. Will they know how to love him? Will they know that he loves the simulated feeling of having an egg cracked gently over his head? That he doesn't have the fine motor skills to twist off a beer cap, so they'll have to do that for him and in a subtle way so no one notices? Will they know? That dropping out of college is his biggest insecurity, so don't ever make too much of that? That he needs to be yelled at sometimes just to get the fucking point? I want to write a manual. Because otherwise, how will they know?

MICHAEL

I feel really far away from you. I feel like we're on different planets. (BEAT) Do you think you love that guy or something?

MAGGIE

He's ten years older than me. He's a snob. (BEAT) No. I do not love him.

MICHAEL

Why didn't you answer the phone when I called? It rang and rang and rang . . .

MAGGIE

I don't know. Let's have some more wine, okay?

MICHAEL

I'm sorry this happened to us, Bruise.

MAGGIE

Me too. (Pause) Me too. (Silence) Don't you want more wine?

MICHAEL

What do you want, Mag?

MAGGIE

(Blurts it out.) I've told you a million times. I don't want to live here. With your parents. I don't want them to drive us everywhere. I want us to take a cab sometimes, or the train or the bus or something. I told you about the free cab service, but you're always so afraid. I hate going everywhere by myself, and I don't want to lie in bed all the time. I want to leave Chicago, Mike. I want to go to graduate school somewhere else and be by myself, and really learn to write. It's the only thing that makes me happy. I don't want to be an actor anymore. (BEAT) I think I want to break up. (Relief and despair.)

MICHAEL

(Calmly.) This is temporary.

MAGGIE

Michael. What if it's not? (Crying her fucking ass off.)

MICHAEL

Do you love me?

MAGGIE

Of course I do. God, this is worse than high school.

MICHAEL

Are you in love with me?

Silence.

MICHAEL

But you said you loved me unconditionally. (Furious.) That's what you always said. (Repeat the phrase "unconditional love" until MAGGIE starts to drown.)

MAGGIE

Maybe I can find a way to make a lot of money and we can hire a nurse part-time.

MICHAEL

No. That means you're giving up. Do not give up. Not now.

MAGGIE

What if this had happened to me?

MICHAEL

(Too quickly.) I would've become an alcoholic. (MICHAEL does a pantomime.)

MAGGIE holds up one empty bottle and starts to open the other one. She offers it to MICHAEL and he waves it away.

RITA (O.S.)

Go get him, Frankie. Please go out there and get him. If he has to take antidepressants now because of this girl, because of this girl . . . She's a friggin' monster, Frank. I have always thought so. Why didn't this happen to her instead? Frank, he's our only son. Please, honey, go and get him.

MAGGIE goes to MICHAEL and sits in his lap. (We hear the violins of R.E.M.'s "Nightswimming," the song they kissed to when they were teenagers.) She buries her head in the crook of his neck and they cry for the deaths of those teenagers who floated toward each other in that swimming pool in the dark so many years ago and kissed each other's chlorine lips, stopping and smiling, then starting again, while the same parents sat in the window and eavesdropped.

NEXT-DOOR NEIGHBOR KID (O.S.)

Mommy! Mommy! Mikey's crying. Ahahahaha. Mikey's crying! Maggie is too! Maggie is too! Aren't they grown-ups?

NEXT-DOOR NEIGHBOR PARENT (O.S.)

Oh my God, Jim. So help me God, if anything ever happens like that to our kids. I swear to God, I think about it all the time now. I imagine every possible scenario. The other day, I thought the baby's head looked kinda big and maybe it was a brain tumor. I even called the doctor. I mean, Jimmy: I pray, I go to church, I'm a good person, but so is Rita. What if this happens to our kids? Oh my God. Poor Rita.

FRANKIE (O.S.)

C'mere, Rita. Honey. C'mere, my beautiful bride-een.

MICHAEL (to MAGGIE)

Everything will be okay in the morning. (Finally and firmly.) I know it.

* * *

We broke up, in part, because I needed to tell the truth now to survive, and Mike still needed imagination. We broke up a year and a half after the stroke, when I was twenty-six and he was twenty-five. We had become an official couple when I was twenty and he was nineteen. We had been friends, or something like it, since I was seventeen and he only sixteen years old.

* * *

The Gift once did a fantastic production of *One Flew Over the Cuckoo's Nest.* In the play, Dale says that people like him go crazy because they feel weak and small, and people like McMurphy go crazy because of people like Dale. When I heard that line, I thought of the night Mike and I broke up, the stroke and RIC, how all of it has left me with my own set of anxieties. I thought of all the things that didn't used to scare me, that now had the power to keep me awake at night. Like skiing or riding a bike, having a high fever or driving a car too fast on the highway. Ending up like all the women at RIC who were paralyzed from high-risk pregnancies and deliveries. Feeling a pain in the back of my neck.

* * *

In the morning, I woke to Frankie's footsteps in the hall. I listened to his morning routine one last time, and missed him already. I listened to him light his first cigarette of the morning and crack a few eggs. I looked over at Mike, who was flat on his back, staring at the ceiling. I knew he hadn't slept at all while I breathed laboriously through the night, drunk enough and empty enough to finally fall asleep. His legs started to spasm involuntarily as they sometimes did in the morning, so I sat up in bed and hugged his legs tightly to me, let them shake my body for a few minutes, until they stopped. I held them for a minute more. I kissed him, probably stinking of spoiled wine, went out to the kitchen, and greeted his father, who was making me breakfast in his underpants. Then I hurried off to Redmoon Theater, that wonderful place, where I could escape into hours upon hours of work.

* * *

As soon as I was settled back at my parents' house, I went to see *The Pavilion* at Victory Gardens. The postcard image: Lynda and Paul sitting on a bench, looking so young, tanned, and thin, literally gazing up at stars—this couple who loved each other so fiercely but never could make the romance work, for whatever reason. I understood them now. In this play about a high school reunion, one of my favorite lines ever: "For us to be together, the universe would have to start all over again . . ." I sat in the audience, knowing I would never act again. I saw my friends after the show and told them all my favorite parts because I knew that's what they needed. I told them what to work on because I knew they needed that too. Then Brendan and Paul looked at their watches and said, "Shouldn't you get back to Mike?"

Lynda said, "Shut up and let her stay if she needs to."

* * *

Because Tabitha was getting married, and I was the maid of honor, there were plans to be finalized. I had planned the bridal shower before I left, but now there was the bachelorette party, which is especially important to a young bride. While I was away, the other bridesmaids wanted my feedback. Does she like strippers, gambling, spa days? I didn't respond right away to their emails, and then I dreaded opening my inbox because one message was worse than the next.

> I can't believe how rude you are, not returning my e-mails. I know you were in Prague, Mag, and I hate to be the master of the obvious, but this is Tabitha's fucking bachelorette party. Stop being so fucking selfish.

I called Tabitha and said I hoped she didn't regret her decision, said she could choose another maid of honor if she wanted. She said she couldn't begin to think about what I'd done to Mike, but she was disgusted at how I treated Shannon in Prague. I emailed Shannon to say I was sorry. We were home now and I realized my mistakes. I should've spent more time with her, but I was working through some things.

> Your "situation" doesn't entitle you to anything . . . Based on the Maggie Andersen Reward System, what does Tabitha get after watching her father die? And my next-door neighbor? She's getting a divorce after struggling with her husband's mental illness for three years. Surely both of them are entitled to more than a month at fantasy camp.
>
> Mag, you told me several things that turned out to be less than truthful, i.e., that your relationship with Rory was platonic (kissing and making out is not platonic) . . . To say it was uncomfortable for me is an understatement (hopefully Mike will shed some more light on that) and rather than address that or understand it, you acted and continue to act self-righteous.
>
> I can only hope that soon, you'll come crashing back to reality . . . Don't forget to tell Mike how genuinely happy you were upon hearing that he stood up three times in a row . . . what a sweetheart.

And I had been happy to hear the news, of course, but I also knew, from experience, not to get my hopes up because they always ended up getting smashed. Let's stop here. Everything they said was true. I had behaved terribly. Even I knew that. I shouldn't have made my friend feel unwelcome, and I had completely betrayed Mike's trust. And the accusations about always needing a man were true enough, though it was difficult to accept this criticism from women who were about to be married, who were about to never be alone again, when I knew somewhere deep inside that I was about to be lonely for a long, long time.

At Tabitha's wedding, I stood on the altar in an eggplant gown and listened to her vow, "In sickness and in health." I felt the congregation's eyes burning holes into me. At the reception, I sat at the head table and Mike sat on the other side of the room with the Gift. I watched as Brendan cut his steak for him (small pieces, I thought) then played cards with him (gin rummy, I thought) while everyone danced the night away. I gave the maid of honor toast, then made my way over to his table.

"You want to dance like we did on the Lokomat?" he said.

We did. He got up and we danced stiffly for a couple minutes, then he sat down, defeated, and said, "Go dance with your friends. Get outta here."

These girlfriends and I were forever changed, but we put on a show for the bride.

* * *

When I told Mike I was worried about my friendship with Tabitha and Shannon, he said, "You'll all get over it, and we will get back together." I tried again, to remember my lines, to play my role with conviction. "But I'm leaving, Mike. I mean it. Please don't try and stop me." Finally, in the middle of the week, he called me at work. From my desk, I could look out a drafty old painted window to the residential city street below. Women were always running with their dogs or running with their babies in strollers or running all alone. That's all I ever really saw: women running. The finale was not dramatic.

Mike said, "You really are leaving me, aren't you?"

I looked over at my boss and smiled politely.

"Yes," I said into the phone.

"I always wanted you to make an unpopular decision, Mag. I practically begged you to." He had to stop for a minute. His voice cracked. "I never knew it would be at my expense."

* * *

Brendan and Lauren took me out that night, probably hoping they could help in some way. We sat in the back of a new, generic restaurant in my neighborhood where they watched me cry until I could barely open my eyes, while my very first cell phone rang and rang. Mike, of course. Every time his number appeared on the screen, I felt like the room was caving in, like I would never be able to escape this despair.

Mike Thornton would have to go back on the dating market now, a twenty-five-year-old man who lived with his parents and collected disability checks and didn't drive. That's what killed me. His life had been a series of humiliations, large and small, and I had never wanted to be a part of that. I had always tried to save him from that, even before the stroke. I did not want him to be lonely like so many of our friends at RIC. But he was talented and handsome and had gotten very good at the art of love. I hoped that would count for something.

CHAPTER 25

2004

I went to my parents' house to tell my sisters I had left Mike. My sisters who had grown from children to women during the course of our relationship. They said what our parents had coached them to say: "Whatever's best for you, Mag. You're my sister." Then they went to their shared bedroom and closed the door, played music that reminded them of Mike and cried. It was like I was a stranger, and one they did not wish to know.

* * *

Frank Maugeri, one of the artistic directors at Redmoon Theater, was probably a genius. He knew about clowns and puppetry and physical theater; he knew the secret music. He had heard the gossip about me and Mike by Monday morning. The news had spread more quickly than I'd expected, and Chicago suddenly felt like a small town. Frank stood beside my desk and looked at my face, and I remembered that someone had told me he was a recovering alcoholic, so I knew he understood real pain. I remembered him saying once that he hated small features, which is maybe why his puppets always had big, giant eyes, like he did. I suddenly felt very self-conscious about my small eyes and thin lips.

"Saw you at rehearsal today," Frank said. "How'd you like it?"

"I liked the train hobos," I said.

"Oh yeah?"

"I understood them," I said. "They just need to get outta here." And then my voice started to betray me.

"Let's go outside," Frank said.

He lit a cigar and we listened to the rumble of the Metra train, watched some guys light up a barbecue under the tracks. We marveled at the Kinzie Corridor—the crumbling factories and vacant lots, the breakfast club for the guys who took lunch at 10 A.M. and the hot dog stands that served beer to the guys who punched out at two. The divey blues clubs and Italian delis, little tiny restaurants with curtains in the windows on residential corners. The trucks everywhere making pickups and drop-offs, the manufacturing facilities that made watches and lamps.

"I know we're supposed to think it's ugly," I said. "But I think it's stunning."

"This will all be gone soon," Frank said. "Pay attention."

I did not want it to change, but I knew, deep down, it would.

"You know what I think?" Frank said. "If he really loves you, he'll understand. I love my wife so much, I wouldn't want her to give up her life and take care of me. I mean that. I really do."

* * *

Mike's mother was furious, of course. Told him not to call me, not to see me, said he should kick me out of the company.

"That's not unconditional love," she said. "She doesn't deserve you. She never has."

Mike asked his father to push him down to Charlotte's, his local bar, and come back in a few hours to pick him up.

"What do *you* think, Dad?" Mike asked, looking straight ahead as his father pushed him over alley cracks and broken glass.

"I think it's sad," Frankie said, and Mike thought he heard him crying.

* * *

Mike refused to kick me out of the company. He said we were *evolved* human beings. But he did call me several times to ask why I left and implore me to change my mind. He wrote letters and sent them through the mail.

> The loneliest day of my life was thinking we may have to go on without each other. I want to walk from this chair and into your heart and kiss it. So if I gotta lose that smile or what your mere entrances do to my brain or your kisses or your tits or your attention for a while, or the only feeling of protection I can offer you currently: pulling up a blanket around your sleepy shoulders, for a while, I'll live and you'll live. But you're what makes living a life. Girlfriend to a wife.
>
> I hate being a reality check, your sad punctuation mark to a wonderful trip free of me and my shadow. I hate being a moral dilemma, a liability, a burden.
>
> I love holding you with my left arm at a party, listening to you talk. Watching you enter the world on Sunday mornings, my favorite part of Sunday football! Talking to you. Yes! Every conversation! The millions of them! And then pow! Zoom! There we are, making love again.

* * *

Shortly after the breakup, I agreed to visit Rory in Michigan, and got off the Amtrak train after I'd been thinking of Mike all day. That first night I made love to him, he fell asleep shortly after, and I sat in a window and cried, hugging my naked knees. But to give him credit, we did have some fun. After all of that grief, I was ready. He made me dinner every night in his kitchen with the vintage wallpaper and antique light fixtures. On Friday night, he made Cornish hens stuffed with dried cherries, and on Saturday, a seafood salad. He mixed up fancy cocktails that I didn't know how to drink (I was more accustomed to Miller Lite), and in the mornings, we went to his local coffee shop and wrote, sitting across from each other, not saying a word for hours. I didn't write about Mike then. I wrote short stories about my family building and all the eccentrics who had lived there. Rory took me to literary readings, taught me that slam poetry and genre fiction are bad, and that writers can be just as crazy as actors: Writers just started drinking earlier. We walked for miles at night until it was time for a pretty cocktail again, or to go back to his drafty apartment and fool around. We agreed to date long-distance after that weekend, but we fought often because he suspected I wasn't in love with him, and that I was still in love with Mike. Frankly, I thought he should've known better, considering he was always bragging about how smart he was and how long he'd been around.

* * *

At the end of that summer, I found myself at a neighborhood street festival with my parents, and saw Tabitha and Shannon from a distance. They were standing on a street corner, laughing, and I knew I could go to them. All we had to do was look at one another's faces and we'd remember our years of friendship. I smiled to myself, trying to think of something witty to say, then told my parents to wait for me as I snuck up behind my old friends. Tabitha and Shannon turned and looked at me with blank expressions, as if I were a stranger, and one they did not wish to know.

The walk back to my parents was agonizing. My father, who had always believed the three of us would be lifelong friends, turned red with helpless embarrassment, and my mother thought as quickly as she could.

"You don't need friends like that," she said unconvincingly.

The ones I'd met in school. We had taken the bus together; we had learned to drive together; we had always believed we'd grow old together. But they said I was selfish and always had been; they decided I didn't deserve them; they chose him over me, in the end. And even though I agreed with everything they said, it broke my goddamn heart.

* * *

At Redmoon, we had a show to put up, and I knew that the show must go on. *Sink, Sank, Sunk* ran for two weekends in late September of 2004. Somehow, through various guerilla-marketing strategies, we convinced many hundreds of people to come down to Ping Tom Park, which was still relatively new. For many years, it had been a Chicago and Western Indiana Railroad yard, but in the late nineties, when I was finishing college, they converted it to green space and added Chinese landscape-design elements because of its proximity to Chinatown. I had only ever gone to Chinatown with my father, who ate lunch there once a week with his coworkers and often took us kids if my mom needed alone time. He took me and my sisters to all the best places, where he knew everyone in the family by name, but he also knew which places had rat infestations and told us to remember. He was friends with the unofficial mayor of Chinatown, who always shook his hand and then whispered with him for a long time while my sisters and I window-shopped and spent our weekly allowances on Hello Kitty pencils and ginger candies. Back then, it had been smaller, but now, hipsters, eccentrics, and urban families came streaming off the Red Line, and local Chinese folks came out of their houses to see what in the hell was happening.

Ping Tom was located on the South Branch of the Chicago River, accessible by train or water taxi, and the year we were there, they hadn't even built a field house or the pool yet, though they had built a really cool pagoda-style pavilion. In the open air, the audience witnessed a visual and totally compelling spectacle narrative. A young woman who had been widowed by thirteen husbands, a bossman who had had his heart broken, and hobos looking for the next train. Once the sky had grown dark, the widow stood with the bossman and the hobos, and looked out at a fleet of small boats coming down the Chicago River, lit with torches. A thirteen-piece band dressed as skeletons started to play a haunting song, and motioned for the audience to follow them down to the riverbank. Every night of the show, I accepted a paper lantern and followed the funeral music. The procession was equal parts mourning and celebration as I walked with the skeletons and hundreds of other Chicagoans. One night, Frank Maugeri sought me out, and together, we moved toward the firelight, feeling a potent mix of hope and despair, as the leaves on the branches threatened to change color.

CHAPTER 26

2005

I can't remember when I really, truly stopped being Mike Thornton's girlfriend. I can't remember that year I was unhinged. After breaking up with him, I literally had nowhere to go. My sister and I had both come home unexpectedly and my parents no longer had space for us. My sister had come home from college because she was homesick, and I had broken my lease and moved out of the apartment, so we slept together in our parents' unrented and empty third-floor apartment. The missing radiators and old windows made it drafty in the winter, but we each had our own bedroom. I fashioned myself an office in the sunroom off the back of the apartment and wrote a series of essays about Chicago, then sent them, along with applications, to a bunch of writing programs. I applied to Iowa because it was the best, Western Michigan because it sponsored the Prague Summer Program, the School of the Art Institute because I loved Chicago and half of me wanted to stay, and Loyola Marymount because Los Angeles was so far away.

By the time I had sent out all my applications, the holidays were coming and I couldn't think about that. Mike wanted to buy me gifts—I told him I couldn't accept them. During this period in our lives, we spoke on the phone regularly, but I wouldn't allow myself to see him. If I could hear his voice, I could live with myself, and if I didn't see his face, I could keep my resolve. Please stop loving me,

I was saying. I am not who you think I am. He asked me to come to Christmas dinner and I declined.

"Do you have other plans?"

"Of course not," I lied.

When Rory asked me to fly to California on Christmas Day and meet his family, I stupidly agreed to it. Three months after the breakup, three months and I was still dealing with some version of PTSD, three months and I still had days where it was difficult to get out of bed. But I needed a distraction. I couldn't sit around on Christmas Day and be reminded of Mike. I did not want to remember all the generosity we had shown each other, all the gifts. It had always been a spectacle with us: Who could outdo the other? Who could make who cry first?

Sometimes I felt like just telling Mike the truth. I am going to California to spend Christmas with a man I just met while you stay here, humiliated and alone. Sometimes I believed the truth would make him stop loving me, and that's what I really wanted. If he stopped loving me, I could handle the heartbreak on my own, and he could just work on walking.

I know what you're thinking. If I felt this way, why not go to him and grovel and tell him I was wrong? But no. I dared myself to do something different with my life. Let's go to Southern California and see what all the fuss is about. Take the free ticket and run. I mean, what choice did I have? I was already convinced that I'd never be forgiven, that I'd never forgive myself, that if there was a hell, I was going, so why not blow it all?

When Christmas Day came, I headed west, dreaming of starting over. My father drove me to the airport and we sat in silence most of the way. I couldn't help looking at other people on the highway—families in their holiday best. Mothers perfectly made-up and fathers wearing neckties, little girls in matching dresses. When I was a child, Christmas Day was reserved for my immediate family. We opened presents from Santa, had a big brunch at home, and stayed in our pajamas all day.

"What does Rory's family do for Christmas?" my father asked, too sweetly.

I knew that Rory's family was dysfunctional, and not in the funny way. His grandparents were some of the wealthiest people in Southern California, but they and his mother had a strained relationship.

His mother and her sister had been spoiled rich girls until they disappointed their father and he cut them off. I knew that this Christmas would be nothing like our own. I'd be shuttling back and forth between trailer parks and oceanside mansions, but I didn't tell my father. He didn't need to know. I think he was hoping as hard as I was that I could find a way to be happy again. Clearly, he was hoping. A man who always said his biggest fear was his daughters moving far away from him was driving his oldest to the airport, helping her get to the land of fruits and nuts for Christmas dinner.

My father pulled up to the concourse, biting his lip and clearing his throat. Finally, he got out of the car, walked around to the trunk, and pushed my hands away when I tried to take out my own suitcase.

"I got it," he said.

He carried the suitcase to the skycap and tipped him.

"Have a good time, babe," he said, sadly. And after I had already walked away: "I love you. Merry Christmas."

A security guard yelled at him then to keep on moving and he spun around. "Blow it out your ass, RoboCop! I *am* the fuckin' police!"

Inside the empty airport, Christmas songs continued to torture me. Pain started slicing through me and I wanted my father to come back and pick me up, force me somehow to stay. *Are you crazy? You just broke up with Mike a few months ago. I haven't said a word until now, but why do you have to meet Rory's family? What are you rushing into? How well do you really know each other? You just don't ever seem like yourself with him. Do you really want to get married to him? These are big decisions, Mag. You are not too old to find love. You are not too fucked up, I promise. I know. All your friends and your sisters are getting married. Okay. Okay.*

At the same time, the pain felt like a perfectly justified punishment. I no longer deserved the world of fireplaces, stockings, and beautifully wrapped presents. I belonged right here with all the other lonely people. There were pockets of grief everywhere, I realized, and the slicing pain was preferable to the heavy, pulling sadness I felt when I worried about missing the opportunity to have a career I loved, marrying Mike for the wrong reasons, being a caretaker instead of a writer. The pain meant I had done something about it, and even if it was the wrong decision, it was a decision nonetheless. I felt a little older than I wanted, as if I had somehow skipped a step. I wrote on the airplane about all of the sad people in the airport. Do you know how many people cry in the airport on Christmas Day?

When Rory met me at the baggage carousel at the Orange County airport, he stuffed his hands deep in his pockets and smiled uncertainly at me.

"I have some bad news," he said. "I should've called you, but things have been pretty hectic."

"What? Rory. Tell me."

"We found my aunt this morning. She hanged herself. She's dead. She did it in the room we were supposed to stay in." He looked away as if it were all too much. "You can go home if you want."

Okay, I thought. Absolutely not, I thought.

Then I put down my suitcase and wrapped my arms around him. We stood there, hugging in the middle of an empty airport. No more arrivals or departures that night—no more Christmas carols. I spent a week with him in that desert where the seasons never changed. We stayed in seedy motels some nights and with his wealthy grandparents part of the time, in a big house jutting out over the ocean. We took a day trip to Hollywood, which I insisted on, and had a sufficiently dramatic argument about that. Predictably, he hated Hollywood. We drank at outdoor bars decorated with twinkle lights and strolled through art galleries on the beach. He helped his mother make funeral arrangements, and every time I stared out at the ocean, I heard the universe telling me to go back to Mike.

* * *

I called him once while I looked out at the ocean, but all he did was ask me to be his girlfriend again and if I could take a look at some of his writing. As always, he cast me in the role of girlfriend and himself as the artist.

"I've been writing again. Really good stuff, I think. Do you have time to read it?"

"Sure."

I used to cry and scream for him to stop when he said things like this. Stop competing with me, let me have my life, why don't you ever ask me about my work?

"I love you," I said. "Talk soon."

I hung up the phone and it was then I understood. I could go back and live with him, but there would be a condition. I'd have to lay down the life I'd lived for the past several months. The writing workshops where I was the star, the trip abroad, the time alone. I'd have to burn it all. That's the price I'd have to pay.

Later that evening, I sat with Rory's mother and the aunt's son, the boy who had unfairly found her. The boy, a teenager, drank several beers and no one seemed to have a problem with it. Rory's mother and I drank white wine with ice cubes and she told me stories of Rory as a baby. He never wanted to snuggle with her, she said; he was always more of a thinker than a feeler.

"We'd better get going," Rory said to me. "We have a drive to the motel."

"You know what I loved most about my mom?" the boy with the dead mother asked. "Well, everything but . . ."

"Rory, I love you," his mother said. "Remember that party I threw when you left for college?"

"That was a good one," he conceded.

"My mom threw me a Chuck E. Cheese party once," the boy with the dead mother said. "Oh, man . . ."

And all I kept thinking was, This is where you belong now. This is where you live. In this barren place where no one listens to one another or loves deeply enough, where tragedy has desensitized them all. Then I asked the boy about the Chuck E. Cheese party, because somebody had to, damn it, and I was not that far gone, yet.

* * *

"I like your mother," I said to Rory as we drove to the motel, hours later.

"I love her," he said. "But she's a selfish woman."

Me too, I thought. Me too.

Rory's mother lived in a patch of California where nothing grew, and I was happy when I was with her, felt like I was helping in some way, like I needed her landscape and its unbearable cruelty. A boy crying for his mother, a woman crying for her sister, a grown man crying for all of them. Poor Rory couldn't save me after all. He was trying to save himself.

* * *

It was a relief to get out of there at the end of the week. As Rory said, these people were not good at life and I really wanted to be. However, the California Christmas was good for me, too. It helped me not to think about a little ranch house in Chicago where there were rosy-faced children and red poinsettias in every room. It helped me not to think about a room with a closed door where a young man was lying in bed, crying for his girlfriend, asking "Why, God?," feeling like he would never be loved again.

I have never told Mike about this trip until now.

Dear Mike: This was my first Christmas without you.

* * *

When I returned home from California, there was a stack of mail for me on the kitchen counter, and in it, a letter from Western Michigan University saying I had been accepted to their MFA program with a teaching assistantship and a stipend. The letter said my writing portfolio was impressive and worthy of their investment. My initial reaction? Hyperventilating. Validation. But then I thought about it. If I said yes, if I signed the contract and returned it, I was committing to three years of my life. Three years of making $11,000 a year and essentially choosing to live at the poverty level after my father had broken the cycle. Three years of living in the same town where Rory lived, and I still felt attracted to him, but also had a feeling we weren't going to last. Three years away from my family and remaining friends, all the people who knew how to love me. And by the time I was done, I'd be thirty, which, for a nice girl from the Midwest, is old. Three years in a place too small for anonymity, and small towns had always felt lonelier and more hostile to me than big cities. But then again, it would be three years of writing in a small city with old Victorian houses, a few good restaurants, and tree-lined streets. I could take the train home on the weekends if I was lonely, and my parents had my sisters for company.

I sat in the third-floor window and looked out over as much city as I could. Goodnight Chicago, I said with a heavy heart. Goodnight art students and famous writers. Goodnight to all the parents who worry for their adult children for reasons we can't imagine. Goodnight to all the hospital patients and theaters. Goodnight, you big city with the soul of a small town. Tomorrow I make arrangements to leave you.

* * *

Of course I remember being Mike Thornton's girlfriend. Of course I remember the year I wasn't anymore. The year of the California suicide. The year I got to know myself, and even started to forgive myself and like myself again.

Actually, I started to like myself more than I ever had.

CHAPTER 27

2005

Classes started in a matter of months, so I began the search for apartments in Kalamazoo, Michigan, and coincidentally, that's when Mike started looking for a permanent space for the Gift. We started to look for home without each other. Our broken hearts, as they often are, were the ones that allowed us to take these necessary risks.

Mike found a space for the theater about the same time I found my apartment. I decided on a small, one-bedroom apartment in a working-class neighborhood, and Mike found an old, vacant shoe store right in the middle of Jefferson Park. Lawrence and Milwaukee had been a popular shopping intersection in the sixties, but was now saddled with empty storefronts. One of our company members checked it out and said he could do all the necessary wiring, get the bathrooms up to code. Everyone else could help with drywall and paint. Mrs. Thornton would convert the concrete basement into dressing rooms. Meanwhile, there were company meetings and heated arguments between Mike and other company members who said the theater should be built in a more "cultured" neighborhood, a place where we might have a built-in audience of theatergoers like Lakeview or Andersonville.

"I mean, Mike," Will said. "I know your grandfather patrolled that corner back in the day. I get that it has sentimental value. It's convenient for you, but let's think business."

Others started to chime in and offer support for Will's argument, and Mike looked like he was beginning to doubt himself, so the pit bull in me came out.

"But you all say you're so goddamn liberal," I said. "Isn't the more socially conscious thing to bring theater to a neighborhood that doesn't have any?"

Defending him in these meetings was the only way I could show love without sending mixed messages. I saw his confidence return then, his sincere belief that the theater didn't belong anywhere but here. Mike announced then that *The Glass Menagerie* would be the first show in the new space, and I was reluctant to audition: Was I really going to travel back and forth between Kalamazoo and Chicago for the entire run of the show?

"Of course you will," Mike said. "It's history in the making."

Sheldon was directing, so I did go to the audition, fully prepared. I took the train downtown and read with Mary Ann Thebus, I as Laura and she as Amanda. She, my mother, pretended like I wasn't disabled, as if I were exactly like everyone else, and that hit me in a visceral way. It made me feel the way I often did when Mike and everyone around us kept saying he would get better even though the medical professionals all so clearly disagreed. I started laughing, awkwardly, then I started laughing really hard, and then I started crying. "But Mother, I'm *crippled*." Mary Ann looked at me for a long time before she gave me her next line. Sheldon offered me the role that night, and I had gone up against several more talented women, so maybe Mike had encouraged him to cast me. Maybe he thought if I had a role like that, I would reconsider graduate school altogether. But no: I think I just might have been that good that night. Now I just had to figure out how to make the trip back and forth.

The next time I saw Mike was at the Gift Theatre fundraiser being held at an office suite in Jefferson Park. The lighting was awful and the view wasn't glamorous, but the purpose was to raise money for the inaugural season in our new space across the street. Mrs. Thornton had planned it, secured all of the silent auction and raffle items, so I tried everything I could to get out of it. It felt inconsiderate to make her uncomfortable at a party she planned, but Mike said I should come anyway.

"We're getting people excited about next season. You'll be reading your audition scene with Mary Ann. You're an ensemble member—you are invaluable to this company. You have to come. The end."

When I arrived the night before the fundraiser to help decorate, I walked into the room and everyone stopped what they were doing to look at me and Mike, as they often did in those days. I had always worked so hard to fill my stage entrances, and now I couldn't make myself invisible. When I bent over to hug him, he pulled me down, and wouldn't let go. Finally, I got up and started crafting, laughing with all my old friends as we cut out paper hearts and strung them around the room. We set up a kissing booth, a stage for the readings, which would be a preview of the upcoming season, and a couple of makeshift bars with fancy champagne glasses and candy bowls. It was destined to be a romantic night, a celebration of love.

The night itself did not feel romantic to me, but that's because I had to deal with Mike's family, and to complicate matters, I had invited my own family and work friends to be an audience for the intense discomfort. Mrs. Thornton and her sisters bustled around the space and refused to look at my face, which distracted me while I tried to talk to my work friends about the upcoming season and how they should totally donate and become subscribers. I did my best to make myself as small as possible, because somewhere deep inside, I knew that I deserved it. Somewhere buried inside were maternal instincts that knew it had to be this way.

When I started to read with Mary Ann, Mrs. Thornton got up and left the audience, quickly finding something else to do.

"Mother, I'm *crippled,"* I cried with snot pouring out of my nose.

After the reading, my own mother came up to me and said loudly, "I cannot believe she left during your reading."

"Mom, be quiet. Please."

Mike's Uncle Jerry came to me and said, "Okay. I understand. You weren't getting laid and you wanted to get laid. I understand. But go and apologize to Rita. She's done a lot for you. She was good to you. She feels betrayed."

"Leave me alone, Jerry," I said. "I love you, but please stop."

Tara, Mike's therapist again, had come to the fundraiser, and after it was all over, when it was just the company members sitting around, having our first drinks because we were finally off the clock, she sat close to Mike, like she was protecting him from me, from the possibility of late-night confessions ("this is not working; this is not fun"), from things I might be tempted to say.

"Did you see my new kicks?" Mike asked. Then he lifted his foot to show me his brightly colored new gym shoes. "Tara bought them for me."

Everyone tried to make Tara feel welcome and appreciated, to help Mikey seal the deal, and I understood then that he was trying to date her. That's why some of the company members were keeping their distance from me. That's not entirely true. John Gawlik teased me relentlessly about the bright-yellow ski jacket I was wearing for a winter coat.

"You look like a bumblebee!" he cried out in what he thought was a Czech accent. "A little baby bumblebee!"

And though he made me laugh like a child again, I just felt like I shouldn't be there anymore, like it wasn't good for Mike or me. He was making me feel guilty all the time while he was clearly pursuing other options, and I was making myself small again to protect his feelings. The point is: Chicago didn't feel like home anymore, for the first time in my life.

As soon as I left the party, my cell phone lit up with a text message. From Mike: *I WILL marry you.* When I got home, I threw away all the paper valentines and conversation hearts from the party, then read Tom's last monologue from *The Glass Menagerie* before going to bed. "I left St. Louis. I descended the steps of this fire escape for a last time . . ."

The following morning, I called Sheldon and asked him to find a replacement, and while I was packing and making preparations to move, our first theater was being built. There are photographs of Paulie high up on a ladder, Lynda smiling with a power drill, Brendan with paint chips in his hair, Frankie and his buddies hauling in drywall, and Mike sitting in his chair and supervising, looking determined. And I was going off to start all over in a brand-new art form with people I had never met.

* * *

Off I went to Kalamazoo. My father drove me there in a small moving truck and Rory met us at my apartment, said he would take it from there, and stiffly shook my father's hand. My father always said I wasn't myself with Rory, but was too afraid to argue with me about it after what I'd been through. Rory spent the good part of an afternoon putting together my bed, and I thought of how Mike wouldn't be able to do this. When I unpacked a framed photograph of Mike wearing an obnoxious Viking helmet and set it on top of my dresser, I noticed Rory noticing it.

"It's funny," I said. "It makes me laugh."

That caused an argument and he stormed out shortly after. Some of the women in the program said they were surprised I was Rory's girlfriend because he was such an old grouch and I was so high-spirited, and then I felt like an imposter in someone else's life.

During those early days, I devoted myself to lesson plans in the mornings, and at night, worked on new essays and stories. I also decided to cook more, so I walked to the grocery store with a list and all the cash left in my bank account. Harding's was a few blocks away, and there were long lines of folks at the can-crushing machines surrounded by moats of stale beer and sticky pop. After cashing out, they headed inside and studied the displays of Little Debbie snacks. This was my new neighborhood. I bought English muffins and oatmeal, and enough ingredients to make myself a simple pasta dish. Noodles and sauce, veggies and spices, sweet Italian sausage. I packed up my groceries, started home and looked up at my old friend, the moon. Truth be told, I felt pretty proud of myself. Look at me, world, killing it. Yes, I'm worried about teaching students who are only a few years younger, and no, I don't think any of the people in the program will ever be real friends, but I live alone now. I take care of myself. I am an artist and the woman I always wanted to be.

A couple of blocks from the apartment, one of my grocery bags started to feel a bit stretched. You'll make it, I told myself repeatedly, until the handle finally snapped, buckling under the weight of the sauce jars, and the bottom of the bag fell out. I chased the jars awkwardly rolling into the street, darted out in front of traffic to save them, snatched up the runaway box of raw noodles, and every last one spilled out while people laid on their horns. Then the second bag broke, and the third. I am a fuckup, I thought, and I will never amount to anything without him.

Meanwhile, in Chicago, *The Glass Menagerie*, the first show at the official Gift Theatre, opened in October of 2005. Critics and audiences came to a dusty storefront theater on Milwaukee Avenue between Lawrence and Foster, a fifty-seat Equity theater that used to be a shoe store, an unassuming storefront with a black awning crunched between Fischman Liquors and a taqueria without a name. Chris Jones, who was quickly becoming the kingmaker of Chicago theater, said this about the space early on: "It's one thing to trust a starry Broadway revival or a major theatrical institution. It's entirely another to wander into a tiny, bowling alley-like storefront in Jefferson Park—a theatrical wasteland before the Gift Theatre took up residence on the rough-hewn corner of Milwaukee and Lawrence." So: We had that to deal with. Also, the opening didn't go as planned.

> Nina Metz, *Chicago Tribune*—"In *The Glass Menagerie* by Tennessee Williams, the lights go out towards the end of the Act Two dinner scene. It's a nifty bit of business that allows for an intimate, candlelit scene in which the long-awaited gentleman caller draws a shy, insecure young woman out of her shell. But on opening night of [the] Gift Theatre's production, the lights went out a bit earlier. Ten minutes into the first act, to be precise.
>
> "Unfortunately, the theater's juice shut down three more times before the lights finally blinked out per the story, lending a special, unexpected humor to a line reading from Mary Ann Thebus as the nattering, overbearing Amanda Wingfield: 'Isn't electricity a mysterious thing?' "

Meanwhile, in Kalamazoo, I was busy with new student gatherings. I'd met Adeena at the teaching training intensive, and she and I quickly became inseparable. I loved her stories of growing up Orthodox Jewish on the East Coast and she loved mine about growing up working-class Chicago. We showed up together to a welcome party at a professor's massive apartment downtown, a block from the art museum and two blocks from the restaurants. Richard Katrovas was director of the Prague Summer Program, and Rory said you should get in good with him if you wanted to be chosen as a teaching assistant in future summers. Richard's wife was Czech, and they had three daughters who spent the academic year in the States and summers in Central Europe. I liked Richard because he had an unironic mullet, and was most comfortable wearing his jujitsu *gi* or T-shirts with the arms cut off. According to him, he'd grown up "poor white trash" in the South, but higher education had saved him. He was an inspired educator and writer, and I loved his classes, and his children, who I ended up nanny-ing. His wife, Dominika, told me about growing up in Communist Prague as we sipped red wine on her midcentury sofa.

People at the party seemed to find me interesting, which I liked because I hadn't felt interesting in a while—for so long, that had been Mike's specialty. But perhaps more important, I found *them* interesting. The theorist from Malaysia who would teach me to play mahjong, the big blond poet proud to be from Texas, and Jaimy Gordon, the beloved fiction professor who loved her dog more than humans. Adeena and I walked home together, as we would for the next three years. We had a nightcap together, as we would for the next three years, and she made me feel like I could risk being loved again. She and I stayed up late and listened to old records. There was a whole world, after all, that had nothing to do with me and Mike, so much music I had never heard.

* * *

When I finally saw *The Glass Menagerie* halfway through the run, Brendan was happy I had come, and I could feel the excitement of the neighborhood folks trickling into our local theater and swelling with a sense of pride and ownership. Downtown and suburban residents were making the trek and thinking it was worth it. Brendan was lovely as Tom Wingfield, and he was getting deeper now, so good. The night I went: a standing ovation. And sure, I felt a little jealous of the actress playing Laura; it would take time to adjust to being a member of the audience.

I took the night train back to Michigan after the show. My father carried my suitcase down the escalator, as he would do every time I came home, and said, "Be good, kid. Make us proud." My father, who had always said that his biggest fear was his children moving far away from him, and in my family, Michigan was too far.

* * *

My favorite bar in Kalamazoo that first year was the Kraftbrau, a big industrial brewery built right in the heart of downtown Kalamazoo, so that the original brewers could send their barrels down the railroad tracks to Chicago. By the time I lived there, they did a good weekend business because of their indie rock concerts, which brought kids from all over the Midwest. But most days, it was a wide-open space with a vintage popcorn machine, an antique piano with a couple of broken keys, creaky wood floors, and a loyal following of professional drinkers. Rory was one of them, and sometimes I met him there when I was lonely, just to hear the train whistle. Whenever we heard it, the bartender paused the music and we all ran outside to the side deck. We all stood there stupidly and watched the Amtrak train rush toward Chicago and waved. I don't know why everyone else did it. Because they would never make it to the big city after all? Because their dreams seemed to be moving farther and farther away? Because life was rushing by like a train? I don't know, but I did it because I had to remind myself that Kalamazoo was my new home and Chicago was too small for me now and I had to stay away and let Mike have it. Goodbye, I waved to the train, drinking a glass of beer on a sunny afternoon when I still felt young enough to dream my way into a new reality. Good luck, Thornton, I thought. If you build it, they will come.

CHAPTER 28

2005

Joy is so much harder to write than grief.

Writing is never easy for me, but I have been able, at times, to find words to sufficiently explain my sadness, and it feels much more challenging to find new ways to express the happiness, especially the kind I found in Michigan. There are only so many ways to say I smiled, I laughed, I laughed really hard. It's the same with the feelings themselves. It was easier then to feel sorry for myself and harder to find joy. But I did find it, finally.

During my first semester, I registered for the required teaching intensive as well as a narrative theory class, a seminar on the literature of 1925, and a fiction workshop with Stuart Dybek, my favorite short-story writer. Stuart had been at Western Michigan for the past thirty years and would soon be retiring. Rory had given me his books back in Prague, said he was sure I'd connect with them because they were Chicago stories, but it ended up being so much more than that. Stu's work made me feel less alone in my life, even though he had grown up in a different generation, in a neighborhood on the other side of the city. Everything felt so familiar, so perfectly authentic and true. The way he wrote heart songs for his father and piano prodigies on the South Side of Chicago, kids playing under viaducts, twenty-two-year-olds kissing on el trains and missing each other while they were still together. His sentences were often lyrical but he never sacrificed the humor, and in his vision, the city was a divided place that could be healed. Studs Terkel called him Chicago's version of James Joyce and our "Blue-Collar Bard." *The New York Times* had recently called him America's greatest living short-story writer. Most of the prose writers had applied to Western's program to study with Stuart—the program was competitive largely because of him.

My new friend Adeena and I smoked cigarettes outside of a beautiful building called Walwood Hall on the evening of our first class with him.

"I'm so nervous I could die," I said to her.

"I'll probably just throw up all over him," she said.

When we entered the classroom, we knew some of the workshop participants from our teaching boot camp, and others I'd met with Rory. There was Annie, the editor of *Third Coast*, the university's esteemed literary magazine. Rachel, a PhD candidate who I remembered from the Prague Summer Program, and Vinny from Northern Michigan. He had returned recently from years of teaching in Korea, and I knew, from Rory, that he was dating Heather, the woman sitting next to him, who was ten years younger and who had already won literary awards and published flash fiction in the best magazines. I recognized the Native poet Mark Turcotte, who had visited my undergraduate poetry class years before. He had already published two books, but needed the degree to teach, so here he was. He shook my hand and smiled, and I felt grateful to be in a class with all of these smart and interesting people. For the next sixteen weeks, we would workshop together, send each other story drafts, and talk about them for hours while the sun set over the quad.

When Stuart walked in, he looked uncannily like my father's former partner from the police department. He sat down in the circle with us and smirked like he'd just thought of something funny, and I'm sure he cracked a joke before telling us to call him Stu. We introduced ourselves one by one.

"I'm Maggie," I heard myself say, when it was my turn, my heart hammering in my ears. "This is my first year and—"

"You have a Chicago accent," he interrupted, and when he saw that it made me insecure, he said, "It's beautiful."

He was a benevolent coach most of the time, drawing diagrams on the chalkboard to help us see the story arcs and central images. He was very naturally funny, but dead serious about reading and writing. He knew exactly how to smile before beginning a story so that everyone would lean in and listen, pronounced the Polish names with the perfect accent and extra love. When I watched him walking up the hill to school, I knew that soon I'd have the name of a new writer to read, a new bit of beauty to take to bed with me. Calvino, he said. Dos Passos. Yehuda Amichai.

On the day of my first workshop, I stood outside an academic building and knew I only had to worry for myself now, which was such an incredible relief. I'd written a semi-autobiographical *Cyrano de Bergerac* story about two middle-school girls, and how one had written the love notes to make her friend believe that the boy she wanted loved her too. I wasn't sure about my story because my classmates were all so good. Mark wrote devastating stories about the reservation, and Heather's flash fiction had already won Pushcart Prizes. Vinny wrote sibling stories in the epistolary form with long, lovely passages about sailing on Lake Michigan. Stuart made it clear when he was a fan, so when he wasn't, the silences were painful. It didn't matter, I told myself, I was ready for feedback. After all, I was just beginning, it was an apprenticeship, and failing along the way didn't scare me anymore. Acting, among other things, had prepared me for this. If I failed, I would fail better this time.

Stu said that mine would be third in line for discussion, and the final piece of the evening was usually his favorite; he saved the best for last so the others wouldn't have to follow praise. Rachel started the conversation, as she often did, by describing the piece and its ambitions like a *New Yorker* book critic. She had always been the smartest person in any room, you could tell, which is why I enjoyed that she was from a small town in Wisconsin. Heather delighted in the moments she considered funniest, and took as much time as she wanted. Vinny read aloud sentences he had underlined, then looked around with bright eyes, and said, "What a line!" Stu waited for several people to speak before offering his opinion, and when he did, he rapped his knuckles on his desk and said, "I love this voice. I love the story. I think it's publishable." Dear reader: It was then that I died a little and went to heaven. He gave me a few editorial notes, like "Here is a paragraph that needs sentence-level work—you're going to have to do more with this minor character or cut her," which felt clearer and more manageable to me than acting notes had ever felt. He rattled off a short list of publications I should pursue, writers I should read.

"Have you read Amy Hempel?" he asked. "You have to read Amy. You're so much like her."

After the workshop, I went out to the bar with my classmates, but I only had half of a drink, then snuck off to the library and checked out the short stories of Amy Hempel. The desire to write, and to read like a writer, became more important than a second beer or being liked, or maybe I just wanted to be liked as a writer, for exactly who I was. Hempel's most widely anthologized story, "In the Cemetery Where Al Jolson Is Buried," was a story of friendship, and Stu was right: She expertly blended pathos and humor. Her use of specific, unusual detail did all the heavy lifting, and I took careful notes. One friend is terminally ill, and the other stays with her and makes jokes until she can't stand it anymore—in the end, she makes her escape. In an interview, Hempel said the story originated from a graduate-school writing prompt: "Write about the thing you will never live down." I finished the story that night in the library, and with the last line, my heart was a freed volcano. When she leaves her friend in the hospital, she becomes "fluent in the language of grief." Maybe that inspired me to write a fictionalized story about Mike for my second workshop.

* * *

Everything felt like a first date in those days—every new person, every new book. I read Amy Hempel and Raymond Carver for the first time; took a class on Louise Erdrich and Toni Morrison. Then I looked out the library windows at the snow and ice, and knew I'd survive the winter. In seminars, we studied the art of the personal essay, and I clung to Michel de Montaigne, the French philosopher who used it as a vehicle for self-awareness. He originally coined the term "essai" (which means an attempt) and this gave me permission, for the first time in my life, to be a writer full of uncertainties. I found something to love in all of the genres: the plays about too much love ending up in the wrong place, the poems about carpe diem, and then seize the day it was.

* * *

Rory left after my first year, thank God. We'd dated on and off, but we were always arguing, suspicious of each other for good reason. We'd started off on a rocky foundation, and didn't belong together, as it turns out. I knew this first, but he convinced me I was wrong, and by the time he realized I was right, I felt more humiliated than he did. He landed a good academic job at a small liberal arts college and I knew he'd go on to change lives. He had certainly changed the course of mine, and for that reason, I couldn't entirely hate him. On his last morning in Kalamazoo, he left me an expensive bottle of champagne, and a card with decaying flowers on the front.

In the spring, I moved into a new apartment with a back deck for the summer and a fireplace for the winter. This neighborhood was called the student ghetto, and I lived there with graduate and undergraduate students, a few of the more interesting professors, and a number of families. For Adeena's birthday, we had a cupcake-and-champagne party. Red velvet, vanilla, chocolate, and pistachio; champagne from pinot gris and chardonnay grapes. We played music on the record player and danced all night long in our favorite dresses. The porch lights all snapped on that first night of spring. The town went silent the day after graduation and didn't come alive again until the start of football season.

We attended literary readings weekly; the even-numbered Fridays were reserved for grad student readings in Sprau Tower and the odds were reserved for famous writers who were usually friends of the faculty. Adeena and I were often invited for dinner with these writers when they visited, and we behaved ourselves at the restaurants, learned how to listen deeply and ask important questions. However, after the readings, we usually drank pepper-infused vodka shots and chased them with pickles at a dark university bar called the Pilsen Klub. We sat with our friends near the fireplace, where the conversations about literature, art, and politics continued late into the night. Adeena and I confessed which writers we'd like to sleep with—always the oldest and ugliest, of course.

* * *

And though I had made the decision to retire from acting, I still did staged readings for all the visiting playwrights who didn't know

Mike Thornton. I played femme fatales and single mothers without worrying about him in the audience, and when I wasn't worried about his being embarrassed of me, I less frequently did embarrassing things. When Stu won the MacArthur "genius" grant, the Kalamazoo Library hosted a celebration in his honor, and he called and asked me to read with him.

On a Friday night, I met him at the city library, that wonderful place, and we rehearsed together in an archival study room. We read one of his more well-known short-shorts, written almost entirely in dialogue. He played the husband with a sleeping wife; I was the ex-girlfriend, calling high in the middle of the night. We also read a short play that he'd written, but never produced, called *Aria*. Most of the play is monologue: A woman hovers in the back of a Roman Catholic church during her former lover's funeral, and breaks out into an aria eventually because she loved him too. We read it once or twice, and he thanked me for helping to make these things fun again.

When I looked down from the balcony, the crowd was in the hundreds.

Library directors from the state university and the private college made remarks about the guest of honor who had been published in *The New Yorker* and *The Paris Review*, who had won the prestigious MacArthur and Rea awards in the same week. Stu's face didn't change; he shuffled his papers and got ready to move. The director of the city library only added to the praise, and reporters from MLive and the *Kalamazoo Gazette* snapped photos. I recognized faculty from Kalamazoo College and Western Michigan, but also celebrated writers from the University of Michigan and Michigan State; my fellow grad students; the wealthy pharmaceutical-company heiresses who kept Kalamazoo a vibrant city, even when it threatened to give up. Stu made his way down a winding, circular staircase and I waited at the top. When it came time for the reading, he thanked everyone for coming—he "reedy" appreciated it, he said in his Chicago accent. He spoke about what Kalamazoo meant to him, this city that had given him a chance before he deserved it, before he'd even published his first book. He meditated on what libraries meant to him as a working-class, first-generation kid from the South Side of Chicago. Then he gave me an unexpected and elaborate welcome, and I was slightly embarrassed by the pomp and circumstance, but also deeply honored. I walked down the stairs filled with performance adrenaline and we locked eyes. It was just us now in this library, standing room only.

He answered the phone, trying to sound composed.

"Yellow!" I said, easily tapping into the feeling of being out-of-my-mind high. "Guess who?"

"I know who."

I tell him that I'm high on the love drug, ask if his wife's in bed with him, if he's wearing pajamas. He looks embarrassed and sad, which makes me feel embarrassed and sad. I ask him to tell his wife it's an old friend and say he has to help with a flat tire; I try so hard to tempt him. I am not thirty years old yet, with a perfect figure, and I know too well the feeling of being the ex-girlfriend who calls crying when she's drunk and lonely. "Baby, baby, baby, baby, baby," I say to my favorite writer. "We'll do *everything*."

He looks at me and becomes a younger man with a battered heart all over again, asks how many people I called before I called him.

I wait. I wait. I wait.

"Just one."

Rapturous applause: that thing you just can't get in your lonely writing room. The painful years of stage acting were all worth it, if only for those evenings of reading him and reading with him, the one who made me feel like an artist, like my heart was wearing a tuxedo. And after reading with him, I didn't lay in bed and dream of performing on a Broadway stage. Instead, I dreamt about a book with my name on it.

This vision felt much more exciting.

* * *

No, I didn't fall in love with Stuart Dybek. I realized, in those days, that I actually liked spending time with myself. I enjoyed writing and creating lesson plans and giving feedback on student writing. When I taught, I heard myself speaking in lecture halls with authority, heard students laughing at my jokes, and saw their hands shooting up all over the room. It was the first job I'd ever had that didn't fill me with dread. In fact, I frequently woke up early to prepare. After my morning classes, I usually read and wrote—in libraries with wing chairs and fireplaces, in smoky coffee shops with indie rock blaring. I spent entire days alone for the first time in my life, then went home to feed myself before going for long runs down abandoned railroad tracks. And when I finally stopped to catch my breath, I realized that everything that had been screaming went quiet. To put it simply, I learned to live alone, and finally had an idea of who I was and what I was supposed to do. Maybe I had wanted to be an actor because I didn't know who I was, but now I knew.

Yes. The harder thing to admit is that many nights I was happy. I fell in love with a smaller city, and still went home occasionally, but most of the time, I lived in Michigan, where I was able to keep myself busy with teaching, workshops, readings, and ill-advised relationships. I was so happy in that time of dream-colored hills and rivers and writers; it is there that my grief went dry.

CHAPTER 29

2008

In our final year, we took the fiction workshop with Jaimy Gordon, which she had always held in her home. Jaimy sat regally in an armchair, dog curled at her feet, while we all vied for her attention as she rewrote sentences right in front of us to show us what she meant by precision of language. She would win the National Book Award, her first big award, that year, at the age of sixty-five, and it confirmed what I'd often suspected: That writing was a profession in which aging could be a blessing. For that reason, and many others, it was so much better for me than acting, but that doesn't mean it wasn't sometimes painful.

Jaimy named, in her living room fiction workshop, several things I didn't yet know of myself, and I was embarrassed that at almost thirty years old, I didn't know. She was from an affluent, highly educated family and seemed to prefer the women in workshop who liked dogs better than humans like she did. She and her husband lived in separate houses, and always had; she was an academic woman of a certain generation, which is maybe why she tended to be less interested in and even impatient with women like me. When I wrote a story about my sister's wedding, she said that my "working class" family was my blessing and my curse, and I wasn't exactly sure what that meant. Was it that my father had been a police officer and my mother a part-time typist? That I had grown up in a family building, everyone on top of one another? Was it that we loved each other too much? That I wanted a marriage like my parents and grandparents, that I wanted to go back to Chicago where all of them lived and seemed to have something to celebrate every weekend? Yes. All of the above. She knew, before I did, that their brand of love had given me invaluable confidence and self-esteem, but she also knew that the obligations that come with a family like that would interrupt my writing time and make me feel agonizing guilt for choosing anything else over them.

When I wrote a story about my ex-dockworker boyfriend, she said it was so working class and *Midwestern*. She always seemed a little disgusted when she said things like that, and it had never occurred to me to be embarrassed of these things. It was only really in her living room that I looked around and realized I was one of the few whose parents weren't paying for the apartment or the car or the computer. It hadn't occurred to me, until I met her, with her Brown University, East Coast pedigree, that the women in my family were maybe not the smartest people in the world, though I had grown up believing they were. I had gone to elementary schools and high schools where everyone was working-class Chicago, then to an undergrad where the demographics were not so different. Seeing myself and my family in this new light was fascinating in some ways, but also made me lonely, and it was then I missed Mike, of course, because only he would understand, and maybe he always had.

"Maggie," Jaimy said from her armchair, "what you have is chutzpah, and ambition, and the things that can't be taught. You're a storyteller already, and now you just have to work on your sentences. Stop writing as a girl now and write as a woman. Put your power here." She pointed to her temple. "Not here." She pointed to her breasts.

All the men in that department had done such a good job of validating me and giving me permission just to be there, but not surprisingly, they left the hardest work to the only woman on faculty. They left it to her to strip me and throw me in the deep end, to see if I could swim.

* * *

When I took the train back to Chicago for the Gift's annual company retreat, I really did think I was ready. The retreat had been planned to keep the ensemble engaged and training together, especially those who hadn't been cast that season. After a challenging semester, I was homesick for old friends with whom I had a shorthand, and wanted the instant gratification that writing did not provide.

When I showed up for the day-long workshop, the man running it said he was going to give birth to us, deliver us into the world. He said we'd be born again, and it could be traumatizing or thrilling. He would spank us as a doctor would a newborn, which I found just unsettling and silly, and then we would exist in the room as babies, unable to speak or walk, until he started calling out numbers. He would call out "One, two, three, four . . ." and our job, as actors, was to become those ages again, to remember those periods in our lives, until he snapped his fingers.

It all sounded a little hokey to me. The man who was leading the exercise, the Walk of Life, was named Eric Forsythe. He had studied with Jerzy Grotowski, the visionary Polish theater director. He had done trust falls in the most terrifying of circumstances and performed all over Eastern Europe, on the street and in taverns, and now he had a cushy job as a university professor who taught acting and directing. He had been one of Mike's mentors at Iowa, so Mike invited him to train our ensemble in the Grotowski method.

Everyone else in the room seemed thrilled, which is how I knew I wasn't supposed to really be an actor anymore. We all lay down on the gymnastics mats with our eyes closed, curled up into the fetal position. Eric narrated the scene—we were in the womb, warm and safe, it was dark, pitch-black, so warm, so soft, such comfort. Initially, I wanted to laugh, but soon enough I wanted to sleep. His voice was so soothing. Then I heard a slapping sound and someone started crying. It took me a minute to realize it was my friend, Lynda. "Faker," I thought. Another slapping sound and another baby wailing. Another and another and another. Suddenly, I was afraid to open my eyes or reconnect with the room. I dreaded Eric's coming for me, and yet I knew, without a doubt, he was coming. When he finally made contact, it did take my breath away. I sat up, opened my eyes, and the room was cold. There was nothing in it but us, a bunch of sleepy-eyed actors, and these ripped blue-and-yellow-striped gymnastics mats; the storefront windows were streaked with dirt; all my friends were crying, really crying. What a bunch of crazy actors, I thought. I didn't feel like crying now, and didn't know if I wanted to play anymore. I saw Mike in the corner of the room, not yet comfortable using his wheelchair; the injury was still new. I wanted to close my eyes again; I didn't want to play anymore.

But I did. And when we became two, three, and four, it got kind of fun because I was flooded with my earliest memories and able to see everyone else's too. Eric snapped his fingers: "Two!" We all toddled around the room, losing our balance, falling down and into one another. Paulie, with his wild curls, drew on the walls and ran with scissors, and that made me laugh; he had transformed right in front of me. Eric snapped his fingers: "Five!" We went to kindergarten and Lynda adjusted to wearing glasses. I could see her discomfort with them and wanted to play with her. We sat in the corner, away from everyone else, and made imaginary cities out of imaginary blocks. The boys mocked us from across the room, but we ignored them, and these kind of pretend games are the reasons I once loved acting. I really could see all of my ensemble members as children, even though I hadn't known them until much later.

At twelve years old, we looked down to examine our newly formed breasts, looked underneath our arms and between our legs. Lynda became a hippie in her teenage years, and I saw her short hair growing long again, her sexuality emerging. John Gawlik drove recklessly around the space and crashed into me again and again, making me feel flattered and a little bit frightened. We all celebrated our college birthdays together, tapped into our muscular memories of being that drunk and that dumb. There was cursing and faux vomiting and faux making out, of course. Those are things that actors will always love doing, but I didn't, necessarily. I can't imagine what we must've looked like to the people passing by.

We must've spent quite a bit of time that way. I don't know. I lost track. Eric snapped his fingers: "Twenty-four!" and my body filled up with a euphoric feeling. Twenty-four: I had an apartment with Mike. I bought my first set of sheets, my first set of towels. I did all of this in pantomime. I rushed around the space, inviting my friends over, serving them drinks, bringing out trays of oven-baked appetizers. I tied on a little apron and showed them around the apartment. *Here is the bathroom, here is the kitchen, this is where we sleep.* Eric snapped his fingers: "Twenty-five!" and something in me snapped too. I promise you: Something in me snapped. My whole body filled with rage and I threw folding chairs across the space, the ones that had been my sofa just a few minutes prior. I kicked them and they went spinning and skidding. I punched the shitty walls, cried and screamed and beat the walls with my fists. I cried for twenty-four, raged and raged at twenty-five. I picked up books and flung them. Eric watched sympathetically for a while, then snapped his fingers and whispered: "Twenty-six." I looked around, and my ensemble looked afraid and sad. They had all been there too. Mike was still in the corner, trying not to look at me. Lynda, I found out later, had followed me around the space and picked up after me, caught the chairs I had thrown, and made sure no one got hurt. At the end of life, Lynda coughed a lot and Paul walked out into the cold winter air without a coat and Gawlik broke down hysterically crying, so I went to him and cradled his head in my hands. I sang him a lullaby.

Once we were all outside on the street, Mike invited me over. "My mom and dad will be out all night," he said. But I didn't go. Instead, I took the train back to Kalamazoo and slept fitfully the whole way home, curled up against a dirty window. When I arrived at my apartment, I found that Adeena had left me a gift wrapped in tissue paper, a little purse made of mismatched buttons and patches that looked just like my rag shop of a heart. "This reminded me of you," she wrote in the card. Thank God for her and all the people like her who had experienced real pain and refused to be immobilized by it, writers who tried to create order from disorder and held themselves to exceptionally high standards, who understood that matters of the heart were complicated and, most important, who didn't give a fuck about Mike Thornton or Chicago theater, those beasts who continued to break my heart.

* * *

During graduate school, I somehow made time to work as a pro bono publicist for the Gift. Mike directed *Hurlyburly* early on, which had been one of our favorite plays in college; we had seen the film version with Sean Penn several times, memorized all the best monologues and recited them to each other for fun. I wrote a press release and emailed and faxed it to a long list of critics, then called and followed up, told them it would be a shame if they had to miss it. Mike really was an up-and-coming director, I said. The story centered on the lives of Hollywood producers and wannabes whose neuroses and romantic entanglements turn catastrophic. It was the perfect play for the Gift, and all the reviewers said so.

The play, full of drinking and bad decisions, inspired us to hang out in the theater after and get drunk with the cast. One of the actors I didn't know asked for my phone number that night, and Mike said, "Jesus Christ! That's Maggie, my Maggie!" The actor looked kind of embarrassed and apologized profusely, and I was proud of my new title of off-limits ex-girlfriend; it felt like progress. But then I asked Mike how he was doing since Paul got nominated for the Jeff Award for Best Actor in *Hurlyburly*.

"You know me too well," Mike said. "What if I never act again?"

"Find a way," I said. "Don't you remember who you are?"

"Yeah," he said dejectedly. "My dad's here to pick me up. Be a good girl, okay?"

"I won't."

"Don't break their hearts."

"I will."

"Don't get too drunk."

"I will."

"I just don't think I'll ever get over you."

With a big lump in my throat: "But you will."

* * *

When I pushed Mike out to his father's car, Frankie looked equally happy and nervous to see me.

"How's school, Little Bit?" he asked. "History major, right?"

"English," I responded. "That's okay."

"Are you back yet?" he asked.

"No. Not yet."

"Got any roommates or anything?"

"No, I live alone."

Then he looked sad, and I called for a cab.

Sometimes I still felt lonely without him.

* * *

After Mike and Frankie left, I took a cab home with Paulie and Brendan.

"We miss you, Maggie," Paulie said drunkenly. "When you comin' home, honey? We need you here, darlin'. Nobody else tells Mike when he's wrong."

The problem was: That couldn't be my life's work. The problem was: I knew Mike was wrong a lot of the time, but right then I could only think about how often he was right. A dispatcher came over the radio and said, "It's a beautiful morning in Chicago. Good morning, American United."

CHAPTER 30

2006

I could tell you about all of the Gift's failures and successes, but I'd rather tell you about *The Good Thief*, the one-man show for which Mike won a Jeff Award. It was the hardest I'd ever worked on publicity, calling every critic in Chicago from my apartment in Michigan, and hounding them until they agreed to come. Our friend John Gawlik directed, and the play began with a man staggering onto the stage in a walker with a bottle of whiskey tucked under his arm. It took so long for him to hobble to the center of the stage that it was agonizing to watch, but then he took his chair in the middle of a blown-out Irish tavern and began his story. He was IRA and had been beaten badly, set up by his best friend who was now married to his ex-girlfriend, Greta. He asked the best friend repeatedly to please, please, just don't fuck her in the arse. That was a laugh line for most, but not for me. Mike told his story for an hour, the story of his injury, the betrayal, him and Greta. The last line, after half a bottle of whiskey, was simple, and Mike fought every ounce of emotion.

"I'm just trying to get out of the rain," he said to the audience. "Just trying to get out of the rain." And then he took his time dragging his legs off the stage and the audience collectively broke into applause, leapt to their feet for him.

Just trying to get out of the rain. Mothers whose little babies have brain tumors and men with elephantiasis arms who whisper in the night, "Sometimes I just get so lonely, Mike. Don't you?" Just trying to get out of the rain.

Standing in the tiny lobby, home from Michigan for the weekend, I tried to compose myself. Mike's return to the stage. He kicked out the stage door with his good leg, stood there in his walker, and I went straight to him, and attacked him, nearly knocked him over with love.

"Was I good?" he asked.

He was so good.

The strangers packed into the lobby started speculating. "Oh, I see. That must be his girlfriend. That's his girlfriend. Don't you think?"

John Gawlik walked past and I reached out for him. "Good job, Coach," I said. "Way to get him up on his feet."

A few months later, Mike called and said, "I've been nominated for the Jeff Award, Bruiser. Please come home."

But I didn't. I thought it might send the wrong message.

* * *

Critics raved about *The Good Thief* and the houses were always packed. It was highly recommended by the *Chicago Tribune*, the *Chicago Sun-Times*, the *Chicago Reader*, *Newcity*, *Windy City Times*, and so many others.

> *Chicago Tribune*—Highly Recommended
>
> Thornton, a founder and artistic director of the company, is making a return to the stage after a pair of spinal strokes in 2003 left him paralyzed. He uses a walker to get around, and his left hand remains crimped. But his voice and his acting instincts have roared back to life, and in John Gawlik's precise direction, this performance is one of the more riveting hours on a local stage this season.
>
> —Kerry Reid

Time Out Chicago—Recommended

As an Irish thug recounting the day his life went to hell, Michael Patrick Thornton delivers what may well be the most interesting performance currently on a Chicago stage.

—Novid Parsi

Chicago Reader—Highly Recommended

Michael Patrick Thornton, making a comeback after life-threatening multiple strokes and years of physical therapy, plays McPherson's unnamed storyteller with remarkable subtlety, never overemphasizing the violence, never punching the many comic lines. Thornton still needs a walker to move about the stage and seems to have only partial use of his hands, but that only makes his stage work all the more remarkable—and moving.

—Jack Helbig

Windy City Times—Highly Recommended

It's not too often that you can get such a heartfelt combination of compassionate caring and frightening chills in one tiny package like *The Good Thief.* It's also the perfect comeback vehicle for Thornton, who triumphs in all aspects of the role. Thornton and everyone involved in this amazing Gift Theatre production deserves respect and admiration for *The Good Thief.*

—Scott C. Morgan

After this production, I had a feeling we would both be okay, and it wasn't only because of the critical response. The critical response means validation, of course, and it helps to sell tickets, but half the time I find myself disagreeing with reviews. Even after good reviews, all actors must return to the world of auditioning and rejection, and all theaters must hustle for sales. Even after a show like this, an actor will not always shine. After being nominated for the Jeff, Mike worried that it was only because he was disabled, but I knew *The Good Thief* had led to his necessary empowerment and my quiet realization that his freedom meant a certain kind of liberation for me too.

"Take your new girlfriend to the ceremony," I said. "I want you to be happy."

* * *

When I got back to Michigan, there was an email waiting for me.

> i want you to be happy, too, but short-term happy not long-term happy, and that may very well be a mind-fuck, but "happiness" without you will always be in lowercase.
>
> i still don't like rory. i wish he and stuart dybek would just move to the north pole and have sex with each other and tell each other how good their novels are.
>
> and i cannot imagine a moment in my life where i would be too busy to make time to see you.
>
> don't write us as a tragedy. we isn't over yet, and we will be a comedy.
>
> you have no idea how much i love you. i could devour entire worlds.

But I did have an idea, and that's what made me feel like I was ruining my life. I called my poor mother in the middle of the night and asked her why I had to be me. She sent me a card the next day that said, "Still thinking of you: in fact, holding you close. As the Jonathan Safran Foer character says, both of us are 'in heavy boots.' I wish crying had the ability to make it all better. In fact, if it wasn't your scourge, it might be a consolation to consider how truly loved you are. And always have been."

The understanding of how much they both loved me, the comprehension of love that could devour entire worlds and make our boots so heavy, got me through graduate school. So many nights, I thought of giving up, and decided against it, because of them. I am Laura and Al Andersen's daughter, I thought. Mike Thornton thinks I'm somebody, I thought. I will get better, I will finish this degree, and I will show them all. After studying with Jaimy, I finally felt ready to send out my first story, and within weeks, it had been accepted by a reputable literary magazine. I shared the news with Mike and my mother first to let them know their loving me had amounted to something, that I had done something to deserve them.

It was then I started listening to the universe, started chronicling my first great love and performing only on the page. It felt like Charles Mee's line: "There are two great loves. The love of another person and the love of books. Anyone who's ever felt like an outsider knows that." At the age of thirty, I started to write the book you're holding in your hands.

CHAPTER 31

2008

At the end of the MFA, it was time to think about what came next. I had gone back to Prague as a teaching assistant, secured a couple of publications, won a teaching award, worked as nonfiction editor for the literary magazine. At the end of three years, I emerged a slightly wiser version of myself who had turned thirty and felt more comfortable in her own skin. It had felt risky to even apply to PhD programs, so I was surprised when the acceptances arrived, and after careful deliberation, I chose Chicago. The stipend was good, is what I told my friends and my family, but the truth was far more complicated.

* * *

Shortly before graduation, the English department faculty hosted a fancy thesis reading for my cohort. What a group. Mark Turcotte, the poet, Louis Khor, an experimental fiction writer from Singapore, my Adeena, who would go on to be editor in chief at *American Short Fiction*. Mark's girlfriend flew in from Atlanta and Adeena's boyfriend came after work. "I'm almost thirty years old," Adeena said. "I mean, I'm not going to ask my parents to come." Meanwhile, my entire family caravanned from Chicago, my father at the wheel.

On the night of the thesis reading, in Walwood Hall, Jaimy Gordon introduced me as the winner of the annual fiction contest. She also revealed that I had been accepted to the PhD program with full funding and they hoped I would accept the offer. She said I wrote about my tight-knit family, which was both a blessing and a curse. I read a story then about my childhood friend and neighbor, which Jaimy said was a story about gentrification, and she was right about that. My father, who hadn't seen me on a stage since I had quit acting five years ago, sat in the back with his arms crossed. My grandmother squinted her eyes and asked her daughters clarifying questions, too loudly. My family took up half the audience and I was reading partially for them, but could also sense that they somehow didn't belong in this room. Their presence in the audience made me feel like a Picasso painting in the surrealist style: disorganized and twisted.

But soon enough, we arrived at the Pilsen Klub, the place we all belonged, the place where our favorite fireplaces and plaid couches waited for us. Usually we gathered there on workshop nights, full of adrenaline, and often after famous authors came to visit, also full of adrenaline. Now I was there with my family, and my aunts and mother had done a Michigan wine tasting before the reading. My father accepted shots of Jameson from my friends. My mother chain-smoked, which was still allowed in bars back then, and rolled her eyes as her husband held court and told "real" Chicago stories. My aunts made fast friends with the bartenders.

"What's your aunt's name again?" one of my friends asked.

"Which one?" I said. "Keith Richards or Mick Jagger?"

Everyone called them Keith and Mick then for the rest of the evening and my grandma turned up her hearing aid.

"Where's Mick Jagger?" she asked. "In this bar?"

She also whispered loudly in my ear that she didn't like the way Jaimy had introduced me.

"A blessing and a curse?" she said. "She was trying to put you down."

I knew that Jaimy was actually giving me the greatest gift: the self-knowledge I needed to be a better writer, and a blueprint for the work to come, but it was no use trying to explain this to my grandmother, a self-educated accountant with a legendary family heart. Instead, I introduced her to the university's theater professor, who spoke more eloquently about plays than she did, but also knew she had started seeing Broadway shows as a teenager in the 1940s. He was right to be enamored with her. They sat in a booth together for hours.

Eventually, I found my way to my father.

"What did you think of the reading?" I asked.

"Why are you cryin' poor mouth?" he said, laughing. "You act like you grew up in the ghetto."

"I said the girls at my high school said we lived in a bad neighborhood. I didn't say it actually was. I said Philip went to prison, and that's true."

"Oh Phil," my dad said, softly, heartsick for my dead friend, just as I was.

He clinked my bottle with his own.

"The story was good, Mag. You're a bohemian like your mother."

She and I ended up at a high-top later in the evening, after we had both had too many.

"What do you think, Mom?" I asked.

"About your story? It was wonderful."

"No. About me turning thirty and being here . . . About me getting a PhD in creative writing."

She didn't say anything.

"I don't know what to do next," I said, searching her face for answers. "I always wanted to get married and have children."

"And I always wanted to write a book," she said. Then she smiled in a way that made me sad.

* * *

The next morning, they all caravanned home to the place where they belonged, the only place that could hold them. My parents dropped my aunties at the bowling alley, my sisters at the tiny World War II houses bought with their high school sweethearts, and my grandma at her senior housing in the forest preserve; then they drove back to their three-flat in Ravenswood where everyone used to live together.

A few weeks after the MFA reading, I went home the same way my family had, but upon my arrival, I couldn't stop seeing them the way Jaimy Gordon had. Which is to say: with a cold and critical eye. Their laughing too loud now, the cigarette smoke too thick, the answers somehow too easy. I had started seeing myself and Chicago as others did, but I also couldn't stop feeling toward my family and the city the way my grandmother did, like without them, I was missing an appendage. So: That's why I chose the PhD program in Chicago. I was able to see with new eyes now, but I still loved it all fiercely, and maybe even more fully. The faculty at UIC were genuinely excited about my memoir in progress, they said, and my mother regretted never writing her book, so it was time for me to write mine.

* * *

"They did a wine tasting *before* the reading?" Mike said, and his laughter erased any residual feelings of embarrassment.

We'd been talking by phone more frequently, since I started writing the book, while I pored over journals and emails.

"I think of Paul's line from *Language of Angels* every time I sit down to write," I said.

"This is how it went."

"This is what I remember."

"You know how I've been taking classes at Second City?" Mike said. "They've asked me to teach the next class."

"I'm coming home this summer. I've been accepted to the program for writers."

"I'm dating again, just so you know."

"Yeah, me too. Just so you know."

"Mag! I've been cast as the Elephant Man at Steppenwolf. Holy shit, huh? The director wants me to use one of those old-school wicker wheelchairs."

"But can you push it?"

"Nope." He laughed weakly. "Embarrassing day at rehearsal."

"Oh God."

"Hey, at least I didn't live back then."

"Thinking of you as the Elephant Man just kills me—your head so heavy with dreams . . ."

* * *

At the end of three years in Michigan, I took the Amtrak train home with my pillow and a rolling suitcase. One last time, I took the train past white churches and aspen trees, through small towns in Michigan, until we arrived in the industrial center of Indiana, the steel mills and smoke of Gary, and then I knew the South Side of Chicago was coming. My heart sped up as the factories, liquor stores, strip clubs, and fast-food restaurants bled into each other, and then I was home. The CTA trains, the cathedrals and Sox Park, the skyline, you beautiful skyline, the lakefront and sailboats and museums, my people, my soul, I was home. Here I am, Chicago—your prodigal daughter has returned. I got off the train downtown and started to walk, ready to just blend back in, but everything looked so different. Everything *was* so different, now that I was going to be a resident again.

Millennium Park, which had opened just before I left, was crowded, and so many of Edward Hopper's *Nighthawks* diners had been replaced with high-end restaurants. The Brown Line, which I was supposed to take, was closed for renovations, and for a minute, I wasn't sure how to get home. I moved back to Chicago in 2008, after the housing bubble had changed the character of my neighborhood. Lincoln Square had lost some of its old-world charm to urgent care centers and high-end athletic retailers; the gentrification had forced out too many longtime residents. My parents had been able to keep their three-flat, because of renters, but they had left their first-floor apartment after living there for thirty years. They moved into a small townhouse in a neighborhood that felt "less yuppie," in their words, and, in their late fifties, had central air for the first time in their lives. I agreed to pay them rent for the apartment and take care of the building in their absence.

This all sounds very spoiled little rich girl, but when I walked into the apartment that I had lived in since infancy, it smelled musty. A window was broken and there were plumbing issues I didn't have money to pay for, mice in the basement. The renters had a long list of complaints, and one of them threatened to sue my father if we didn't do something soon. My father scoffed at my complaints and said, "I ain't payin' for it. You wanna live in that yuppie neighborhood, *you* take care of it. Otherwise, I'll sell it." I knew he wouldn't, but also knew he wouldn't fix anything, so resigned myself to trying to scrub the cigarette stains from the walls, addressing the renter complaints, and setting new mousetraps in the basement.

At UIC, I met my PhD cohort, and in 2008, most of them lived in apartments in Pilsen and Wicker Park, so they all made fun of my living in Ravenswood, which had already become pretty gentrified while their neighborhoods were supposedly more hip. No one in my cohort was from Chicago. They were from Italy and Korea, Ohio and Arizona, but they all believed they knew more about the city than I did. Occasionally, that was true.

"Oh wow, you're coming from the suburbs," they would say, which made me want to set them on fire, but I kept my mouth shut and promised myself to succeed in spite of them. Ten years after graduating from UIC as an undergrad, I was back as a doctoral student. The brutalist architecture was the same, and the student population still remarkably diverse, but the gentrification trends did mean the university had attracted more out-of-state students and succeeded in raising their reputation. We had both gotten a little fancier, I guess.

* * *

A few months after I moved home, I attended the Gift's annual company retreat. I walked into the storefront theater, where every poster, for every show, hung in the black box lobby. Since I'd moved back, I'd been volunteering in the box office, and sometimes a patron would ask if I was an actor. My stock response: "I used to be." Then I would lock the door, listen for the show to begin, listen to my friends become sick women and despicable men, people I had never met. And then the posters would all seem to come alive; the ghosts would all seem to wake up. *Boys' Life*: 2001. *Orestes 2.0*: 2002. *Language of Angels*: 2003. *A Young Man in Pieces*: 2004. I knew why I continued to volunteer, but wasn't sure why I had agreed to attend the company retreat that year. I knew I was done with acting, and they had all moved on without me anyway. Brendan and Lauren had moved to New York to give it a go and Lynda had gone back to Boston to help take care of her father. Paulie was still here, as were Connolly and Alex and John Gawlik, but they had friends I didn't know now, new actors they were in love with, jokes I just didn't understand anymore. The space wasn't even new anymore—they'd been living in it for years without me.

"Tell your scene partner something that happened to you recently," Mike said from the front row of the theater.

Alex and I sat at a table for two on the stage. I hadn't acted with my company in years, and never in this space.

"One more thing," Mike said. "Tell her the story in gibberish."

His dimples emerged, and he leaned forward to watch me sweat. I looked into Alex's eyes, big and sweet; she had played the role of my mother in more than one production.

"Go ahead," she whispered.

I told her about the day of my sister's wedding, in my own invented language, the nonsense words I needed to tell the complicated truth. I stumbled at first, stopped and started, made paddling motions with my hands.

"That sounds too much like English!" Mike said.

I clenched my teeth and returned to Alex's eyes, searched them to make sure she understood. Here is a translation:

> Listen. I know I'm supposed to be more evolved after three years of higher education but the point is, I still want someone to love, and I still want someone to laugh with. I was very jealous at my sister's wedding and I hated that about myself. It's easy to fall for people, and easier to fall out of love when they don't match up to him. Happy people make me sad lately and sad people make me sadder. I'm not sure about this doctoral program, Alex. I just don't know if I'm up for it. We're expected to know Marx and Foucault, economics, and political philosophy. What if I can't catch up? None of my girlfriends have time for me anymore. They all have babies now—some have two and three. And since when is my neighborhood a destination for designer diaper bags? Are there any single people left in the city? I'm so goddamn sick of sleeping with the TV on for company. He's hardening toward me, I know, and while that's what I've wanted, now that it's actually happening, it hurts. I hate that I will always remind him of painful things, Alex. I feel like I don't have a real friend in the world. Tell him not to be mean to me.

Mike called for us to cut and Alex charged at me with kindness, as if she had understood every word I said. Then I sat down next to Johnny Gawlik, who patted my shoulder. Maybe he'd understood me, too. "You back for good now?" he said. "We should go for a beer sometime."

* * *

While I was gone, Mike had gained a certain amount of popularity at The Second City, the comedy institution Sheldon had helped to start fifty years prior. Mike asked the producers if they might consider a play he'd written. He called it *The Princess and the Bear*, and dedicated it to me: *For Maggie, who went through it, too*. He asked me to do a table reading of it at Second City, and hungry for an artistic life in Chicago, I agreed.

At North and Wells on a Saturday afternoon, I sat at a long table with some of the most promising young improvisers and a couple of the most veteran. I hadn't read the play in advance because I wanted it to be fresh and spontaneous. In the play, Mike, the main character, has had a spinal stroke. His ex-girlfriend (me) is a children's author who left a few months in. Tara, the therapist he fantasizes about, is teaching him how to do a sit-to-stand-to-kneel so he can propose to the ex-girlfriend, and his various crushes tap-dance from scene to scene, tempting him with silly songs. His nervous system is a mail carrier who gets confused about where to deliver the envelopes, and God is a yogi in a Hawaiian shirt, sipping on a coconut drink. Throughout, Mike imagines the ex-girlfriend (me) having sex with other men in arguably funny and irreverent sequences. He is also haunted by panic attacks and nightmares of children dying. At a crucial point, he tells God that his ex-girlfriend's family never visited him in the hospital and that he always had to beg for sex. During that reading, I realized how different our stories had become, and that's when you know any relationship is over.

At the end, after the applause, as I was packing up, I heard the director, Norm Holly, say to Mike, "Okay, she's really good. Can we have her?" (Words I once could've lived on for weeks.) "Is that the real girl?"

"Yup."

"Damn Thornton, you got bigger balls than I do, asking her to read that part."

Mike wheeled over to me and whispered, "When did you learn to act like that? I had a hard time keeping up with you." Maybe this seems like a given, but when I was acting, I couldn't touch roles that were too much like me. I had to play women with different hair and different accents, women who had grown up with trust funds, women who were nothing like me. And now that I had learned to play myself, I didn't want to rely on someone else's text; I only wanted to create my own.

"Give it to someone else," I said. "I don't want it."

"Did you like it?"

I wiped the mascara from my face and said, "It's great. I have a few notes."

Mike thanked all the actors and the director for coming, then I pushed him across the street to the Old Town Ale House. We'd been there in the before times, and both loved it, of course, because it was divey and as close to the Old Town of the sixties as you were ever going to get. The jukebox played the lesser-known albums and never the greatest hits, and the walls were papered with Lautrec-style paintings of Chicago writers and Second City performers. The regulars held a variety of professions (including none) and always seemed to be the just-right mix of winners and losers, and the smartest ones, who always know they're both. It was like the ghosts of the old newspaper men stuck around just to haunt and protect the place. Mike grabbed a table while I ordered drinks at the bar, and at first, I made jabs.

"A children's author?" I said. "You still don't give me any credit, Thornton. And you've ripped off a bunch of my stuff."

After a beer on an empty stomach, I started to get angry. We weren't married when he had the stroke, and if we had been, it might have been different. He's the one who had said, "Not until we're older, not until we make some money." He had had an affair just months prior to the stroke, and now he wanted an audience to feel compassion for him for having the *idea* to propose? I didn't even know he was looking at rings. The anger grew until my hands shook until I finally exploded and screamed, "How can you paint me like an absolute monster and God gets to be a yogi in a fucking Hawaiian shirt? Really? *God?*" So loudly that the regulars turned around and looked at us.

He asked me, again, why I left, and I tried, again, to explain. To be worthy of a life of my own. Even before the stroke, you and the theater required so much that there was very little left for me. I went straight from my father's house to yours, and I needed to learn to take care of myself. That's when Mike asked if it wasn't the best thing that had ever happened to me.

"I mean, look at you," he said. "You're so confident. A teacher, an artist. All the things you wanted to be."

And then I didn't want to argue anymore. I would've done anything to erase what had happened to him, but it's true: I was proud of the people we'd become.

"Nothing will make it in without your permission," he said.

And I made the same promise. Everything you've read here has been approved by him. There are ethics in storytelling, after all.

"What did I hear over and over again while I was in the coma?" he asked.

"There's only love," we said at the same time.

"There's only love," we repeated.

Then we got to work on the script, and I knew this was our currency now. Artistic feedback, validation and standards, a refusal to accept mediocrity from each other. Maybe it was after that night, after poring over his script for hours, that he asked me to be literary manager at the Gift. For once, he had given me something I knew I deserved.

CHAPTER 32

2009

John Gawlik texted me: *Meet me at Simon's. 6:57. I'll buy you a glogg.* Simon's: a perfect choice for a cold fall day. They made the best mulled wine and had the comfiest, rattiest couches. Simon's was an anchor in Andersonville, the neighborhood where I'd bombed my audition with Jon Berry just five years prior. Now I was a published writer in a doctoral program. I walked toward the neon fish sign, and there he was, Kennedy handsome, long legs and wide swimmer's shoulders, green eyes, killer good looks without any of the accompanying asshole. I had liked John, in a way, since I'd first seen him, and now here I was, already dreaming about him driving me home.

"What's shakin'?" he said, and I knew he was nervous and trying to be cool.

We drank glogg at Simon's as fall turned to winter while sitting on a ratty couch together in the back of the barroom. I told him about the audition where I sang "Sixteen Going on Seventeen" because I knew it would make him laugh, and I loved to make that happen. I pointed out Calo, my grandma's favorite Italian restaurant down the street, and Alamo, where we bought new school shoes every year. He liked imagining the neighborhood in bygone eras, so I filled his head with stories. When I told him stories about growing up with German Christmas at the Brauhaus and the pervert German Santa Claus who started grabbing our asses when we were only eleven, he laughed, as he always did, at my irreverence. We somehow managed *not* to kiss each other that night, though he did unzip my knee-high boots once while I was in the middle of a sentence, and that doesn't mean he wasn't listening. He was the best listener I'd ever met, so I told him about the PhD program, all the things I was reading and learning and grappling with, and he was interested in all of it. He was that kind of person, endlessly curious, then clear-eyed and insightful without an ounce of pretension. Every time I walked out of my night class and saw the skyline lit up, I wanted to see him. As soon as it was dark outside, I wanted to see him, but I waited until he initiated. At first, it was once every couple weeks, and then he started to lose his restraint.

He was a director and actor, and when I saw him in a David Rabe play about the Vietnam War at the Gift, I was particularly impressed by his scenes with Connolly, how easily they could transform into men on the edge of oblivion. But in the end, when he sat alone and sang "Beautiful Dreamer" in Vietnamese, I was overcome with crying. He was a man on the edge of oblivion, and I wanted him to know I was safe.

When I wasn't working box office at the Gift or having secret meetings with John, I went to campus without him and performed in classrooms without him. I tried to contribute thoughtfully in literature seminars, spent hours every day just reading, thinking, walking, writing. In workshops, I was most myself, in the land of creatives without the snobbery of the theorists. (That's where I worked on the book.) Occasionally, I met my fellow grad students at a Taylor Street staple called Little Joe's, a dark tavern with red-and-white-checked tablecloths and Christmas lights, where you could actually meet the holdouts from the old Italian neighborhood, and also the holdouts from the Mexican neighborhood that came later. My favorite party tricks included fucking with the regulars. The doctoral candidates, high on Marxist theory, would bother them with questions and they would all make fun of us for too much college and not enough high school. Then I would say, "What do you think about Gus Mauro buyin' up all the property?"

"How the fuck do you know Gus Mauro?"

"I used to hang out with his son in high school!"

While I liked reading about Florence Scala and gentrification with Marxist academics, I also wanted to hear stories from the people who had actually known her, who had actually seen her stand in front of the bulldozers when they came to raze half the neighborhood to build the university we all attended.

I waited a long time before inviting John into my apartment, the place where I'd grown from a child to a teenager to a woman, where I once played spin the bottle in the front hall closet. I invited him in, knowing the Marshall Field's carpet that my parents had once been so proud of was no longer fashionable and probably saturated with cigarette smoke. The wing chairs where they read their newspapers on Sunday mornings were worn now, and the vintage wallpaper beginning to curl in places. When I showed him the cement square that we called a backyard, I knew he saw the ugliness but also felt the potential beauty and luxury of it, like I did. He knew what should be preserved and what could be made more beautiful. He was an artist, after all, a director who understood complex character as well as he did aesthetic beauty. I served him a charcuterie board one night and hoped he liked it, and late that night, after too much wine, I finally asked, "What are we going to do about Mike?"

"Don't we deserve to be happy?" he said.

I hadn't known I needed him to say it, but I had needed him to say it.

* * *

With John Gawlik, Chicago became alive with possibility again. I was already crazy about him, but hadn't told Mike yet. I don't even know when it started. When I first saw him in *Flanagan's Wake* and thought he looked like a young Ted Kennedy? No. I was still in love with Mike then. When he looked at me at Si and Lia's after I'd found out about Suzanne? No. That was more brotherly than romantic. Was it during *Language of Angels*, when he chased me around in his sheriff's costume and shot at me with a prop gun? Or during the Walk of Life exercise when we got to the end of life and he broke down crying and I went to him and held him like a baby? The way he did a Czech accent and made me laugh until I was five years old again? I honestly don't know. But I did love him now, enormously, in that teenage way I hadn't felt since Mike, but also in a grown-up, unselfish way.

* * *

That's exactly when Mike did a really nice thing and got a TV job in Los Angeles. He returned Chicago to me so it could become the city in which I loved John Gawlik. We took walks where Mike and I never had, ate dinner in different restaurants, and saw new plays. We had different kinds of conversations and power dynamics and chemistry; it was an explosion of fresh-start love. We went to the Checkerboard Lounge on the South Side to see live blues, danced to a Willie Nelson song at the California Clipper, lingered for hours in the small museums, and he came to my readings at UIC and then to Little Joe's after to meet my classmates and the regulars. He was happy to let me lead sometimes, and he liked the regulars as much as the artists, just like me.

* * *

When Mike first got the news about his first television role on *Private Practice*, a spin-off of *Grey's Anatomy*, the ensemble gathered in a Jefferson Park beer garden to celebrate. It wasn't like the old days. We were calmer now, drank our beer more slowly, laughed easily but not as loudly as we used to. Others had had cameos and one-offs, but Mike was the first one to get a recurring role, the kind that would get him a table at restaurants where most people had to make reservations three months out. He told us about the state-of-the-art wheelchair they'd give him on set—all he would have to do is push a button and the chair would raise him up to a standing position. (I still want to know why he couldn't keep it.) I gave him a tube of sunscreen and a card that said I was proud. He talked a lot about his girlfriend, Lindsey, that night, and I held John's hand under the table.

While Mike was in Los Angeles, staying in a hotel room with his mother, I watched his first episode at the gym. I wrote him an email afterward, saying how sorry I was to hear that they hadn't been able to find an accessible apartment. Then I told him the show was a glorified soap opera, but he was pretty good. I was so sorry about our past, I said, and so excited about our futures, even though the show should really get new writers, or America should get better taste. His response was the last letter he wrote to me.

You didn't do anything terrible, and I'll always be in your life. Thank you for getting me to this point; trying to have fun and be free out here amidst the wonderful insanity swirling around. It's odd: I feel quite at home on a tv set. Everything's so inexplicably, beguilingly familiar.

Bruiser, I want only the best for you, and while I'll never (or at least have decided to never) love you the way I used to, I love you in a new, slowly articulating way. You didn't fuck anything up and I wish you could, soon, forgive yourself for it all. Life happened. And we not only survived, we triumphed. Our greatest act of courage was not trying to put the pieces back together, telling each other that endless story of "someday," the waiting for which nearly killed me. No. Our greatest act of courage was the bold, quiet, admittance that we didn't love each other the same way. For whatever reasons.

But look where we are. We are "successful": PhD, Hollywood, etc. All forms, all illusion . . . we're doing okay. We still have our sense of humor, and our friendship. And while it seems often the right thing to say, that we'd trade it all to go back to the day before the parade to simpler, lighter days, I'd wager to say that privately, in the deep dark purple true part of our hearts, we wouldn't. I'd wager to say that through all the pain and hellfire, we're quite proud of the people we've become. And we should be. We goddamn better well be.

And now I think I'm in love with someone else and you have a very scared, often locked-up, but beautiful, intelligent, and funny man waiting in the wings to love you, to make his entrance.

Let him. Just let him and let him and love him and love him. He's the one to save from the fire, and he'll pull you out, too, for he is not a box of letters; he's a man. Breathing, waiting, standing—just as awed and confusedly as I imagine we often are—at this majestic perplexing thing called Life.

* * *

I took Mike's advice one last time and told John Gawlik the truth, which was that I loved him madly, and one last time, Mike was right. It was time for new stories to be told, finally, and our old friend Johnny Gawlik became my husband. My husband, who is always my first reader and values me as an artist, and I him. My husband, who has made Chicago feel like home again. My husband, who directed Mike in *The Good Thief* and coached him to be brave enough to walk out on the stage, no matter how long it took; my husband, who pushed him up a ramp to the stage where he accepted his first Jeff Award; my husband, who understands that I was once in love with Mike and I'm not anymore, but we survived a hell of a war together and so will always love each other, in a way. My husband, who I will do the Walk of Life with, in sickness and in health. The one who proudly walked into Mike and Lindsey's wedding with me, and danced with me all night there. I love him for all of these reasons, and countless others.

* * *

Brendan Donaldson married Lauren Sharpe in an idyllic little town called New Harmony that had been built with the intention of creating a utopian community. Mike was doing a show at Steppenwolf at the time, so he couldn't come, but he sent Lindsey in his place. How nervous she must've been driving all that way and showing up to a wedding of old friends who had so many years of shared history. John and I drove up with Paul, and Lindsey drove up with Connolly, who, she reported, did not stop talking for the entire five-hour drive.

When we arrived in New Harmony, it was one hundred degrees and we were shown to the wedding campus. Lauren and Brendan would marry in the middle of the field under a white tent, and we would all stay at the historic guest house on the property, each with our own rooms and an open common space with lots of light. John and I checked into our bedrooms and found homemade goody bags from Brendan and Lauren with snacks and water, tiny puppets from the bride and groom. When we heard Lindsey and Connolly pulling up on the gravel road, we rushed to greet them. Lindsey asked if I liked her dress, and I asked if she liked mine. Then we ironed them beside each other in the common area while the men around us filled up the room with noise. She was seven years younger than me, and the age difference didn't bother me that day when I still felt pretty in my sleeveless dress with the belt. The problem was my hair; I'd always had bad hair, and it was an especially humid day. I looked at this woman in the communal bathroom, this woman who had rescued my first love, who hadn't allowed him to call me or text me in the first year of their relationship. (Honestly, it made me feel slightly flattered.) I looked at her and decided that we were going to be friends for life, so we'd better get started now.

"Lindsey, this is a little weird, but can you do something with my hair?" I asked.

"I'm not very good at that," she said. "But I'll try."

She took the hair dryer from the wall unit, turned it on low. She ran her fingers through my hair, uncertainly but gently.

We spent time that weekend without her husband, which seemed important, because we both knew how good he could be at eclipsing other people. At the wedding, Lindsey and John sat on either side of me, and squeezed my hands before I went up to give my reading. They both told me how moving it was when I had finished. We wept together when Brendan and Lauren gave their vows, and drank too much over the course of the evening. I introduced Lindsey to all the people she didn't know yet—the bride and groom's sisters and their parents.

"Have you met Mike's wife?" I asked. "We're crazy about her."

After the wedding, back at the guest house, Brendan and Lauren's mothers and aunts moved all the couches and chairs to make a dance floor, and someone played really good Motown. Lindsey and I watched at first, unsure if we should join in, unsure if we knew each other well enough to take this social risk together. Diana Ross was singing "Ain't No Mountain High Enough" and I looked around the room. Brendan in a rumpled dress shirt, dancing with Lauren in a white ballerina dress. Paulie and Connolly close-talking in the corner with their ties loosened. All the friends who had been there at my lowest, all the tender cobwebs of my aging heart. No mountain high enough.

I looked at my soon-to-be husband, who still had black hair as he high-kicked on the dance floor and made everyone laugh like crazy.

He danced with Brendan's grandmother and gave her a twirl, and I couldn't wait to marry him.

I sang along to the song. Lindsey sang along to the song.

Then we joined hands, Lindsey and I, in preparation for the pivotal moment in the song where Diana Ross just screams, because language is no longer sufficient for the unsayable. We threw our heads back and screamed, "Ahh-ahh-ahh-ahh!" We howled at the skylight moon. We both knew the man's selfishness and generosity in ways that no one else ever would, and I wanted to support her through it. Tell her she was an artist too. Make sure she took her self-care days. Be an audience for their lives.

After that song, a few of us went outside, and she and I sat on a picnic blanket on the lawn and looked up at the stars we couldn't see in the city. I knew she still worried about my place in his heart, but that it was shrinking because of her, and that's the way it had to be. I knew I would have to be loved less by him and that she would replace me in every way, and that's the way it had to be. I studied her dewy skin and suspected she was a woman who would only get better with age; she was prettier than me already. She had heard me give Brendan and Lauren's wedding speech so she knew I held the past, but I knew she held the future. And I knew, under that bowl of stars, that I would love her. We didn't say any of this, but I took her hand and she grabbed mine back tightly, in the pitch-black night in that utopian town as we listened to a night chorus of wailing loons.

I trust that Mike and Lindsey have a good marriage because he bought himself a first-floor condo when he met her, in Jefferson Park, of course. Because she is artistic director of her own performance art theater company and they have created some of the most emotionally moving, innovative theater I've seen in Chicago. Because she was an artist long before she met him, and had already traveled the world, and then she fell in love. She fell in love with him, knowing he used a wheelchair, and on their honeymoon, she pushed him around London and Paris and made the necessary accommodations. In return, he made those cities more exciting and beautiful, as he does. In return, he worked on his independence and promised her he'd buy her a New York apartment and take her to the Tonys someday, which he did. Mike and Lindsey Thornton danced in his walker on their wedding day, and it was a happy song.

* * *

Over the next few years, John and I pulled up the carpet in the living room together and hired a Romanian refugee (who used to be a chemistry professor) to restore the hardwood floors. We painted the dining room a bright yellow that wasn't quite right, then repainted it a perfect shade of grey. The technical director of the Gift made us a rosewood railing for the sunroom and a butcher-block table so we could entertain in the yard. John planted rose bushes where there hadn't been any, filled ceramic pots with flowers and ferns, and strung up Italian lights. I argued with my father about the things that needed to be fixed, and created budgets so those things got fixed, one at a time. I filled the cabinets with mismatched china, a mix of my family's dishes and pieces we found at thrift stores. Occasionally, I remembered John breaking down at the end of the Walk of Life exercise, and always, I promised myself I would make the journey until then worth it. We chose each other again and again.

CHAPTER 33

2012

The afternoon of my doctoral exams, the sky was cobalt blue, and Sheldon Patinkin waited for me in the lobby of University Hall, a skyscraper on Morgan Street, where my office on the twenty-seventh floor seemed to tremble and shake on windy days. My committee consisted of our most intellectually rigorous American literature professors. Every committee needed an outside reader, and my list included several postwar American plays, so we invited Sheldon Patinkin, one of the foremost experts in the city. I walked toward him and perhaps because he'd known me for years, he sensed the fear. Or maybe he just knew how high the stakes were—today they would decide if I had what it took to be a PhD.

"Do you want a cigarette?" he asked.

"No," I said. "I can't go in there reeking like smoke."

We took the elevator up together and didn't say a word. I think we both worried that that would be cheating. All I could think of was a man in the program who had recently failed his preliminary exams, a woman who had left the room crying in the middle of hers. All I could think of were the other members of my cohort, whose parents were wealthy entrepreneurs and highly regarded academics. My father had gone to community college on the G.I. Bill and my mother had gone so she'd be paid more in the typing pool. We were not a family of advanced degrees. All I could think of was failing.

Sheldon introduced himself to the committee, and when they treated him with reverence, I was glad. A few weeks prior, I had submitted my thirty-page research paper, which had taken months to write, and two essay exams, which I had to complete over the course of a weekend. My professor, Luis Urrea, had written one of the essay questions, which asked about marginalized writers and the memoir form: "Was there a correlation between diasporic texts and women's writing?" Sheldon's question focused on memory plays: "In *Old Times*, which I know is not on your list, Pinter has one of his characters say, 'There are some things one remembers even though they may never have happened.' How does this match up with your ideas about magical realism?"

Magical realism, in basic terms, is a genre in which reality and magic exist side by side, without explanation. Some of the most famous practitioners of the subgenre have been Latin American and Catholic, which makes sense for a form where angels and spirits are very much real characters. However, unlike fantasy and fairy tales, magical realism and memory plays allow for multiple truths while refusing to completely abandon reality. I wrote about these practitioners being the guardians of competing memories and the ways in which competing memories have the ability to challenge dominant myths. I celebrated a form that makes space for the possibility of complicating narratives beyond positivity and progress, something that felt especially important to me when reading and writing disability. "I maintain that magical realism allows for the flexibility that memory requires to represent the various layers of truth in its embellishments, vilifications, and glorifications. While the realities of these texts often represent trauma and loss, the magic becomes a healing agent for those remembering as well as those watching the remembrance." After writing about texts I had not written, I understood better why Mike had written in his own play that I had left after only a few months. He needed his memories for healing, and I needed mine. The audience needed both, and for us to change the poison into medicine, and we were happy to oblige.

I never did ask Sheldon if there were things in the book that we remembered differently, but I do know that when one of the professors said she found Mike unlikeable and wasn't sure why I stayed as long as I did, Sheldon looked at me, smiled wryly, and said, "Well, that's very complicated." We sat around a seminar table and for three hours, they asked questions about my reading lists, which included approximately fifty plays, fifty memoirs, and several critical and theoretical texts. They also described the first draft of this book, why it was a valuable contribution, and which revisions I might consider in future drafts. At the end of it all, they asked me to wait in the hall for a few minutes, where I leaned against the cinderblock wall and tried to replay every response I'd given. Had I been clear enough in my Kushner response? Did I link him properly to Miller? Oh, Jesus fucking Christ.

When Sheldon came out of the room first, I dragged myself up off the wall. I looked at him, and tried to read his face. Maybe they had sent him to deliver the bad news, I thought, but I wanted to remember him in this moment—his back that was starting to hunch, a snazzy knit blazer, as always, eyes wet behind his glasses.

"Passed with high distinction," he said.

Passed with high distinction, he said. In an ivory tower, to the girl who had cried every night after *Boys' Life* rehearsal because she knew she wasn't good enough. The girl who fell asleep on his shoulder watching television in his living room. The girl who said, "Mother, I'm crippled," in her *Glass Menagerie* audition and then bawled her eyes out, now fluent in the language of grief. The girl who answered the phone in the hospital, twenty-five years old, and said, "Sheldon, they just read last rites." And here she was, not a girl anymore at all. A woman with the beginnings of crow's feet and forehead lines, wearing a pencil skirt and her hair in a bun.

"Passed with high distinction," he said and then I leaned over his walker and kissed him all over his face.

It's possible there are things I remember that never really happened, but I swear on my firstborn child that's exactly how it went.

* * *

In the elevator with Sheldon, he told me how much he enjoyed reading my research paper, said the argument was original and tightly constructed, but he really wanted to talk about the book. "It's good," he said. "It's really good." He asked about our wedding preparations too—said the invitations were lovely and he hoped he could make it, but he hadn't been feeling himself lately and driving long distances was only getting harder. We stood outside and looked up at the Chicago skyline, and he said, "You earned it, Professor. Now finish that goddamn book."

CHAPTER 34
2012

After we tell the bar waitress some stories, Lynda and Paulie head to the bus stop, and Mike asks, "You want one more, Italian model?" I push him out of the bar and across the street to the theater, grab a couple Miller High Lifes from the basement fridge, and then sit cross-legged in the art deco foyer, right next to his chair, as we look out at a quiet night. It's a perfect weather compromise tonight: seventy degrees for him, warm breeze for me. We haven't been alone together in a long time, and it feels painfully awkward, but also like the most natural thing in the world. In the foyer of our theater, we are framed by storefront windows, and in them, a display of the ensemble's head-shots, a scroll list of donors, blown-up press reviews, raving about the current production. Carefully chosen pull quotes from *The Guardian*, *The Washington Post*, the *Chicago Tribune*, the *Chicago Sun-Times*, and *The New York Times*. All of them have been here.

"So what will I call you?" Mike asks. "Dr. Andersen? Mrs. Gawlik? Dr. Gawlik?"

I shrug my shoulders.

"I like living with Lindsey," he says, finished with his beer already. "Maybe I'll have another stroke in a few months, huh?"

"Not funny," I say.

A silence washes over us and then I give him unsolicited advice.

"Be nice to her during football season," I say.

"I was always nice to you!"

"Just be nice to her on Sunday. Sundays are important."

I look at the big old-fashioned bank clock on the corner and it says it's late and I don't want my fiancé to worry.

"I'll send you the manuscript soon," I say.

"Don't be afraid of sentimentality," he says. "The problem with everything is that we're afraid of sentimentality."

"I know. Everyone thinks it's weird that John asked you to be best man. My mom and dad think it's weird."

"Do you think it's weird?" he asks.

"Nah. I think it's cool."

When I crush the beer cans and take them to the trash can on the corner, I hear airplanes in the sky, and wonder if they're arriving or departing. I look around the foyer again, see a framed article from *The Guardian* titled "Chicago Is No Longer American Theater's Second City." In it, the writer cites Steppenwolf, Black Ensemble Theater, and storefronts, specifically the Gift and our "astounding work" in a tiny space, in and for a working-class community. "That the rest of the world is finally catching on to Chicago's theatrical breadth is just the icing on the cake."

A long time ago, we started this company in somebody's studio apartment. Mike chose the play and cast himself in the lead, and I photocopied the scripts and took a supporting role. We sat on milk crates and imagined we were other people. Now the urban planners and newspaper writers say this theater is the most promising economic development for the Northwest Side of Chicago. Mayor Rahm Emanuel once said to us that he couldn't believe the quality of the work out here in "Copland."

"Can you push me to my car?" Mike asks.

Of course I can.

"See ya soon," I say to his back in my childish monster voice, the one we invented together.

He manufactures laughter for me.

He presses a button on his keychain and the van door slides open, slowly. The ramp rolls out for him and he wheels up and away from me, drives home with his hands instead of his feet. He, too, is independent now. I take a taxi away from the neighborhood where we once lived and worked together, and think of him in our high school auditorium, singing. The Bob Dylan postcard he gave me when he left for college, with the line on the back about meeting again as friends.

Our storefront theater on Milwaukee Avenue is one of my favorite places in the world, and even it won't last. We have a string of new ensemble members. They don't like it, but we call them Gift 2. They are award-winning actors and directors, playwrights who write for TV. They are Black and white, gay and straight, very young and very old. It's a place where I coordinate a storytelling series and staged readings, trying to give new writers a chance, a place where we all work with Northwest Side neighborhood kids in our giftED program, trying to convince them that art is for them, too.

We were once those kids, I think, as the window lights blink off up and down Milwaukee Avenue. I see our dreams floating up into the sky, coloring the clothesline sheets, the billboards and storefronts and alleys. Then the city goes to sleep and forgets us, the writer and the actor who learned together that it's always best to go out on a high note, who have always known that the show must go on.

* * *

In the fall of 2013, one hundred and fifty people drove to a resort town two hours outside the city for our wedding. Me in a cream-colored mermaid wedding dress, the most elegant gown I've ever worn. John wore a charcoal-gray suit, looking like an old-fashioned movie star, and outside the Riviera Ballroom, it was peak color season on the shores of Lake Geneva, and the leaves looked like fire, gold and scarlet.

Mike stood nervously in his walker, in the middle of the ballroom, and gave the best man speech. "First, I'd like to thank the Andersen and Gawlik families for producing and raising two of my best friends. There is no Irish or Polish proverb, no stock wedding toast found online that even scratches the surface of how deeply honored I am to call John and Maggie my friends." On the day of our wedding, I was so grateful to my parents for all their quirks and eccentricities, their particular brand of love and bad habits, for making me the person I was. And I was equally grateful for John's family, for making him. Mike said, "I've known John for a dozen years—at the beginning of our Chicago careers we became friends performing the improvised Irish comedy *Flanagan's Wake*; those were deliciously blurry evenings of pints of beer and professing our love for each other deep into the wee hours at the great Chicago pub, O'Rourke's.

"I've known Maggie since high school, back when I was the popular kid and she needed help making friends. (Wait a minute, I got that totally reversed.) Maggie was the first friend I had who not only saw her friends for who they were, but pushed them to go further. Without Maggie, the theater many of us here tonight serve—the Gift—may have never been born. Maggie was a bright North Star during the darkest of life's nights and her friendship literally and figuratively put me back on my feet." Instead of a head table, John and I had decided to sit at a round table in the center of the room, and everyone at that table was a member of our company. They wore suits and vintage dresses, cried the hardest, drank the most, and danced the longest. You should always invite your theater people to a wedding—they understand the importance of the performance.

"And once back on my feet, John got me walking. It was John who decided I should make my return to the stage by *walking* in a walker, and even though I didn't know if I could do it, I said yes, 'cuz I trust John like a brother. John has held me up and carried me past obstacles without even being in the same *room*. He is another bright star in life's dark nights, a man whose exactitude of mind is eclipsed only by his magnitude of heart." Yes, I thought, as I sat there holding John's hand. That's exactly right. But still, I liked what I said better.

John and I wrote our own vows, and while his were elegant and brief, mine were predictably long and winding. I stood before him in a mermaid dress and read with absolute confidence.

> There's a book that's been written by the wife of a famous playwright and she tells about the first night she and her husband met and the question he asked her: "Must you go?" If we have children, I will tell them, I fell in love with your father because he grilled for your grandparents in our tiny backyard—he wore a *Polska* jacket to the Copernicus Center and a snazzy hat to the Arlington Racetrack. I loved the way he put his arm around his father in public places, took such pride in his very different sisters, spent entire nights just

dreaming for his niece and nephew. The way he swam with great splashing and played men trapped in blizzards. And then again, I loved him when he handled enormous successes with not an ounce of ego and when he was a really good coach who'd just had a losing season. I loved the way he decorated for Christmas, a tree in every room, and the way he signed gift tags. *To: My Love, From: Your Love . . .*"

John Gawlik and I danced until midnight in the Riviera Ballroom. The oldest guest at the wedding was a great-aunt, and when she came to us at the end of the evening to say goodnight, we asked for her marital advice.

"Be nice to each other," she said.

We looked at each other and smiled with relief, knowing we could do that.

EPILOGUE

2022

In 2022, Mike decided to step down and make space for new artistic directors, Brittany Burch and Jennifer Glasse, two ensemble members we all loved. Mike was headed off to Broadway again and couldn't responsibly do the job anymore. Brittany and Jenn were younger and talented, and had the energy and vision for it. We had outgrown the space on Milwaukee, and it seemed like a natural time for new leadership, for new stories to be told.

In 2022, we marked twenty years as a Chicago theater company and had a fancy party to celebrate at the historic Copernicus Center in Jefferson Park. If you're old enough, you might remember the Copernicus Center when it was the Gateway Cinema, but otherwise, you might have lived here your whole life and missed it. The building is unassuming from the outside, but inside, you'll find yourself transported to vintage elegance.

I walked in, after a long day of teaching at a local university, wearing a wool camel coat over my cocktail dress. Inside the golden doorway, I saw Frank and Rita Thornton first, and suddenly I was sixteen and twenty-five and twenty-seven and forty-four, all the ages I had ever been. They came walking toward me, genuinely happy to see me, and I looked at the woman who had taught me about the cruelty of motherhood, the heroics of endurance, and ageless beauty. In some ways, I thought, maybe we had inadvertently helped form the current versions of ourselves. She drank a little more wine these days and cared just a little less what God thought, and I had become a mother whose heart ached anytime anyone didn't love my son as much as I thought they should. I had become the mother in the doctor's waiting rooms, always prepared for the bad news and profoundly grateful for the good.

She and I had been friends for years now, but I still sometimes thought about the letter I wrote when I first moved back to Chicago, and wondered if she'd kept it. "Dear Rita and Frankie, I'm writing to wish you a merry Christmas. I've been wanting to write for some time now, to say all the things I should've said. I always hope it's not too late." Sending that letter had sealed us together, I think, in a friendship that suited us better than in-laws.

Rita hugged me first, and I could see us at RIC together, her struggling to hold me up in the elevator. I could see her standing next to that priest reading last rites and looking straight ahead at a storm. I could see her slowly taking her grown-up son's clothes from the closet of his apartment, knowing he could no longer button his buttons the way she had taught him to when he was a tiny child. She was still that woman to me, but she was also the woman I now called for her taco salad recipes, the one who hearted all the posts of my son on Instagram, who invited us to her husband's seventieth birthday party, and who gossiped with me in the corner at every Gift event.

"Hi, honey," she said, helping me out of my coat.

There are people who will always call you honey, and that makes the world a better place.

"We saw the prince," Frankie said, kissing the top of my head. "He's getting so big!"

My son, Archie, the prince, came running to me then. He was eight years old at the time and looked like a Polish immigrant circa 1925. All cerulean eyes and seriousness, excited to be wearing his navy-blue communion suit.

"Are you being a good boy?" I asked, reaching my arms out to him.

"There are stars in the ceiling!" he cried.

It was true. The theater had classic red theater seats and a midnight-blue ceiling made to give the illusion of a star-filled sky. The stars were always lit on performance nights. This is where we had our twenty-year birthday party, and where we said farewell to an era. I greeted my husband, dapper in his own blue suit.

"Three hundred tickets sold," he said. (He is a unicorn of a man who can do the numbers and books as well as he can direct a show or perform a monologue.) "Archie's having a great time, and your students have been very helpful."

John got back to business and Archie said he was going to find his grandparents. (His grandmother, my mother, was outside smoking, of course, and his grandfather had cornered the alderman.)

A few of my favorite students worked the lobby. I'd asked them to help because they were writers, and I had a feeling they'd enjoy it. They took tickets, worked coat check, blew up balloons, and wrote poems on typewriters for guests while chatting with our subscribers, who asked them questions and took them very seriously. I made sure to introduce them to Lindsey Thornton, who had, for a long time, been our director of giftED. She was an inspired and good-hearted educator. Her face tonight was dewy and glowing, and she looked especially lovely in a green lace dress.

"They have a signature cocktail called the Gift," she said, widening her eyes.

"Twist my arm," I said.

We hurried to the 1930s vintage bar.

"I heard you're reading tonight," she said.

"Totally nervous," I said.

"You'll be great." She squeezed my hand.

Many artists say things like this to each other, but when Lindsey and I say it to each other, we mean it.

At the bar, I saw Brendan, in from New York, Lynda from Boston, and Will from Los Angeles. We looked at each other, laughed in disbelief, and shook our heads. Brendan picked me up and spun me round and round. Not many people light up when I enter a room, but Brendan, Lynda, and Will still do. We hadn't seen each other since Connolly's funeral, just before the pandemic hit.

After cocktail hour and passed appetizers, we, the ensemble, sat in a half-circle on the stage, some of us wearing masks, all of us gussied up and gimlet-eyed in the space where we lived most purely. I had occasionally felt old and isolated with the newer ensemble members, but now, the combination of generations made us all feel extra powerful.

Everyone took turns, giving speeches about Mike, making toasts to the new artistic directors, singing nostalgic and celebratory songs, playing videos from out-of-town ensemble members, reciting monologues and scenes from shows we had done, once upon a time. Brendan did his monologue from *Boys' Life* twenty years later, and he looked the same, with a little more gray in his hair maybe and the wiser, crinklier eyes of a father. Lynda also had more gray, but was still the belle of the ball. She was wearing a black dress and telling everyone how she bought it on clearance. The wonderful thing is? They will always be young to me. Our board president says it's so clear how much we all really like each other, and maybe personal chemistry really is the most crucial ingredient for any lasting theater company. The stars twinkled in the ceiling and I thought of a favorite Ada Limón poem called "Dead Stars":

> Look, we are not unspectacular things.
> We've come this far, survived this much. What
>
> would happen if we decided to survive more? . . .

The director of the evening had asked me to go last, said she didn't need to see my speech ahead of time; she trusted me. The rest of the ensemble cleared the stage and I missed them already as I watched them return to their seats one by one. The theater was charged with post-pandemic meaning, crowded with living, breathing people and their post-pandemic ghosts. I looked up and tried to find Sheldon and Connolly in the ceiling, thought I recognized them in the shapes of the stars. Sheldon gone the year I became a mother, and Connolly just moments after I realized Archie could read. It would take a small thing to undo me tonight, so I returned my attention to the audience.

From the podium, I looked out and the place was packed, everyone in suits and dresses and full makeup. Artistic directors and managing directors from other theaters, our board and subscribers and their friends. Politicians, restaurant owners, and venture capitalists. They were all waiting so patiently for me to tell them a story, and that, I knew I could do.

"Hi," I said into the microphone.

That was all I said, and they all started wildly applauding.

Now it was just me in a spotlight, and Mike, sitting in his chair a few feet away. I looked for Brendan, Lynda, Will, and Paulie, because even twenty years later, I felt safer with them in the room. Even twenty years later, I could see them smoking in the window of Brendan's studio apartment, rushing across the quad in the snow to see Sheldon at the University of Chicago, standing above a hospital bed at RIC with the saddest faces, fluent now in the language of grief.

"Mike and I met each other doing high school theater," I said into the microphone.

"I was the kind of dork who went to poetry club after school. He was the kind of dork who did dance routines to *The Pajama Game*'s soundtrack. The year after I graduated, he did *The Fantasticks*, and when he sang 'Try to Remember,' well, I had a feeling I would remember it for the rest of my life. I had just turned seventeen and he was sixteen years old.

"Shortly after, Mike decided that he would start mounting his own shows instead of participating in the beneath-him high school productions. As you might imagine, most kids in the high school theater program thought he was a class-A dick, but I was in college already, so I agreed to help him. He cast himself as an old drunk and me as his nagging wife in a Sam Shepard play called *Buried Child*.

"We rehearsed every day, because that's all we wanted to do, and there's a scene in which the stage direction tells me to slap him. This was the nineties, before intimacy directors and violence choreographers. Anyway, I told the director I didn't want to do that. 'But you should,' Mike said. 'If you want to, you should hit me.'

"He wore one of Frankie's old flannels and I wore one of my mom's most hideous dresses, and we sprayed gray in our shiny hair, painted wrinkles on our fresh faces. And when we went out onstage, the entire theater was full. When it came time to slap him, I did it, because he was cruel to me, and when I saw the mark on his cheek, I burst into tears. When they gave us a standing ovation, I didn't know if they were clapping for me or for him.

"He told me, after *Buried Child*, in Frank and Rita's kitchen, that he was going to go to college and figure out how to start a theater company and I would always have a place in it.

" 'But I mean,' I said, 'we can do that? Like, people like us do that?'

"'Yes,' he said, drinking a can of 50/50. 'People like us do that.'"

I looked out to see Rita and Frank Thornton, holding each other's arms, Lindsey Thornton beside them in her green lace dress. She nodded at me and winked, and then I kept on going.

"I became part of the audience," I said, "which is still where I sit most days. I left acting a long time ago, but the Gift still fuels me sometimes. When I had to deal with literary agents and qualifying exams, when I needed bravery and discipline? I called on Brittany Burch as Girleen. Whenever I need artistic inspiration, I think of Jennifer Glasse and Greg Fenner in *Hang Man*. It's Alex in *Wit* when I teach poetry, and when I need to advocate for students, I call on Cyd Blakewell in *Doubt*. *Mine* prepared me for early motherhood, and *Wolf Play* urgently reminded me to be a better advocate for other mothers. Whenever I suffer from imposter syndrome, it's Mike Thornton in my ear, saying: 'Yes. People like us do that.'

"Happy birthday to those kids who were smart enough to know they would need their dreams when they were older.

"I still don't know, won't know, when you're clapping, if you're clapping for me or him. Our new artistic team will wonder if you're clapping for them, or him. It doesn't matter anymore. He sure as shit couldn't have done it without us and we sure as shit couldn't have done it without him. To our new dynamic leaders: Art quite literally saved us from despair, and I hope it will save you too. We forgave each other betrayals, and hope you will do the same. We put up the drywall, hoping you would come, and we're all so glad you're here. I hope the story of the past serves your future in some way.

"Happy Birthday, Mike Thornton," I said, and that is when my voice broke.

I looked out into the audience and saw my mother, dabbing at her eyes, and my father who may have been put on this earth to be a grandfather. Archie sat beside them in his own father's lap, for once not wiggly and distracted. My God, I had gotten lucky. My God, they were worth the wait. Don't start crying now, I told myself. Finish strong.

I thought of *Ulysses*, the book Mike had read to me a long time ago. The character Molly Bloom who had been unfaithful, and who had gotten the final word in the book. I thought of Joyce's lack of punctuation, the repeated "yes" in the final chapter. He had once said that "yes" was a feminine word, the acquiescing word, the end of resistance, and maybe that's why I had stopped saying it. And now I was so many women, the one who had been pretty in bed in Dublin, the one who had buried herself in books there, the one who had become a wife and mother hiking with her kid and husband across the history of oppression and taking in the wonders of the natural world. I heard the jigging music and the keening music, and there was a flash of a photograph of me and Mike racing to the top of Sheatrim Hill, me and John with Archie, sweaty and triumphant at the peak of Croagh Patrick, me alone on top of Bray Hill, smiling, if only just for myself. What do you mean, what's the meaning of life? What do people mean when they ask that?

"Happy Birthday, Mike Thornton," I repeated, and it was easier to recover when I remembered that he was right beside me, when I realized we had never been strangers and never would be. He reached out his hand and I held it without looking at him for the rest of the speech. Instead, I looked at my students sitting together in the back row, huddled together in shadow, backlit by a lobby of golden light. Caitlin, Clare, Shaina, Day, Io, Sofia, Vero, Rebekah, Yaritza, Riley. All of them haloed, all of the wonderful and impossible dreams inside their heads. I wanted to tell them so many things, but mostly I wanted to tell them to never, ever give up.

"We don't need the spray paint in our hair anymore or the painted-on wrinkles," I said softly into the microphone. "But we earned them. Thank you, Mike, for the difficult conversations, the exceedingly high standards, and for littering the world with beauty.

"People like us do that? *Yes*. People like us do that."

ACKNOWLEDGMENTS

I would like to thank Jim McCarthy, the first industry professional who believed in this book, and Megan Stielstra, who made my dreams come true. (This book is so much better because of her.) Thanks also to the entire team at Northwestern University Press, who worked so hard for me. Special shout-out to Maddie, Charlotte, Mary, and Ari.

This book took a long time to make, so I have to thank the teachers and writer-friends who read the earliest, ugliest pages: Robert Eversz, Richard Katrovas, Stuart Dybek, Cris Mazza, Luis Urrea, Lisa Freeman, Melinda Moustakis, Jessi Phillips, Adeena Reitberger, Rachel Swearingen, Jody Keisner, Kris Peterson, Robert Kirkbride, Laura Krughoff, and Mike Levine. Also, the friends who read the most recent versions, including Sam Bailey, Jennifer Rumberger, Heather Slomski, and my sister Jeanne Andersen-Bakula, whose comments were invaluable.

Thank you to Dominican University, especially the Faculty Development Committee and the English Department, for your support on this project. Thanks to the Dairy Hollow Writers' Colony for the revision time and space, and to Jana for her inspired cooking. Love to my students who were so happy for me when I told them this book would be published. Love to all of the employees and patients at the Rehab Institute of Chicago for teaching me about grit and a life of purpose and making the impossible possible. Love to all of the theater companies in Chicago. Every single one.

Without the Gift, there would be no story, so a huge shout-out to the Gift family, old and new. Especially though: Brendan Donaldson,

Lauren Sharpe, Lynda Newton, Paul D'Addario, David Pries, Alex Main, Brittany Burch, Jennifer Glasse, Sheldon Patinkin, John Kelly Connolly, Claire Demos, Cyd Blakewell, Michael Patrick Thornton, and John Gawlik.

Thank you to my family for the self-esteem and no-nonsense love required to pursue an artistic life: my parents, Laura and Alan Andersen; my sisters, Jeanne and Mary; my grandmother Charmaine; my aunties and cousins. To my friends Becky O'Hearn, Wendy Sammons, Michelle Gebhardt, and Meghan Janda, who loved me through it all, even when that was an unpopular decision.

Rita and Frank Thornton: Thank you for being my family, too. Michael and Lindsey Thornton: You are artists of true friendship and I'm so glad and deeply honored you're mine. *"Here's to us. Who's like us? Damn few."*

Archie and Johnny Gawlik: I will never be able to thank you enough for loving me, all my past and present selves. You were both so worth the wait. God only knows what I'd be without you.